**W9-CFV-619**

# grzimek's
## Student Animal Life Resource

• • • •

# grzimek's
# Student Animal Life Resource

• • • •

## Mammals
## volume 1

### Echidnas to Armadillos

THOMSON

GALE

Detroit • New York • San Francisco • San Diego • New Haven, Conn. • Waterville, Maine • London • Munich

**THOMSON**
™
**GALE**

Grzimek's Student Animal Life Resource
Mammals

**Project Editor**
Melissa C. McDade

**Editorial**
Julie L. Carnagie, Madeline Harris,
Elizabeth Manar, Heather Price

**Indexing Services**
Synapse, the Knowledge Link
Corporation

**Rights and Acquisitions**
Sheila Spencer, Mari Masalin-Cooper

**Imaging and Multimedia**
Randy Bassett, Michael Logusz, Dan
Newell, Chris O'Bryan, Robyn Young

**Product Design**
Tracey Rowens, Jennifer Wahi

**Composition**
Evi Seoud, Mary Beth Trimper

**Manufacturing**
Wendy Blurton, Dorothy Maki

**LIBRARY OF CONGRESS CATALOGING-IN-PUBLICATION DATA**

Grzimek's student animal life resource. Mammals / Melissa C. McDade, project
editor.
        p. cm.
    Includes bibliographical references and index.
    ISBN 0-7876-9183-6 (set hardcover : alk. paper) — ISBN 0-7876-9184-4
    (volume 1) — ISBN 0-7876-9185-2 (volume 2) — ISBN 0-7876-9187-9 (volume 3)
    — ISBN 0-7876-9188-7 (volume 4) — ISBN 0-7876-9234-4 (volume 5)
    1. Mammals—Juvenile literature.   I. Grzimek, Bernhard. II. McDade, Melissa C.
    QL703.G79 2005
    599—dc22                                                    2004015604

ISBN 0-7876-9402-9 (21-vol set), ISBN 0-7876-9183-6 (Mammals set),
ISBN 0-7876-9184-4 (v.1), ISBN 0-7876-9185-2 (v.2), ISBN 0-7876-9187-9 (v.3),
ISBN 0-7876-9188-7 (v.4), ISBN 0-7876-9234-4 (v.5)

This title is also available as an e-book
Contact your Thomson Gale sales representative for ordering information.

Printed in Canada
10 9 8 7 6 5 4 3 2 1

# Contents

## MAMMALS: VOLUME 3

# Reader's Guide

*Grzimek's Student Animal Life Resource: Mammals* offers readers comprehensive and easy-to-use information on Earth's mammals. Entries are arranged by taxonomy, the science through which living things are classified into related groups. Order entries provide an overview of a group of families, and family entries provide an overview of a particular family. Each entry includes sections on physical characteristics; geographic range; habitat; diet; behavior and reproduction; animals and people; and conservation status. Family entries are followed by one or more species accounts with the same information as well as a range map and photo or illustration for each species. Entries conclude with a list of books, periodicals, and Web sites that may be used for further research.

## ADDITIONAL FEATURES

Each volume of *Grzimek's Student Animal Life Resource: Mammals* includes a pronunciation guide for scientific names, a glossary, an overview of Mammals, a list of species in the set by biome, a list of species by geographic location, and an index. The set has 540 full-color maps, photos, and illustrations to enliven the text, and sidebars provide additional facts and related information.

## NOTES

The classification of animals into orders, families, and even species is not a completed exercise. As researchers learn more about animals and their relationships, classifications may change. In some cases, researchers do not agree on how or whether to make a change. For this reason, the heading "Number of species" in the introduction of an entry may read "About 36 species" or "34 to 37 species." It is not a question of whether some animals exist or not, but a question of how they are classified. Some researchers are more likely to "lump" animals into the same species classification, while others may "split" animals into separate species.

*Grzimek's Student Animal Life Resource: Mammals* has standardized information in the Conservation Status section. The IUCN Red List provides the world's most comprehensive inventory of the global conservation status of plants and animals. Using a set of criteria to evaluate extinction risk, the IUCN recognizes the following categories: Extinct, Extinct in the Wild, Critically Endangered, Endangered, Vulnerable, Conservation Dependent, Near Threatened, Least Concern, and Data Deficient. These terms are defined where they are used in the text, but for a complete explanation of each category, visit the IUCN web page at http://www.iucn.org/themes/ssc/redlists/RLcats2001booklet.html.

## ACKNOWLEDGEMENTS

Special thanks are due for the invaluable comments and suggestions provided by the *Grzimek's Student Animal Life Resource: Mammals* advisors:

- Mary Alice Anderson, Media Specialist, Winona Middle School, Winona, Minnesota
- Thane Johnson, Librarian, Oklahoma City Zoo, Oklahoma City, Oklahoma
- Debra Kachel, Media Specialist, Ephrata Senior High School, Ephrata, Pennsylvania
- Nina Levine, Media Specialist, Blue Mountain Middle School, Courtlandt Manor, New York
- Ruth Mormon, Media Specialist, The Meadows School, Las Vegas, Nevada

## COMMENTS AND SUGGESTIONS

We welcome your comments on *Grzimek's Student Animal Life Resource: Mammals* and suggestions for future editions of this work. Please write: Editors, *Grzimek's Student Animal Life Resource: Mammals*, U•X•L, 27500 Drake Rd., Farmington Hills, Michigan 48331-3535; call toll free: 1-800-877-4253; fax: 248-699-8097; or send e-mail via www.gale.com.

# Pronunciation Guide for Scientific Names

*Abrocoma cinerea* AB-ruh-KOH-muh sin-EAR-ee-uh
**Abrocomidae** ab-ruh-KOH-muh-dee
*Acomys cahirinus* ak-OH-meez kay-hih-RYE-nuhs
*Acrobates pygmaeus* ak-CROW-bah-teez pig-MEE-uhs
**Acrobatidae** ak-crow-BAH-tuh-dee
*Agouti paca* ah-GOO-tee PAY-cuh
**Agoutidae** ah-GOO-tuh-dee
*Ailuropoda melanoleuca* AYE-lur-uh-POD-uh MEL-uh-noh-
    LYOO-kuh
*Ailurus fulgens* AYE-lur-uhs FULL-jens
*Alces alces* AL-ceez AL-ceez
*Alouatta seniculus* ah-loo-AH-tuh se-NIH-kul-uhs
**Anomaluridae** ah-nuh-mah-LOOR-uh-dee
*Anomalurus derbianus* ah-nuh-MAH-loor-uhs der-BEE-an-uhs
*Antilocapra americana* AN-til-uh-KAP-ruh uh-mer-uh-KAN-uh
**Antilocapridae** an-til-uh-KAP-ruh-dee
*Antrozous pallidus* an-tro-ZOH-uhs PAL-uh-duhs
**Aotidae** ay-OH-tuh-dee
*Aotus trivirgatus* ay-OH-tuhs try-VER-gah-tuhs
*Aplodontia rufa* ap-loh-DON-shuh ROO-fah
**Aplodontidae** ap-loh-DON-tuh-dee
*Arctocephalus gazella* ARK-tuh-SEFF-uh-luhs guh-ZELL-uh
**Artiodactyla** AR-tee-uh-DAK-til-uh
*Asellia tridens* ah-SELL-ee-uh TRY-denz
*Ateles geoffroyi* ah-TELL-eez JEFF-roy-eye
**Atelidae** ah-TELL-uh-dee

*Babyrousa babyrussa* bah-bee-ROO-suh bah-bee-ROO-suh

*Balaena mysticetus* bah-LEE-nuh mis-tuh-SEE-tuhs

**Balaenidae** bah-LEE-nuh-dee

*Balaenoptera acutorostrata* bah-lee-NOP-teh-ruh uh-KYOOT-uh-ROS-trah-tuh

*Balaenoptera musculus* bah-lee-NOP-teh-ruh muhs-KU-luhs

**Balaenopteridae** bah-lee-nop-TEH-ruh-dee

*Barbastella barbastellus* bar-buh-STELL-uh bar-buh-STELL-uhs

**Bathyergidae** bath-ih-ER-juh-dee

*Bettongia tropica* bee-ton-JEE-uh TROP-ik-uh

*Bison bison* BI-sun BI-sun

**Bovidae** BOH-vuh-dee

**Bradypodidae** brad-ih-POD-uh-dee

*Bradypus variegatus* BRAD-ih-puhs vair-ee-uh-GAH-tuhs

*Bubalus bubalis* BYOO-bal-uhs BYOO-bal-is

**Burramyidae** bur-ruh-MY-uh-dee

*Cacajao calvus* KA-ka-jah-oh KAL-vuhs

*Caenolestes fuliginosus* kee-NOH-less-teez fyoo-li-JEH-noh-suhs

**Caenolestidae** kee-noh-LESS-tuh-dee

*Callicebus personatus* kal-luh-SEE-buhs per-SON-ah-tuhs

*Callimico goeldii* kal-luh-MEE-koh geel-DEE-eye

**Callitrichidae** kal-luh-TRIK-uh-dee

**Camelidae** kam-EL-uh-dee

*Camelus dromedarius* KAM-el-uhs drom-uh-DARE-ee-uhs

**Canidae** KAN-uh-dee

*Canis lupus* KAN-is LYOO-puhs

*Caperea marginata* kay-per-EE-uh mar-JIN-ah-tuh

*Capricornis sumatraensis* kap-rih-KOR-nis soo-mah-TREN-sis

**Capromyidae** kap-roh-MY-uh-dee

*Capromys pilorides* KAP-roh-meez pi-LOH-ruh-deez

**Carnivora** kar-NIH-voh-ruh

*Castor canadensis* KAS-tor kan-uh-DEN-sis

**Castoridae** kas-TOR-uh-dee

**Caviidae** kave-EYE-uh-dee

**Cebidae** SEE-buh-dee

*Cebuella pygmaea* see-boo-ELL-uh pig-MEE-uh

*Cebus capucinus* SEE-buhs kap-oo-CHIN-uhs

*Cebus olivaceus* SEE-buhs ah-luh-VAY-see-uhs

*Ceratotherium simum* suh-rah-tuh-THER-ee-um SIM-um

*Cercartetus nanus* ser-kar-TEE-tuhs NAN-uhs

*Cercopithecidae* ser-koh-pith-EEK-uh-dee

*Cervidae* SER-vuh-dee

*Cervus elaphus* SER-vuhs EL-laff-uhs

*Cetacea* sih-TAY-she-uh

*Cheirogaleidae* KY-roh-GAL-uh-dee

*Cheiromeles torquatus* ky-ROH-mel-eez TOR-kwah-tuhs

*Chinchilla lanigera* chin-CHILL-uh la-NIJ-er-uh

*Chinchillidae* chin-CHILL-uh-dee

*Chironectes minimus* ky-roh-NECK-teez MIN-ih-muhs

*Chiroptera* ky-ROP-ter-uh

*Chlamyphorus truncatus* klam-EE-for-uhs TRUN-kah-tuhs

*Choloepus hoffmanni* koh-LEE-puhs HOFF-man-eye

*Chrysochloridae* krih-soh-KLOR-uh-dee

*Chrysocyon brachyurus* krih-SOH-sigh-on bra-kee-YOOR-uhs

*Civettictis civetta* sih-VET-tick-tis SIH-vet-uh

*Coendou prehensilis* SEEN-doo prih-HEN-sil-is

*Condylura cristata* KON-dih-LUR-uh KRIS-tah-tuh

*Connochaetes gnou* koh-nuh-KEE-teez NEW

*Craseonycteridae* kras-ee-oh-nick-TER-uh-dee

*Craseonycteris thonglongyai* kras-ee-oh-NICK-ter-is thong-LONG-ee-aye

*Cricetomys gambianus* kry-see-TOH-meez GAM-bee-an-uhs

*Cricetus cricetus* kry-SEE-tuhs kry-SEE-tuhs

*Crocuta crocuta* kroh-CUE-tuh kroh-CUE-tuh

*Cryptomys damarensis* krip-TOH-meez DAM-are-en-sis

*Cryptoprocta ferox* krip-TOH-prok-tuh FAIR-oks

*Cryptotis parva* krip-TOH-tis PAR-vuh

*Ctenodactylidae* ten-oh-dak-TIL-uh-dee

*Ctenomyidae* ten-oh-MY-uh-dee

*Ctenomys pearsoni* TEN-oh-meez PEAR-son-eye

*Cyclopes didactylus* SIGH-kluh-peez die-DAK-til-uhs

*Cynocephalidae* sigh-nuh-seff-UH-luh-dee

*Cynocephalus variegatus* sigh-nuh-SEFF-uh-luhs VAIR-ee-uh-GAH-tus

*Cynomys ludovicianus* SIGH-no-mees LOO-doh-vih-SHE-an-uhs

*Dasypodidae* das-ih-POD-uh-dee

*Dasyprocta punctata* das-IH-prok-tuh PUNK-tah-tuh

*Dasyproctidae* das-ih-PROK-tuh-dee

*Dasypus novemcinctus* DAS-ih-puhs noh-VEM-sink-tuhs

**Dasyuridae** das-ih-YOOR-uh-dee

**Dasyuromorphia** das-ih-yoor-oh-MOR-fee-uh

**Daubentoniidae** daw-ben-tone-EYE-uh-dee

*Daubentonia madagascariensis* daw-ben-TONE-ee-uh mad-uh-GAS-kar-EE-en-sis

*Delphinapterus leucas* del-fin-AP-ter-uhs LYOO-kuhs

**Delphinidae** del-FIN-uh-dee

*Dendrohyrax arboreus* den-droh-HI-raks are-BOHR-ee-uhs

*Dendrolagus bennettianus* den-droh-LAG-uhs BEN-net-EE-an-uhs

**Dermoptera** der-MOP-ter-uh

*Desmodus rotundus* dez-MOH-duhs ROH-tun-duhs

*Dicerorhinus sumatrensis* die-ser-uh-RHY-nuhs soo-mah-TREN-sis

**Didelphidae** die-DELF-uh-dee

**Didelphimorphia** die-delf-uh-MOR-fee-uh

*Didelphis virginiana* DIE-delf-is ver-JIN-ee-an-uh

**Dinomyidae** die-noh-MY-uh-dee

*Dinomys branickii* DIE-noh-meez BRAN-ick-ee-eye

**Dipodidae** dih-POD-uh-dee

*Dipodomys ingens* dih-puh-DOH-meez IN-jenz

**Diprotodontia** dih-pro-toh-DON-she-uh

*Dipus sagitta* DIH-puhs SAJ-it-tuh

*Dolichotis patagonum* doll-ih-KOH-tis pat-uh-GOH-num

*Dromiciops gliroides* droh-MISS-ee-ops gli-ROY-deez

*Dugong dugon* DOO-gong DOO-gon

**Dugongidae** doo-GONG-uh-dee

**Echimyidae** ek-ih-MY-uh-dee

*Echinosorex gymnura* EH-ky-noh-SORE-eks JIM-nyoor-uh

*Echymipera rufescens* ek-ee-MIH-per-uh ROO-fehs-sens

*Ectophylla alba* ek-toh-FILE-luh AHL-buh

**Elephantidae** el-uh-FAN-tuh-dee

*Elephas maximus* EL-uh-fuhs MAX-im-uhs

**Emballonuridae** em-bal-lun-YOOR-uh-dee

**Equidae** EK-wuh-dee

*Equus caballus przewalskii* EK-wuhs CAB-uh-luhs prez-VAL-skee-eye

*Equus grevyi* EK-wuhs GREH-vee-eye

*Equus kiang* EK-wuhs KY-an

*Eremitalpa granti* er-uh-MIT-ahl-puh GRAN-tie

*Erethizon dorsatum*  er-uh-THY-zun DOR-sah-tum

**Erethizontidae**  er-uh-thy-ZUN-tuh-dee

**Erinaceidae**  er-ih-nay-SIGH-dee

*Erinaceus europaeus*  er-ih-NAY-shuhs yoor-uh-PEE-uhs

**Eschrichtiidae**  ess-rick-TIE-uh-dee

*Eschrichtius robustus*  ess-RICK-shuhs roh-BUHS-tuhs

*Eubalaena glacialis*  yoo-bah-LEE-nuh glay-SHE-al-is

**Felidae**  FEE-luh-dee

**Furipteridae**  fur-ip-TER-uh-dee

**Galagidae**  gal-AG-uh-dee

*Galago senegalensis*  GAL-ag-oh sen-ih-GAHL-en-sis

*Galidia elegans*  ga-LID-ee-uh EL-uh-ganz

*Gazella thomsonii*  guh-ZELL-uh TOM-son-ee-eye

*Genetta genetta*  JIN-eh-tuh JIN-eh-tuh

**Geomyidae**  gee-oh-MY-uh-dee

*Giraffa camelopardalis*  JIH-raf-uh KAM-el-uh-PAR-dal-is

**Giraffidae**  jih-RAF-uh-dee

*Glaucomys volans*  glo-KOH-meez VOH-lans

*Glossophaga soricina*  glos-SUH-fag-uh sore-ih-SEE-nuh

*Gorilla gorilla*  guh-RILL-uh guh-RILL-uh

*Hemicentetes semispinosus*  hemi-sen-TEE-teez semi-PINE-oh-suhs

**Herpestidae**  her-PES-tuh-dee

*Heterocephalus glaber*  HEH-tuh-roh-SEFF-uh-luhs GLAH-ber

**Heteromyidae**  HEH-tuh-roh-MY-uh-dee

*Hexaprotodon liberiensis*  hek-suh-PRO-tuh-don lye-BEER-ee-en-sis

**Hippopotamidae**  HIP-poh-pot-UH-muh-dee

*Hippopotamus amphibius*  HIP-poh-POT-uh-muhs am-FIB-ee-uhs

**Hipposideridae**  HIP-poh-si-DER-uh-dee

**Hominidae**  hom-IN-uh-dee

*Homo sapiens*  HOH-moh SAY-pee-enz

**Hyaenidae**  hi-EE-nuh-dee

**Hydrochaeridae**  hi-droh-KEE-ruh-dee

*Hydrochaeris hydrochaeris*  hi-droh-KEE-ris hi-droh-KEE-ris

*Hydrodamalis gigas*  hi-droh-DAM-uhl-is JEE-guhs

*Hylobates lar*  hi-loh-BAY-teez lahr

*Hylobates pileatus*  hi-loh-BAY-teez pie-LEE-ah-tuhs

**Hylobatidae**  hi-loh-BAY-tuh-dee

*Hylochoerus meinertzhageni* hi-loh-KEE-ruhs MINE-ertz-hah-gen-eye

*Hyperoodon ampullatus* hi-per-OH-uh-don am-PUH-lah-tuhs

**Hypsiprymnodontidae** HIP-see-PRIM-nuh-DON-shuh-dee

*Hypsiprymnodon moschatus* hip-see-PRIM-nuh-don MOS-kah-tuhs

**Hyracoidea** HI-rah-koy-DEE-uh

**Hystricidae** hiss-TRIK-uh-dee

*Hystrix africaeaustralis* HISS-triks AF-rik-ee-au-STRA-lis

*Hystrix indica* HISS-triks IN-dik-uh

*Indri indri* IN-dri IN-dri

**Indriidae** in-DRY-uh-dee

*Inia geoffrensis* in-EE-uh JEFF-ren-sis

**Iniidae** in-EYE-uh-dee

**Insectivora** IN-sek-TIV-uh-ruh

*Kerodon rupestris* KER-uh-don ROO-pes-tris

*Kogia breviceps* koh-JEE-uh BREV-ih-seps

**Lagomorpha** LAG-uh-MOR-fuh

*Lagothrix lugens* LAG-uh-thriks LU-jens

*Lama glama* LAH-muh GLAH-muh

*Lama pacos* LAH-muh PAY-kuhs

*Lemmus lemmus* LEM-muhs LEM-muhs

*Lemur catta* LEE-mer KAT-tuh

*Lemur coronatus* LEE-mer KOR-roh-nah-tuhs

**Lemuridae** lee-MYOOR-uh-dee

*Lepilemur leucopus* lep-uh-LEE-mer LYOO-koh-puhs

*Lepilemur ruficaudatus* lep-uh-LEE-mer ROO-fee-KAW-dah-tuhs

**Lepilemuridae** LEP-uh-lee-MOOR-uh-dee

**Leporidae** lep-OR-uh-dee

*Lepus americanus* LEP-uhs uh-mer-uh-KAN-uhs

*Lepus timidus* LEP-uhs TIM-id-uhs

*Lipotes vexillifer* lip-OH-teez veks-ILL-uh-fer

**Lipotidae** lip-OH-tuh-dee

**Lorisidae** lor-IS-uh-dee

*Loxodonta africana* LOK-suh-DON-tuh AF-rih-kan-uh

*Loxodonta cyclotis* LOK-suh-DON-tuh SIGH-klo-tis

*Lutra lutra* LOO-truh LOO-truh

*Lynx rufus* LINKS ROO-fuhs

*Macaca mulatta* muh-KAY-kuh MYOO-lah-tuh

*Macroderma gigas* ma-CROW-der-muh JEE-guhs

**Macropodidae** ma-crow-POD-uh-dee

*Macropus giganteus* ma-CROW-puhs jy-GAN-tee-uhs

*Macropus rufus* ma-CROW-puhs ROO-fuhs

**Macroscelidea** MA-crow-sel-uh-DEE-uh

**Macroscelididae** MA-crow-sel-UH-duh-dee

*Macrotis lagotis* ma-CROW-tis la-GO-tis

*Macrotus californicus* ma-CROW-tuhs kal-uh-FORN-uh-kuhs

*Madoqua kirkii* ma-DOH-kwah KIRK-ee-eye

*Mandrillus sphinx* man-DRILL-uhs SFINKS

**Manidae** MAN-uh-dee

*Manis temminckii* MAN-is TEM-ink-ee-eye

*Marmota marmota* MAR-mah-tuh MAR-mah-tuh

*Massoutiera mzabi* mas-soo-TEE-er-uh ZA-bye

**Megadermatidae** meg-uh-der-MUH-tuh-dee

**Megalonychidae** meg-uh-loh-NICK-uh-dee

*Megaptera novaeangliae* meg-uh-TER-uh NOH-vee-ANG-lee-dee

*Meles meles* MEL-eez MEL-eez

*Mephitis mephitis* MEF-it-is MEF-it-is

**Microbiotheria** my-crow-bio-THER-ee-uh

**Microbiotheriidae** my-crow-bio-ther-EYE-uh-dee

*Microcebus rufus* my-crow-SEE-buhs ROO-fuhs

*Micropteropus pusillus* my-crop-TER-oh-puhs pyoo-SILL-uhs

*Miniopterus schreibersi* min-ee-OP-ter-uhs shry-BER-seye

*Mirounga angustirostris* MIR-oon-guh an-GUHS-tih-ROS-tris

**Molossidae** mol-OS-suh-dee

*Monachus schauinslandi* MON-ak-uhs SHOU-inz-land-eye

*Monodon monoceros* MON-uh-don mon-UH-ser-uhs

**Monodontidae** mon-uh-DON-shuh-dee

**Monotremata** mon-uh-TREEM-ah-tuh

**Mormoopidae** mor-moh-UP-uh-dee

*Moschus moschiferus* MOS-kuhs mos-KIF-er-uhs

*Muntiacus muntjak* mun-SHE-uh-kuhs MUNT-jak

**Muridae** MUR-uh-dee

*Mustela erminea* MUS-tuh-luh er-MIN-ee-uh

**Mustelidae** mus-TUH-luh-dee

*Myocastor coypus* MY-oh-KAS-tor COI-puhs

**Myocastoridae** MY-oh-kas-TOR-uh-dee

*Myotis lucifugus* my-OH-tis loo-SIFF-ah-guhs

*Myoxidae* my-OKS-uh-dee
*Myoxus glis* MY-oks-uhs GLIS
**Myrmecobiidae** mur-mih-koh-BYE-uh-dee
*Myrmecobius fasciatus* mur-mih-KOH-bee-uhs fah-SHE-ah-tuhs
*Myrmecophaga tridactyla* mur-mih-KOH-fag-uh try-DAK-til-uh
**Myrmecophagidae** mur-mih-koh-FAJ-uh-dee
*Mystacina tuberculata* miss-tih-SEE-nuh too-ber-KYOO-lah-tuh
**Mystacinidae** miss-tih-SEE-nuh-dee
*Myzopoda aurita* my-zoh-POD-uh OR-it-uh
**Myzopodidae** my-zoh-POD-uh-dee
*Nasalis larvatus* NAY-zal-is LAR-vah-tuhs
**Natalidae** nay-TAL-uh-dee
*Natalus stramineus* NAY-tal-uhs struh-MIN-ee-uhs
**Neobalaenidae** nee-oh-bah-LEE-nuh-dee
*Noctilio leporinus* nok-TIHL-ee-oh leh-por-RYE-nuhs
**Noctilionidae** nok-tihl-ee-ON-uh-dee
*Notomys alexis* noh-TOH-meez ah-LEK-sis
**Notoryctemorphia** noh-toh-rik-teh-MOR-fee-uh
*Notoryctes typhlops* noh-TOH-rik-teez TIE-flopz
**Notoryctidae** noh-toh-RIK-tuh-dee
**Nycteridae** nik-TER-uh-dee
*Nycteris thebaica* NIK-ter-is the-BAH-ik-uh
*Nycticebus pygmaeus* nik-tih-SEE-buhs pig-MEE-uhs
*Nyctimene robinsoni* nik-TIM-en-ee ROB-in-son-eye
*Ochotona hyperborea* oh-koh-TOH-nuh hi-per-BOHR-ee-uh
*Ochotona princeps* oh-koh-TOH-nuh PRIN-seps
**Ochotonidae** oh-koh-TOH-nuh-dee
*Octodon degus* OK-tuh-don DAY-gooz
**Octodontidae** ok-tuh-DON-tuh-dee
**Odobenidae** oh-duh-BEN-uh-dee
*Odobenus rosmarus* oh-DUH-ben-uhs ROS-mahr-uhs
*Odocoileus virginianus* oh-duh-KOI-lee-uhs ver-JIN-ee-an-nuhs
*Okapia johnstoni* oh-KAH-pee-uh JOHNS-ton-eye
*Ondatra zibethicus* ON-dat-ruh ZIB-eth-ih-kuhs
*Onychogalea fraenata* oh-nik-uh-GAL-ee-uh FREE-nah-tuh
*Orcinus orca* OR-sigh-nuhs OR-kuh
**Ornithorhynchidae** OR-nith-oh-RIN-kuh-dee
*Ornithorynchus anatinus* OR-nith-oh-RIN-kuhs an-AH-tin-uhs
**Orycteropodidae** or-ik-ter-uh-POD-uh-dee
*Orycteropus afer* or-ik-TER-uh-puhs AF-er

*Otariidae*  oh-tar-EYE-uh-dee

*Otolemur garnettii*  oh-tuh-LEE-mer GAR-net-ee-eye

*Ovis canadensis*  OH-vis kan-uh-DEN-sis

*Pagophilus groenlandicus*  pa-GO-fil-luhs GREEN-land-ih-cuhs

*Pan troglodytes*  PAN trog-luh-DIE-teez

*Panthera leo*  PAN-ther-uh LEE-oh

*Panthera tigris*  PAN-ther-uh TIE-gris

*Paucituberculata*  paw-see-too-ber-KYOO-lah-tuh

*Pedetidae*  ped-ET-uh-dee

*Peramelemorphia*  per-uh-mel-eh-MOR-fee-uh

*Peramelidae*  per-uh-MEL-uh-dee

*Perameles gunnii*  PER-uh-MEL-eez GUN-ee-eye

*Perissodactyla*  peh-RISS-uh-DAK-til-uh

*Perodicticus potto*  per-uh-DIK-tuh-kuhs POT-toh

*Perognathus inornatus*  PER-ug-NAH-thuhs in-AWR-nah-tuhs

*Peropteryx kappleri*  per-OP-ter-iks KAP-ler-eye

*Peroryctidae*  per-uh-RIK-tuh-dee

*Petauridae*  pet-OR-uh-dee

*Petauroides volans*  pet-or-OY-deez VOH-lanz

*Petaurus breviceps*  PET-or-uhs BREV-ih-seps

*Petrogale penicillata*  pet-ROH-gah-lee pen-ih-SIL-lah-tuh

*Petromuridae*  pet-roh-MUR-uh-dee

*Petromus typicus*  PET-roh-muhs TIP-ih-kuhs

*Phalanger gymnotis*  FAH-lan-jer jim-NOH-tis

*Phalangeridae*  fah-lan-JER-uh-dee

*Phascogale tapoatafa*  fas-KOH-gah-lee TAP-oh-uh-TAH-fuh

*Phascolarctidae*  fas-koh-LARK-tuh-dee

*Phascolarctos cinereus*  fas-KOH-lark-tuhs sin-EAR-ee-uhs

*Phocidae*  FOE-suh-dee

*Phocoena phocoena*  FOE-see-nuh FOE-see-nuh

*Phocoena spinipinnis*  FOE-see-nuh SPY-nih-PIN-is

*Phocoenidae*  foe-SEE-nuh-dee

*Pholidota*  foe-lih-DOH-tuh

*Phyllostomidae*  fill-uh-STOH-muh-dee

*Physeter macrocephalus*  FY-se-ter ma-crow-SEFF-uh-luhs

*Physeteridae*  fy-se-TER-uh-dee

*Piliocolobus badius*  fill-ee-oh-KOH-loh-buhs BAD-ee-uhs

*Pithecia pithecia*  pith-EEK-ee-uh pith-EEK-ee-uh

*Pitheciidae*  pith-eek-EYE-uh-dee

*Plantanista gangetica*  plan-TAN-is-tuh gan-JET-ik-uh

*Platanistidae* plan-tan-IS-tuh-dee

*Pongo pygmaeus* PON-goh pig-MEE-uhs

*Pontoporia blainvillei* pon-toh-POR-ee-uh BLAIN-vill-ee-eye

*Pontoporiidae* PON-toh-por-EYE-uh-dee

*Potoroidae* pot-uh-ROY-dee

*Primates* PRY-maytes

*Proboscidea* proh-BOS-see-uh

*Procavia capensis* proh-CAVE-ee-uh KAP-en-sis

*Procaviidae* proh-kave-EYE-uh-dee

*Procyon lotor* proh-SIGH-on LOH-tor

*Procyonidae* proh-sigh-ON-uh-dee

*Proechimys semispinosus* proh-EK-ih-meez sem-ih-SPY-noh-suhs

*Propithecus edwardsi* proh-PITH-eek-uhs ED-werds-eye

*Proteles cristatus* PROH-tell-eez KRIS-tah-tuhs

*Pseudocheiridae* soo-doh-KY-ruh-dee

*Pseudocheirus peregrinus* soo-doh-KY-ruhs PEHR-eh-GRIN-uhs

*Pteronotus parnellii* ter-uh-NOH-tuhs PAR-nell-ee-eye

*Pteropodidae* ter-uh-POD-uh-dee

*Pteropus giganteus* ter-OH-puhs jy-GAN-tee-uhs

*Pteropus mariannus* ter-OH-puhs MARE-ih-an-uhs

*Pudu pudu* POO-doo POO-doo

*Puma concolor* PYOO-muh CON-kuh-luhr

*Puripterus horrens* PYOOR-ip-TER-uhs HOR-renz

*Pygathrix nemaeus* PIG-uh-thriks neh-MEE-uhs

*Rangifer tarandus* RAN-jih-fer TAR-an-duhs

*Rhinoceros unicornis* rye-NOS-er-uhs YOO-nih-KORN-is

*Rhinocerotidae* rye-NOS-er-UH-tuh-dee

*Rhinolophidae* rye-noh-LOH-fuh-dee

*Rhinolophus capensis* rye-noh-LOH-fuhs KAP-en-sis

*Rhinolophus ferrumequinum* rye-noh-LOH-fuhs FEHR-rum-EK-wy-num

*Rhinopoma hardwickei* rye-noh-POH-muh HARD-wik-eye

*Rhinopomatidae* rye-noh-poh-MAT-uh-dee

*Rhynchocyon cirnei* rin-koh-SIGH-on SIR-neye

*Rodentia* roh-DEN-she-uh

*Rousettus aegyptiacus* ROO-set-tuhs ee-JIP-tih-kuhs

*Saccopteryx bilineata* sak-OP -ter-iks BY-lin-EE-ah-tuh

*Saguinus oedipus* SAG-win-uhs ED-uh-puhs

*Saimiri sciureus* SAY-meer-eye sigh-OOR-ee-uhs

*Sarcophilus laniarius* SAR-kuh-FIL-uhs lan-ee-AIR-ee-uhs

*Scalopus aquaticus*   SKA-loh-puhs uh-KWAT-ik-uhs

**Scandentia**  skan-DEN-she-uh

**Sciuridae**  sigh-OOR-uh-dee

*Sciurus carolinensis*  SIGH-oor-uhs kar-uh-LINE-en-sis

*Sigmodon hispidus*   SIG-muh-don HISS-pid-uhs

**Sirenia**   sy-REEN-ee-uh

*Solenodon paradoxus*  so-LEN-uh-don PAR-uh-DOCKS-uhs

**Solenodontidae**  so-len-uh-DON-shuh-dee

*Sorex palustris*  SOR-eks PAL-us-tris

**Soricidae**  sor-IS-uh-dee

*Stenella longirostris*  steh-NELL-uh LAWN-juh-ROS-tris

**Suidae**  SOO-uh-dee

*Sus scrofa*  SOOS SKRO-fuh

*Sylvilagus audubonii*  SILL-vih-LAG-uhs AW-duh-BON-ee-eye

*Symphalangus syndactylus*  SIM-fuh-LAN-guhs sin-DAK-til-uhs

**Tachyglossidae**  TAK-ih-GLOS-suh-dee

*Tachyglossus aculeatus*  TAK-ih-GLOS-suhs ak-YOOL-ee-ah-tuhs

*Tadarida brasiliensis*  ta-DARE-ih-dah bra-ZILL-ee-en-sis

**Talpidae**  TAL-puh-dee

*Tamias striatus*   TAM-ee-uhs stry-AH-tuhs

**Tapiridae**  tay-PUR-uh-dee

*Tapirus indicus*  TAY-pur-uhs IN-dih-kuhs

*Tapirus terrestris*   TAY-pur-uhs TER-rehs-tris

**Tarsiidae**  tar-SIGH-uh-dee

**Tarsipedidae**  tar-sih-PED-uh-dee

*Tarsipes rostratus*  TAR-si-peez ROS-trah-tuhs

*Tarsius bancanus*  TAR-see-uhs BAN-kan-uhs

*Tarsius syrichta*   TAR-see-uhs STRIK-tuh

*Tasmacetus shepherdi*  taz-muh-SEE-tuhs SHEP-erd-eye

*Tayassu tajacu*  TAY-yuh-soo TAY-jah-soo

**Tayassuidae**  tay-yuh-SOO-uh-dee

*Tenrec ecaudatus*   TEN-rek ee-KAW-dah-tuhs

**Tenrecidae**  ten-REK-uh-dee

*Thomomys bottae*  TOM-oh-meez BOTT-ee

**Thryonomyidae**  thry-oh-noh-MY-uh-dee

*Thryonomys swinderianus*  THRY-oh-NOH-meez SWIN-der-EE-an-uhs

**Thylacinidae**  thy-luh-SEEN-uh-dee

*Thylacinus cynocephalus*  THY-luh-SEEN-uhs sigh-nuh-SEFF-uh-luhs

*Thyroptera tricolor* thy-ROP-ter-uh TRY-kuh-luhr

**Thyropteridae** thy-rop-TER-uh-dee

**Tragulidae** tray-GOO-luh-dee

*Tragulus javanicus* TRAY-goo-luhs jah-VAHN-ih-kuhs

**Trichechidae** trik-EK-uh-dee

*Trichechus manatus* TRIK-ek-uhs MAN-uh-tuhs

*Trichosurus vulpecula* TRIK-uh-SOOR-uhs vul-PEK-yoo-luh

**Tubulidentata** toob-yool-ih-DEN-tah-tuh

*Tupaia glis* too-PUH-ee-uh GLIS

**Tupaiidae** too-puh-EYE-uh-dee

*Tursiops truncatus* tur-SEE-ops TRUN-kah-tuhs

*Uncia uncia* UN-see-uh UN-see-uh

**Ursidae** UR-suh-dee

*Ursus americanus* UR-suhs uh-mer-uh-KAN-uhs

*Ursus maritimus* UR-suhs mar-ih-TIME-uhs

**Vespertilionidae** ves-puhr-TEEL-ee-UHN-uh-dee

**Viverridae** vy-VER-ruh-dee

**Vombatidae** vom-BAT-uh-dee

*Vombatus ursinus* VOM-bat-uhs ur-SIGH-nuhs

*Vulpes vulpes* VUHL-peez VUHL-peez

**Xenarthra** ZEN-areth-ruh

*Yerbua capensis* YER-byoo-uh KAP-en-sis

*Zalophus californianus* ZA-loh-fuhs kal-uh-FORN-uh-kuhs

*Zalophus wollebaeki* ZA-loh-fuhs VOLL-back-eye

**Ziphiidae** ziff-EYE-uh-dee

# Words to Know

## A

**Aborigine:** Earliest-known inhabitant of an area; often referring to a native person of Australia.

**Adaptation:** Any structural, physiological, or behavioral trait that aids an organism's survival and ability to reproduce in its existing environment.

**Algae:** Tiny plants or plantlike organisms that grow in water and in damp places.

**Anaconda:** A large snake of South America; one of the largest snakes in the world.

**Aphrodisiac:** Anything that intensifies or arouses sexual desires.

**Aquatic:** Living in the water.

**Arboreal:** Living primarily or entirely in trees and bushes.

**Arid:** Extremely dry climate, with less than 10 inches (25 centimeters) of rain each year.

**Arthropod:** A member of the largest single animal phylum, consisting of organisms with segmented bodies, jointed legs or wings, and exoskeletons.

## B

**Baleen:** A flexible, horny substance making up two rows of plates that hang from the upper jaws of baleen whales.

**Biogeography:** The study of the distribution and dispersal of plants and animals throughout the world.

**Bipedal:** Walking on two feet.

**Blowhole:** The nostril on a whale, dolphin, or porpoise.

**Blubber:** A layer of fat under the skin of sea mammals that protects them from heat loss and stores energy.

**Brachiation:** A type of locomotion in which an animal travels through the forest by swinging below branches using its arms.

**Brackish water:** Water that is a mix of freshwater and saltwater.

**Burrow:** Tunnel or hole that an animal digs in the ground to use as a home.

## C

**Cache:** A hidden supply area.

**Camouflage:** Device used by an animal, such as coloration, allowing it to blend in with the surroundings to avoid being seen by prey and predators.

**Canine teeth:** The four pointed teeth (two in each jaw) between the incisors and bicuspids in mammals; designed for stabbing and holding prey.

**Canopy:** The uppermost layer of a forest formed naturally by the leaves and branches of trees and plants.

**Carnivore:** Meat-eating organism.

**Carrion:** Dead and decaying animal flesh.

**Cecum:** A specialized part of the large intestine that acts as a fermentation chamber to aid in digestion of grasses.

**Cervical vertebrae:** The seven neck bones that make up the top of the spinal column.

**Clan:** A group of animals of the same species that live together, such as badgers or hyenas.

**Cloud forest:** A tropical forest where clouds are overhead most of the year.

**Colony:** A group of animals of the same type living together.

**Coniferous:** Refers to evergreen trees, such as pines and firs, that bear cones and have needle-like leaves that are not shed all at once.

**Coniferous forest:** An evergreen forest where plants stay green all year.

**Continental shelf:** A gently sloping ledge of a continent that is submerged in the ocean.

**Convergence:** In adaptive evolution, a process by which unrelated or only distantly related living things come to resemble one another in adapting to similar environments.

**Coprophagous:** Eating dung. Some animals do this to extract nutrients that have passed through their system.

**Crepuscular:** Most active at dawn and dusk.

**Critically Endangered:** A term used by the IUCN in reference to a species that is at an extremely high risk of extinction in the wild.

## D

**Data Deficient:** An IUCN category referring to a species that is not assigned another category because there is not enough information about the species' population.

**Deciduous:** Shedding leaves at the end of the growing season.

**Deciduous forest:** A forest with four seasons in which trees drop their leaves in the fall.

**Deforestation:** Those practices or processes that result in the change of forested lands to non-forest uses, such as human settlement or farming. This is often cited as one of the major causes of the enhanced greenhouse effect.

**Delayed implantation:** A process by which the fertilized egg formed after mating develops for a short time, then remains inactive until later when it attaches to the uterus for further development, so that birth coincides with a better food supply or environmental conditions.

**Den:** The shelter of an animal, such as an underground hole or a hollow log.

**Dentin:** A calcareous material harder than bone found in teeth.

**Desert:** A land area so dry that little or no plant or animal life can survive.

**Digit:** Division where limbs terminate; in humans this refers to a finger or toe.

**Digitigrade:** A manner of walking on the toes, as cats and dogs do, as opposed to walking on the ball of the feet, as humans do.

**Dingo:** A wild Australian dog.

**Diurnal:** Refers to animals that are active during the day.

**Domesticated:** Tamed.

**Dominant:** The top male or female of a social group, sometimes called the alpha male or alpha female.

**Dorsal:** Located in the back.

**Dung:** Feces, or solid waste from an animal.

# E

**Echolocation:** A method of detecting objects by using sound waves.

**Ecotourist:** A person who visits a place in order to observe the plants and animals in the area while making minimal human impact on the natural environment.

**Electroreception:** The sensory detection of small amounts of natural electricity by an animal (usually underwater), by means of specialized nerve endings.

**Elevation:** The height of land when measured from sea level.

**Endangered:** A term used by the U. S. Endangered Species Act of 1973 and by the IUCN in reference to a species that is facing a very high risk of extinction from all or a significant portion of its natural home.

**Endangered Species Act:** A U. S. law that grants legal protection to listed endangered and threatened species.

**Endemic:** Native to or occurring only in a particular place.

**Erupt:** In teeth, to break through the skin and become visible.

**Estivation:** State of inactivity during the hot, dry months of summer.

**Estuary:** Lower end of a river where ocean tides meet the river's current.

**Eutherian mammal:** Mammals that have a well-developed placenta and give birth to fully formed live young.

**Evergreen:** In botany, bearing green leaves through the winter and/or a plant having foliage that persists throughout the year.

**Evolve:** To change slowly over time.

**Extinct:** A species without living members.

**Extinction:** The total disappearance of a species or the disappearance of a species from a given area.

# F

**Family:** A grouping of genera that share certain characteristics and appear to have evolved from the same ancestors.

**Feces:** Solid body waste.

**Fermentation:** Chemical reaction in which enzymes break down complex organic compounds into simpler ones. This can make digestion easier.

**Forage:** To search for food.

**Forb:** Any broad-leaved herbaceous plant that is not a grass; one that grows in a prairie or meadow, such as sunflower, goldenrod, or clover.

**Fragment:** To divide or separate individuals of the same species into small groups that are unable to mingle with each other.

**Frugivore:** Animal that primarily eats fruit. Many bats and birds are frugivores.

**Fuse:** To become joined together as one unit.


## G

**Genera:** Plural of genus.

**Genus (pl. genera):** A category of classification made up of species sharing similar characteristics.

**Gestation:** The period of carrying young in the uterus before birth.

**Gland:** A specialized body part that produces, holds, and releases one or more substances (such as scent or sweat) for use by the body.

**Gleaning:** Gathering food from surfaces.

**Grassland:** Region in which the climate is dry for long periods of the summer, and freezes in the winter. Grasslands are characterized by grasses and other erect herbs, usually without trees or shrubs, and occur in the dry temperate interiors of continents.

**Grooming:** An activity during which primates look through each other's fur to remove parasites and dirt.

**Guano:** The droppings of birds or bats, sometimes used as fertilizer.

**Guard hairs:** Long, stiff, waterproof hairs that form the outer fur and protect the underfur of certain mammals.

**Gum:** A substance found in some plants that oozes out in response to a puncture, as plant sap, and generally hardens after exposure to air.

# H

**Habitat:** The area or region where a particular type of plant or animal lives and grows.

**Habitat degradation:** The diminishment of the quality of a habitat and its ability to support animal and plant communities.

**Hallux:** The big toe, or first digit, on the part of the foot facing inwards.

**Harem:** A group of two or more adult females, plus their young, with only one adult male present.

**Haul out:** To pull one's body out of the water onto land, as when seals come out of the water to go ashore.

**Herbivore:** Plant-eating organism.

**Hibernation:** State of rest or inactivity during the cold winter months.

**Hierarchy:** A structured order of rank or social superiority.

**Home range:** A specific area that an animal roams while performing its activities.

# I

**Ice floe:** A large sheet of floating ice.

**Incisor:** One of the chisel-shaped teeth at the front of the mouth (between the canines), used for cutting and tearing food.

**Indigenous:** Originating in a region or country.

**Insectivore:** An animal that eats primarily insects.

**Insulate:** To prevent the escape of heat by surrounding with something; in an animal, a substance such as fur or body fat serves to retain heat in its body.

**Invertebrate:** Animal lacking a spinal column (backbone).

**IUCN:** Abbreviation for the International Union for Conservation of Nature and Natural Resources, now the World Conservation Union. A conservation organization of government agencies and nongovernmental organizations best known for its Red Lists of threatened and endangered species.

# K

**Keratin:** Protein found in hair, nails, and skin.

**Krill:** Tiny shrimp-like animals that are the main food of baleen whales and are also eaten by seals and other marine mammals.

## L

**Lactate:** To produce milk in the female body, an activity associated with mammals.

**Larva (pl. larvae):** Immature form (wormlike in insects; fishlike in amphibians) of an organism capable of surviving on its own. A larva does not resemble the parent and must go through metamorphosis, or change, to reach its adult stage.

**Leprosy:** A disease of the skin and flesh characterized by scaly scabs and open sores.

**Lichen:** A complex of algae and fungi found growing on trees, rocks, or other solid surfaces.

**Litter:** A group of young animals, such as pigs or kittens, born at the same time from the same mother. Or, a layer of dead vegetation and other material covering the ground.

## M

**Malaria:** A serious disease common in tropical countries, spread by the bites of female mosquitoes, that causes complications affecting the brain, blood, liver, and kidneys and can cause death.

**Mammae:** Milk-secreting organs of female mammals used to nurse young.

**Mammals:** Animals that feed their young on breast milk, are warm-blooded, and breathe air through their lungs.

**Mangrove:** Tropical coastal trees or shrubs that produce many supporting roots and that provide dense vegetation.

**Marsupial:** A type of mammal that does not have a well-developed placenta and gives birth to immature and underdeveloped young after a short gestation period. It continues to nurture the young, often in a pouch, until they are able to fend for themselves.

**Matriarchal:** Headed by a dominant female or females; said of animal societies.

**Mechanoreceptor:** Sensory nerve receptor modified to detect physical changes in the immediate environment, often having to do with touch and change of pressure or turbulence in water or air. In the platypus, mechanoreceptors in its bill may detect prey and obstacles.

**Megachiroptera:** One of the two groups of bats; these bats are usually larger than the microchiroptera.

**Melon:** The fatty forehead of a whale or dolphin.

**Membrane:** A thin, flexible layer of plant or animal tissue that covers, lines, separates or holds together, or connects parts of an organism.

**Microchiroptera:** One of two categories of bats; these make up most of the bats in the world and are generally smaller than the megachiroptera.

**Migrate:** To move from one area or climate to another as the seasons change, usually to find food or to mate.

**Migratory pattern:** The direction or path taken while moving seasonally from one region to another.

**Molar:** A broad tooth located near the back of the jaw with a flat, rough surface for grinding.

**Mollusk:** A group of animals without backbones that includes snails, clams, oysters, and similar hard-shelled animals.

**Molt:** The process by which an organism sheds its outermost layer of feathers, fur, skin, or exoskeleton.

**Monogamous:** Refers to a breeding system in which a male and a female mate only with each other during a breeding season or lifetime.

**Muzzle:** The projecting part of the head that includes jaws, chin, mouth, and nose.

**Myxomatosis:** A highly infectious disease of rabbits caused by a pox virus.

## N

**Near Threatened:** A category defined by the IUCN suggesting that a species could become threatened with extinction in the future.

**Nectar:** Sweet liquid secreted by the flowers of various plants to attract pollinators (animals that pollinate, or fertilize, the flowers).

**Neotropical:** Relating to a geographic area of plant and animal life east, south, and west of Mexico's central plateau that includes Central and South America and the West Indies.

**New World:** Made up of North America, Central America, and South America; the western half of the world.

**Nocturnal:** Occurring or active at night.

**Non-prehensile:** Incapable of grasping; used to describe an animal's tail that cannot wrap around tree branches.

**Noseleaf:** Horseshoe-shaped flap of skin around the nose.

**Nurse:** To feed on mother's milk.

## O

**Old World:** Australia, Africa, Asia, and Europe; in the eastern half of the world.

**Omnivore:** Plant- and meat-eating animal.

**Opportunistic feeder:** An animal that eats whatever food is available, either prey they have killed, other animals' kills, plants, or human food and garbage.

## P

**Pack ice:** Large pieces of ice frozen together.

**Patagium:** The flap of skin that extends between the front and hind limbs. In bats, it stretches between the hind legs and helps the animal in flight; in colugos this stretches from the side of the neck to the tips of its fingers, toes, and tail.

**Phylogenetics:** Field of biology that deals with the relationships between organisms. It includes the discovery of these relationships, and the study of the causes behind this pattern.

**Pinnipeds:** Marine mammals, including three families of the order Carnivora, namely Otariidae (sea lions and fur seals), Phocidae (true seals), and Odobenidae (walrus).

**Placenta:** An organ that grows in the mother's uterus and lets the mother and developing offspring share food and oxygen through the blood.

**Placental mammal:** Any species of mammal that carries embryonic and fetal young in the womb through a long gestation period, made possible via the placenta, a filtering organ passing nutrients, wastes, and gases between mother and young.

**Plantigrade:** Walking on the heel and sole of the foot, instead of on the toes. Plantigrade species include bears and humans.

**Plate tectonics:** Geological theory holding that Earth's surface is composed of rigid plates or sections that move about the surface in response to internal pressure, creating the major geographical features such as mountains.

**Poach:** To hunt animals illegally.

**Pod:** In animal behavioral science (and in some zoology uses) the term pod is used to represent a group of whales, seals, or dolphins.

**Pollen:** Dust-like grains or particles produced by a plant that contain male sex cells.

**Pollination:** Transfer of pollen from the male reproductive organs to the female reproductive organs of plants.

**Pollinator:** Animal which carries pollen from one seed plant to another, unwittingly aiding the plant in its reproduction. Common pollinators include insects, especially bees, butterflies, and moths; birds; and bats.

**Polyandry:** A mating system in which a single female mates with multiple males.

**Polyestrous:** A female animal having more than one estrous cycle (mating period) within a year.

**Polygamy:** A mating system in which males and females mate with multiple partners.

**Polygyny:** A mating system in which a single male mates with multiple females.

**Predator:** An animal that eats other animals.

**Prehensile:** Able to control and use to grasp objects, characteristically associated with tails. Prehensile tails have evolved independently many times, for instance, in marsupials, rodents, primates, porcupines, and chameleons.

**Prey:** Organism hunted and eaten by a predator.

**Primary forest:** A forest characterized by a full-ceiling canopy formed by the branches of tall trees and several layers of smaller trees. This type of forest lacks ground vegetation because sunlight cannot penetrate through the canopy.

**Promiscuity:** Mating in which individuals mate with as many other individuals as they can or want to.

**Puberty:** The age of sexual maturity.


# Q

**Quadruped:** Walking or running on four limbs.


# R

**Rabies:** A viral infection spread through the bite of certain warm-blooded animals; it attacks the nervous system and can be fatal if untreated.

**Rainforest:** An evergreen woodland of the tropics distinguished by a continuous leaf canopy and an average rainfall of about 100 inches (250 centimeters) per year.

**Regurgitate:** Eject the contents of the stomach through the mouth; to vomit.

**Rookery:** A site on land where seals congregate to mate and raise the young.

**Roost:** A place where animals, such as bats, sit or rest on a perch, branch, etc.

## S

**Savanna:** A biome characterized by an extensive cover of grasses with scattered trees, usually transitioning between areas dominated by forests and those dominated by grasses and having alternating seasonal climates of precipitation and drought.

**Scavenger:** An animal that eats carrion, dead animals.

**Scent gland:** Formed from modified, or changed, sweat glands, these glands produce and/or give off strong-smelling chemicals that give information, such as marking territory, to other animals.

**Scent mark:** To leave an odor, such as of urine or scent gland secretions, to mark a territory or as a means of communication.

**Scrotum:** The external pouch containing the testicles.

**Scrub forest:** A forest with short trees and shrubs.

**Scrubland:** An area similar to grassland but which includes scrub (low-growing plants and trees) vegetation.

**Seamount:** An underwater mountain that does not rise above the surface of the ocean.

**Seashore:** When referring to a biome, formed where the land meets the ocean.

**Secondary forest:** A forest characterized by a less-developed canopy, smaller trees, and a dense ground vegetation found on the edges of forests and along rivers and streams. The immature vegetation may also result from the removal of trees by logging and/or fires.

**Semiaquatic:** Partially aquatic; living or growing partly on land and partly in water.

**Semiarid:** Very little rainfall each year, between 10 and 20 inches (25 to 51 centimeters).

**Sexually mature:** Capable of reproducing.

**Solitary:** Living alone or avoiding the company of others.

**Species:** A group of living things that share certain distinctive characteristics and can breed together in the wild.

**Spermaceti:** A waxy substance found in the head cavity of some whales.

**Steppe:** Wide expanse of semiarid relatively level plains, found in cool climates and characterized by shrubs, grasses, and few trees.

**Streamline:** To smooth out.

**Succulent:** A plant that has fleshy leaves to conserve moisture.

**Suckle:** To nurse or suck on a mother's nipple to get milk.

**Syndactyly:** A condition in which two bones (or digits) fuse together to become a single bone.


## T

**Tactile:** Having to do with the sense of touch.

**Talon:** A sharp hooked claw.

**Taxonomy:** The science dealing with the identification, naming, and classification of plants and animals.

**Teat:** A projection through which milk passes from the mother to the nursing young; a nipple.

**Temperate:** Areas with moderate temperatures in which the climate undergoes seasonal change in temperature and moisture. Temperate regions of the earth lie primarily between 30 and 60° latitude in both hemispheres.

**Terrestrial:** Relating to the land or living primarily on land.

**Territorial:** A pattern of behavior that causes an animal to stay in a limited area and/or to keep certain other animals of the same species (other than its mate, herd, or family group) out of the area.

**Thicket:** An area represented by a thick, or dense, growth of shrubs, underbrush, or small trees.

**Threatened:** Describes a species that is threatened with extinction.

**Torpor:** A short period of inactivity characterized by an energy-saving, deep sleep-like state in which heart rate, respiratory rate and body temperature drop.

**Traction:** Resistance to a surface to keep from slipping.

**Tragus:** A flap of skin near the base of the external ear.

**Tributary:** A small stream that feeds into a larger one.

**Tropical:** The area between 23.5° north and south of the equator. This region has small daily and seasonal changes in temperature, but great seasonal changes in precipitation. Generally, a hot and humid climate that is completely or almost free of frost.

**Tundra:** A type of ecosystem dominated by lichens, mosses, grasses, and woody plants. It is found at high latitudes (arctic tundra) and high altitudes (alpine tundra). Arctic tundra is underlain by permafrost and usually very wet.

**Turbulent:** An irregular, disorderly mode of flow.

## U

**Underfur:** Thick soft fur lying beneath the longer and coarser guard hair.

**Understory:** The trees and shrubs between the forest canopy and the ground cover.

**Ungulates:** Hoofed animals, such as deer and elk.

**Urine washing:** A monkey behavior in which it soaks its hands with urine, then rubs the liquid on its fur and feet so as to leave the scent throughout its forest routes.

**Uterus:** A pear-shaped, hollow muscular organ in which a fetus develops during pregnancy.

## V

**Vertebra (pl. vertebrae):** A component of the vertebral column, or backbone, found in vertebrates.

**Vertebrate:** An animal having a spinal column (backbone).

**Vertical:** Being at a right angle to the horizon. Up and down movements or supports.

**Vestigial:** A degenerate or imperfectly developed biological structure that once performed a useful function at an earlier stage of the evolution of the species.

**Vibrissae:** Stiff sensory hairs that can be found near the nostrils or other parts of the face in many mammals and the snouts, tails, ears, and sometimes feet of many insectivores.

**Vocalization:** Sound made by vibration of the vocal tract.

**Vulnerable:** An IUCN category referring to a species that faces a high risk of extinction.

## W

**Wallaby:** An Australian marsupial similar to a kangaroo but smaller.

**Wean:** When a young animal no longer feeds on its mother's milk and instead begins to eat adult food.

**Wetlands:** Areas that are wet or covered with water for at least part of the year and support aquatic plants, such as marshes, swamps, and bogs.

**Woodlands:** An area with a lot of trees and shrubs.

## Y

**Yolk-sac placenta:** A thin membrane that develops in the uterus of marsupials that does not fuse with the mother's uterus and results in short pregnancies with the young being born with poorly developed organs.

# Getting to Know Mammals

## MAMMALS

Mammals are found on all continents and in all seas. It isn't easy to tell that an animal is a mammal. A combination of special features separates mammals from other animals.

### Mammal milk

Only mammals can feed their young with milk produced by their body. This milk comes from special glands called mammae. A female may have two mammary glands or as many as a dozen or more. Mammal milk is very healthy for infants and immediately available.

### Body temperature

Mammals are warm-blooded, meaning they keep a constant body temperature. To keep their temperature fairly constant, a mammal needs some protective covering. Hair, made of a protein called keratin, serves several functions. One function is insulation, controlling the amount of body heat that escapes into the mammal's environment through the skin.

### Mammal hair

All mammals have hair at some time of their life. Some have a lot, such as gorillas, and some have very little, such as the naked mole rats. There are three types of hair: a coarse long topcoat, a fine undercoat, and special sensory hairs, or whiskers.

In some mammals, hair has unusual forms. Porcupines have stiff, sharp, and thickened hairs called quills. Anteaters have

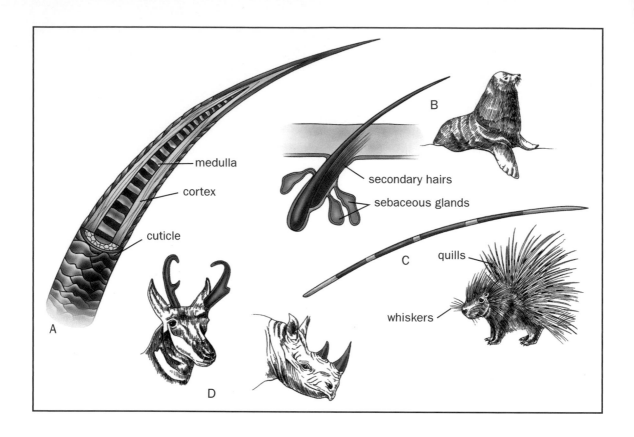

medulla

cortex

cuticle

A

B

secondary hairs

sebaceous glands

C

quills

whiskers

D

sharp-edged scales made of modified hairs. These modified, or changed, hairs are protective against predators.

Mammals that live all or most of their lives in water, such as sea otters, may have a lot of dense, long hair, or fur. Others have much less hair, but a very thick hide, or skin, plus a thick layer of fat or blubber underneath the hide.

Hair color and pattern may vary. Males and females may have different fur colors. Special color patterns, such as a skunk's black and white fur, act as warnings. Hair color can also serve as camouflage, enabling the mammal to blend into its background.

Some mammals have fur color changes in summer and winter. Colors can be entirely different. Snowshoe rabbits and weasels can be brownish in summer, and almost pure white in winter. But this only happens if there is snow where they live. If it seldom snows, weasels and snowshoe rabbits stay brown.

**Grzimek's Student Animal Life Resource**

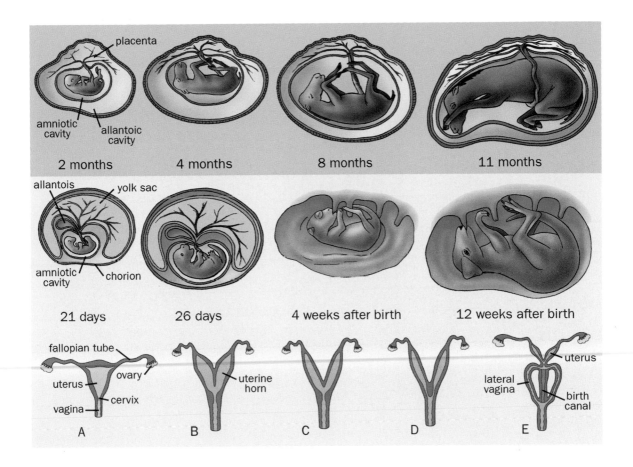

Top: Placental mammal development. Middle row: Marsupial mammal development. Types of uterus: A. Simplex; B. Bipartito; C. Bicornuate; D. Duplex; E. Marsupial. (Illustration by Patricia Ferrer. Reproduced by permission.)

## Reproduction

Mammals have two genetic sexes, male and female. Ninety percent of mammals are placental (pluh-SENT-ul). In placental mammals, the baby develops, or grows, within the mother's body before it enters the world. What about the other 10 percent? These mammals lay eggs. There are only three egg-laying mammals alive today.:

## Other mammal features

Other bodily mammal features include their ability to breathe air through their lungs. Water-dwelling mammals, such as the whale and porpoise, do this too. Mammals have jaws, usually with teeth. Mammals usually have four limbs. Mammals have a four-chambered heart. Mammals have vertebrae, or back bones, unlike invertebrates such as insects, in which there is an outside shell or structure called an exoskeleton.

*This life-sized woolly mammoth model is kept in the Royal British Columbia Museum. Woolly mammoths were as tall as 10 feet (3 meters). (© Jonathan Blair/Corbis. Reproduced by permission.)*

## FOSSIL MAMMALS

Fossils are body parts of animals that lived very long ago. Not many long-ago mammals are preserved as fossils. But some entire mammal fossils have been discovered, such as a 10-foot (3-meter) woolly mammoth preserved in Siberian frozen ground, and an Ice Age woolly rhinoceros discovered in Poland, preserved in asphalt.

Many long-ago mammals lived in a warm, wet world. They ate soft, leafy plants. The earliest known mammals were possibly shrew-like creatures living about 190 million years ago. Later larger mammals occurred, then disappeared, or became extinct. These include the mesohippus, a three-toed horse only 24 inches (60 centimeters) high; a giant pig with a head that was 4 feet (1.22 meters) in length; and the smilodon, a huge saber-toothed cat with canine teeth that were 8 inches (20.3

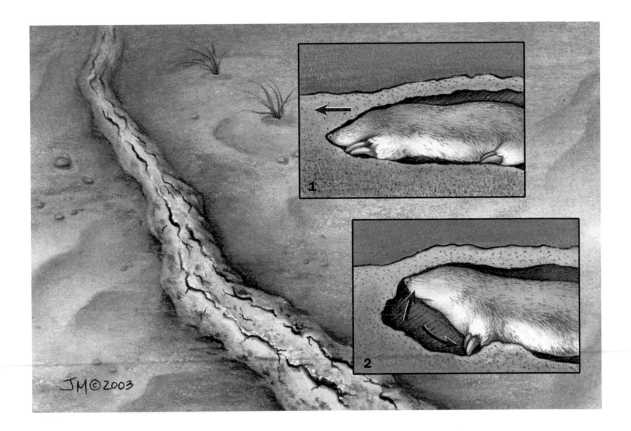

centimeters) in length. By about 15,000 years ago, long-ago people were hunting mammals with stone-pointed spears. Most of the animals they hunted are extinct for various reasons, some known, and some unknown.

## WHERE MAMMALS LIVE

### Underground mammals

Some small mammals spend all or most of their lives living underground. These include many species of prairie dogs, chipmunks, moles, groundhogs, Greenland collared lemmings, and Peruvian tuco-tucos. Each of these mammals has a special body design enabling it to survive underground.

Moles have large, powerful shoulders and short, very powerful forelimbs. Spade-like feet have claws, enabling quick digging. Hind feet have webbed toes, enabling the mole to kick soil backwards effectively. Velvety-type fur enables a mole to slip easily through its tunnels. And, although moles

*The Grant's desert mole uses its powerful forelimbs to burrow through the sands of the Namib Desert in southern Africa. The golden mole moves forward (1), and enlarges the tunnel by pushing dirt up with its head and back with its claws (2). (Illustration by Jacqueline Mahannah. Reproduced by permission.)*

**A RECENT DISCOVERY**

A bright orange, mouse-like mammal, weighing 0.5 ounces (15 grams) and measuring 3.12 inches (8 centimeters) plus a long tail, has recently been discovered in the Philippines. It has whiskers five times longer than its head. It can open and eat very hard tree nuts that no other mammal in the area can eat.

have almost no eyes, they can rely on touch, smell, and sensitivity to vibration to find underground insects and earthworms.

## Sea mammals

Some mammals live in the sea, including manatees, whales, seals, and dolphins. While some need air every few minutes, a sperm whale can remain underwater for an hour and a half. How is this possible? Some sea mammals have a very low metabolism. They don't use up the their oxygen quickly and can store large amounts of oxygen in their bodies.

## Tree mammals

Some mammals spend all or most of their lives in trees. Tree-dwelling mammals are often hidden from sight by leaves, vines, and branches. Tree-dwelling mammals include the Eastern pygmy possum, which nests in small tree hollows; the koala; Lumholtz's tree kangaroo, which leaps from branch to branch; the three-toed sloth; and the clouded leopard.

## Flying mammals

The only truly flying mammals are bats. The sound of bat wings was first heard about 50 million years ago. Some bats are large, with a wingspan almost 7 feet (21.3 meters) wide. Some are small, as the Philippine bamboo bat, whose body is just 2 inches (5.08 centimeters) long.

Other mammals only appear to fly, such as the southern flying squirrel and the colugo, or Malayan flying lemur. These mammals have gliding membranes, skin folds from body front to legs, that, when spread out, act almost like a parachute. For example, the feathertail glider, a tiny possum, crawls along narrow branches. At branch end, it leaps out and slightly downward. Spreading its gliding membranes, it speeds through the air, landing on a nearby tree.

## Mountain mammals

Some mammals spend most of their lives on mountain peaks. These include Asian corkscrew-horned markhor goats, North

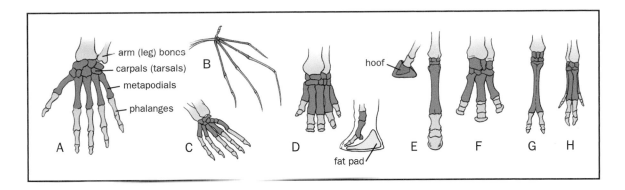

A. hominid hand; carpals (tarsals); metapodials; phalanges; arm (leg) bones. B. bat wing. C. pinniped flipper. D. elephant foot; fat pad. E. equid foot; hoof. F. odd-toed hoofed foot. G. two-toed hoofed foot. H. four-toed hoofed foot.

American Rocky Mountain bighorn sheep, and Siberian ibex. Siberian ibex can stand anyplace on any pinnacle with just enough room for its four feet. North American mountain goats can climb up a mountain peak, almost going straight up. Specially shaped hooves help.

Other high mountain dwelling mammals include snow leopards and Asian pikas that can survive at 19,685 feet (6,000 meters). Gunnison's prairie dogs do well up to 11,500 feet (3,505 meters).

## Desert mammals

Some mammals spend most of their lives in arid, or very dry areas. Not all deserts are sandy like Death Valley or the Sahara. Some are rocky. Other arid areas are mountainous. Desert dwelling mammals include the North African elephant shrew, white-tailed antelope squirrel, and the desert kangaroo rat. No mammal can live without water. Desert rodents have a way to extract, or get, water from their own body functions. Rodents may also get water by eating plants, seeds, roots, and insects that contain water.

Larger mammals live in arid regions too. The striped hyena can survive in stony desert as long as it is within 6 miles (9.7 kilometers) of water. Fennecs, a very small fox living near sand dunes, can go a long time without drinking. Camels can use body fluids when no water is available.

## WHAT DO MAMMALS EAT?

### Insect-eaters

Some mammals have mostly insect meals. Insect-eating mammals include the moles, aye-ayes and aardvarks. The aardvark

Mammals' hands and feet differ depending on where the animal lives and how it gets around. A. A hominid hand is used for grasping objects; B. A bat's wing is used for flight; C. A pinniped's flipper helps move it through the water. Hoofed animals move around on all fours: D. Elephant foot; E. Equid (horse family) foot; F. Odd-toed hoofed foot; G. Two-toed hoofed foot; H. Four-toed hoofed foot. (Illustration by Patricia Ferrer. Reproduced by permission.)

has a sticky tongue that can reach out as long as 1 foot (0.3 meters) to capture its ant and termite meals.

### Plant eaters

Some mammals eat nothing but plants. Plant eaters include pandas, the West Indian manatee, and the red-bellied wallaby. Some mammals have a single stomach that breaks the plant food down into small pieces. Other mammals, such as cows and camels, have a large stomach made of several parts. Each part does a separate job of breaking down difficult-to-digest plants.

Some mammals eat both plants and fruit. These include the 14-ounce (400-gram) Eurasian harvest mouse, the 100-pound (45-kilogram) South American capybara, and the African elephant. An elephant can eat up to 500 pounds (227 kilograms) of grass, plants, and fruit per day.

### Meat eaters

Mammals eating mostly meat or fish are carnivorous. Carnivorous mammals have long, pointed, and very strong incisor teeth. Carnivores include polar bears, hyenas, walruses, and Eu-

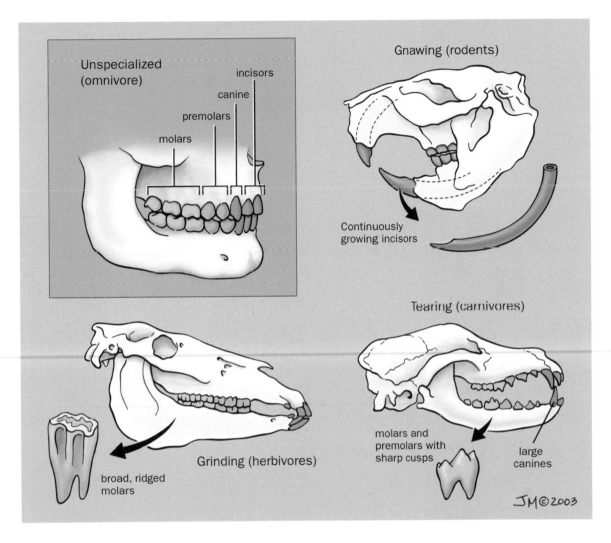

Unspecialized
(omnivore)

incisors

canine

premolars

molars

Gnawing (rodents)

Continuously
growing incisors

Tearing (carnivores)

Grinding (herbivores)

broad, ridged
molars

molars and
premolars with
sharp cusps

large
canines

JM©2003

ropean wild cats. The European wild cat may be an ancestor of
our house cats.

## Omnivores

Some mammals eat just about anything. They are omnivorous. Omnivorous mammals include wolverines, raccoons, and
wild pigs. Wild pigs are the ancestors of our domestic pigs.

## MAMMAL SLEEPING HABITS

### Day or night

Some mammals sleep during the night, others sleep during
the day. The night sleepers are diurnal, active during the day.

*Mammals have different tooth
shapes for different functions.
Herbivores typically have large,
flattened teeth for chewing
plants. Rodents' ever-growing
incisors are used for gnawing.
Carnivores have teeth for
holding and efficiently
dismembering their prey.
(Illustration by Jacqueline
Mahannah. Reproduced by
permission.)*

## THE BIGGEST, THE TALLEST, AND THE SMALLEST

The largest and heaviest mammal alive today is the blue whale. One adult female measured 110.2 feet (33.6 meters). Blue whale weight can reach 268,400 pounds (121,853 kilograms).

The largest living land animal is the African bush elephant. From trunk tip to tail tip, a male has measured 33 feet (10 meters). Body weight was 24,000 pounds (10,886 kilograms).

The smallest non-flying mammal is the Savi's white-toothed pygmy shrew. An adult's head and body together measure only 2 inches (5.1 centimeters) long. Maximum weight is 0.09 ounces (2.5 grams).

How small is this? This pygmy shrew can travel through tunnels left by large earthworms!

The smallest flying mammal is the rare Kitti's hog-nosed bat, or "bumblebee bat," from Thailand. Head and body length is just 1.14 to 1.29 inches (29 to 33 millimeters). Weight is just 0.06 to 0.07 ounces (1.75 to 2 grams). This tiny bat was only discovered in 1973.

The tallest living animal is the giraffe. The average adult male, or bull, is 16 feet (4.9 meters) high, from front hoof to head horn tip. This size male weighs 2,376 to 2,800 pounds (1,078 to 1,270 kilograms).

The day sleepers are nocturnal, active at night. They may have special night vision. Many desert animals are nocturnal, moving about when it is cooler.

### Hibernation

Some bat species hibernate through an entire winter. Hibernation is like a very long deep sleep. When a mammal hibernates, it uses up body fat that has accumulated from food eaten in good weather. Hibernators include the North African jird, groundhogs or woodchucks, and several dormice species. Dormice enter a tree hollow or ground burrow in autumn, and don't come out until springtime.

Bears don't truly hibernate. Their sleep isn't deep. They slow down quite a bit, and nap a lot, but do not sleep through an entire winter.

A new hibernating pattern has just been discovered. Madagascar fat-tailed lemurs hibernate in tree holes when winter daytime temperatures rise above 86° Fahrenheit (30° Celsius). They sleep for seven months. Scientists belief these dwarf lemurs find less food in what is the dry season in Madagascar, so they go to into deep sleep to preserve energy until a better food supply appears.

## REPRODUCTION

### Mating

Some mammals mate for life, such as wolves and sometimes coyotes. More commonly, a male may mate with several females each breeding period. Or a female may mate with several males.

Some mammals have one litter each year. Others have a litter only every two or three years. But the North American meadow mouse can have seventeen litters per year. That's a group of babies about every three weeks!

There may be one or more infants in a litter. Bats, giraffes, and two-toed sloths have just one baby per year. However, the Madagascar tenrec can produce thirty-two babies in just one litter.

*Opossums are marsupial animals. The mother has a pouch in which the young continue to develop after they're born. (© Mary Ann McDonald/Corbis. Reproduced by permission.)*

## Child care

All mammal infants need protection. They are very small compared to their parents. They may be blind and hairless. Usually females provide care. However, in a few mammal species, such as the golden lion marmoset, the male does most of the care.

Female marsupial mammals, such as opossums, koalas, and kangaroos, have a pouch, like a pocket, on the front or under the body. Their tiny babies are incompletely developed when they are born. At birth, an opossum baby is about the size of a dime. It crawls immediately into its mother's pouch and stays there until ready to survive outside. The pouch contains mammary glands so babies can feed.

## SOCIAL LIFE

### Solitary mammals

Some mammals are solitary. They keep company with another of the same kind only when mating or when raising young. Solitary mammals include the giant anteaters, European bison, and right whales.

Japanese macaques are social animals, and groom each other regularly. (© Herbert Kehrer/OKAPIA/Photo Researchers, Inc. Reproduced by permission.)

## Group living

Many mammals live in groups. In large groups, some eat, some rest, and some keep guard. Baboons, for example, may have from twenty to 300 animals in a group. One or more adult males lead each group. If a predator, such as a leopard, approaches, the males take action against it, while the females and young escape.

Some mammals travel in herds. Musk oxen travel in closely packed herds of fifteen to 100 individuals. These herds include males and females. Bighorn sheep females travel in herds of five to fifteen, with a dominant ewe, or female, as the leader.

Pack mammals get their food by cooperation. They work together to bring down much larger prey. Dingoes, killer whales, and lions hunt in packs.

## MAMMALS AND PEOPLE

### Domesticated mammals

About 14,000 years ago, humans began controlling, or domesticating, certain animals. This made humans' lives easier.

Horses have been domesticated for practical uses, such as transportation, and for entertainment, such as horse riding and racing. (© Kevin R. Morris/Corbis. Reproduced by permission.)

The earliest domesticated mammal was probably the dog. Some scientists think hunters adopted wolf cubs and trained them to smell out game, animals they hunted for food.

People use mammals for many purposes. Cows provide meat, milk, cheese, butter, and hide. Camels, yaks, and Indian elephants carry or pull heavy items. Water buffaloes do hauling and can provide milk. Horses provide transportation and racing activities. Other domesticated animals include rabbits, pigs, goats, sheep, cavies, and capybaras.

People keep animals as pets. Common mammal pets are dogs, cats, guinea pigs, and hamsters.

### Pest mammals

Some mammals are considered pests. These include rats, mice, and, depending where they live, gophers, rabbits, and ground squirrels. Rats can transmit disease-carrying fleas. Rabbits and gophers eat garden and food plants.

## ENDANGERED MAMMALS

### Mammals in danger

Of about 5,000 mammal species currently existing, over 1,000 are seriously endangered. Few wild mammals can live outside their natural habitat. When land is cleared for farming or housing, animals making homes there must leave, if there is any place for them to go. If not, they die from starvation or (because they are easily seen) from predators. Slowly, or quickly, the mammal species disappears.

Many human habits lead to endangerment. Hunting for amusement, killing for fur or body parts, native and commercial killing for food, fishing gear entrapment, land-destructive wars, and the illegal pet trade all take their toll. So do chemicals.

Some mammals are probably on the way to extinction, or total elimination. There are only about sixty Java rhinoceros left in the world. The Seychelles sheath-tailed bat has only about fifty individuals remaining. Yellow-tailed woolly monkeys number no more than 250 individuals. Mediterranean monk seals may be killed by scuba divers, and number only 600 individuals.

## Saving endangered animals

Today many people are trying to save endangered animals. Methods include zoo breeding, establishing forest reserves, and training native populations that animals can be an economic benefit. Ecotourism, people visiting a country to see its animals in their natural habitat, is increasing. There are laws against importing and exporting endangered species. And, in some parts of the world, there are laws against land destruction.

Some mammals have possibly been rescued from immediate extinction. The American bison once roamed the North American prairies, numbering about 50 million. After slaughter by soldiers and settlers for food and sport, by 1889 only 541 remained alive. Now, in the United States, there are about 35,000 in protected areas. California northern elephant seals were once reduced to fewer than 100 members due to hunting. Today, protected, there are about 50,000. The ibex was once hunted for supposedly curative body parts and few were left. But in 1922, a National Park was established in the Italian Alps, where several thousand now live. The Mongolian wild horse, once thought to be extinct, now has a special reserve in Mongolia.

## Too late to save

Some mammals became extinct only recently. Recently extinct animals include Steller's sea cows, which became extinct in about 1768. The Tasmanian wolf was last seen in 1933, eliminated by bounty hunters. The African bluebuck disappeared from Earth in 1880. The quagga, from southern Asia, was hunted for hides and meat. The last known quagga, a relative of the zebra, died in a Dutch zoo in 1883.

## FOR MORE INFORMATION

### Books

Boitani, Luigi, and Stefania Bartoli. *Guide to Mammals*. New York: Simon and Schuster, 1982.

Booth, Ernest S. *How to Know the Mammals*. Dubuque, IA: Wm. C. Brown Company Publishers, 1982.

Embery, Joan, and Edward Lucaire. *Joan Embery's Collection of Amazing Animal Facts*. New York: Dell Publishing, 1983.

Jones, J. Knox Jr., and David M. Armstrong. *Guide to Mammals of the Plains States*. Lincoln, NE: University of Nebraska Press, 1985.

Kite, L. Patricia. *Raccoons*. Minneapolis: Lerner Publications Company, 2004.

Kite, L. Patricia. *Blood-Feeding Bugs and Beasts*. Brookfield, CT: Millbrook Press, 1996.

Line, Les, and Edward Ricciuti. *National Audubon Society Book of Wild Animals*. New York: H. L. Abrams, 1996.

Nowak, Ronald M., and John L. Paradiso. *Walker's Mammals of the World*. Baltimore and London: The Johns Hopkins University Press, 1983.

Vogel, Julia, and John F. McGee. *Dolphins (Our Wild World*. Minnetonka, MN: Northword Press, 2001.

Walters, Martin. *Young Readers Book of Animals*. New York, London, Toronto, Sydney, and Tokyo: Simon & Schuster Books for Young Readers, 1990.

Whitaker, John O. Jr. *National Audubon Society Field Guide to North American Mammals*. New York: Alfred A. Knopf, 2000.

Wilson, D. E., and D. M. Reeder. *Mammal Species of the World*. Washington, DC: Smithsonian Institution Press, 1993.

Wood, Gerald L. *Animal Facts and Feats*. New York: Sterling Publishing, 1977.

Woods, Samuel G., and Jeff Cline. *Amazing Book of Mammal Records: The Largest, the Smallest, the Fastest, and Many More!* Woodbridge, CT: Blackbirch Press, 2000.

**Periodicals**

Allen, Leslie. "Return of the Pandas." *Smithsonian Magazine* (April 2001): 44–55.

Chadwick, Douglas H. "A Mine of Its Own." *Smithsonian Magazine* (May 2004): 26–27.

Cheater, Mark. "Three Decades of the Endangered Species Act." *Defenders* (Fall 2003): 8–13.

Conover, Adele. "The Object at Hand." *Smithsonian Magazine* (October 1996).

Gore, Rick. "The Rise of Mammals." *National Geographic* (April 2003): 2–37.

Mitchell, Meghan. "Securing Madagascar's Rare Wildlife." *Science News* (November 1, 1997): 287.

Pittman, Craig. "Fury Over a Gentle Giant." *Smithsonian Magazine* (February 2004): 54–59.

"Prehistoric Mammals." *Ranger Rick* (October 2000): 16.

Sherwonit, Bill. "Protecting the Wolves of Denali." *National Parks Magazine* (September/October 2003): 21–25.

Sunquist, Fiona. "Discover Rare Mystery Mammals." *National Geographic* (January 1999): 22–29.

Weidensaul, Scott. "The Rarest of the Rare." *Smithsonian Magazine* (November 2000): 118–128.

"Wildlife of Tropical Rain Forests." *National Geographic World* (January 2000): 22–25.

**Web sites**

Animal Info. http://www.animalinfo.org/ (accessed on June 6, 2004).

"Class Mammalia." Animal Diversity Web. http://animaldiversity.ummz.umich.edu/site/accounts/information/Mammalia004 (accessed on June 5, 2004).

"Hibernating Primate Found in Tropics." CNN Science & Space. http://www.cnn.com/2004/TECH/science/06/24/science.hibernation.reuit/inex.html (accessed on June 24, 2004).

"Ice Age Mammals." National Museum of Natural History. http://www.mnh.si.edu/museum/VirtualTour/Tour/First/IceAge/index.html (accessed on June 6, 2004).

"Mammary Glands." Animal Diversity Web. http://animaldiversity.ummz.umich.edu/site/topics/mammal_anatomy/mammary_glands.html (accessed on June 6, 2004).

**MONOTREMES**
**Monotremata**

**Class:** Mammalia
**Order:** Monotremata
**Number of families:** 2 families

## PHYSICAL CHARACTERISTICS

"Monotreme" means "one opening" and refers to the single rear orifice, or opening, that these animals have for getting rid of wastes, laying eggs, and mating. The lower intestine, excretory system (system that gets rid of wastes), and reproductive system all end at this opening, called the cloaca (kloh-AY-kah). This feature is common in reptiles and birds but extremely rare among mammals.

Trying to describe a "typical" monotreme (MAHN-ah-treem) is difficult, since the only two living types, the platypus and the echidna (ih-KID-nah), do not look much alike at first glance. The platypus is built in a streamlined manner, like an otter, has soft fur, and its snout resembles a duck's bill, while the echidna looks like a pudgy, waddling watermelon covered with fur and sharp spines, with a narrow, hornlike snout. Although echidnas may look overweight, most of the soft tissue mass that might be mistaken for blubber is muscle, lots of it. The platypus is semi-aquatic, hunting animal food underwater but sheltering in a dry burrow, but the echidnas are land animals that forage, or search, in the soil for insects and worms.

Adult platypus are about the size of house cats, while echidnas range from twice to three times as large as a house cat. An adult platypus weighs from 3 to 5 pounds (1.4 to 2.3 kilograms), and its adult head and body length runs 12 to 18 inches (30 to 46 centimeters), the tail adding another 4 to 6 inches (10 to 15 centimeters). The short-beaked, or short-nosed, echidna can grow up to 14 pounds (6.4 kilograms), with a head and body

phylum

class

subclass

● **order**

monotypic order

suborder

family

length of up to 21 inches (53 centimeters), the stubby tail adding another 3 or 4 inches (7.6 to 10 centimeters). The long-beaked, or long-nosed, echidna weighs up to twenty pounds, with a head and body length ranging from 18 to 31 inches (45 to 77.5 centimeters), while the tail, like that of the short-nosed echidna, is a mere stubby shoot. Male platypus and male echidnas are larger than females.

Platypus and echidnas are often called "primitive" because they carry a number of reptilian, or reptile-like, characteristics along with typically mammalian features. Ever since the first discovery of monotremes by Europeans in the late 1700s, zoologists, scientists who study animals, have been busy studying this mix of details in order to place the monotremes properly in the framework of mammalian evolution. Even more confusing is that the living monotremes have a number of modified, or changed, features all their own, examples being the snouts of platypus and echidnas.

The most well-known and special feature of the monotremes, and the one that seems most reptilian, is that the females lay eggs rather than giving live birth. Monotremes are the only living, egg-laying mammals. Other characteristics that platypus and echidnas have in common are similar skeletons and highly modified snouts equipped with nerves whose endings are sensitive to pressure and to natural electricity. Monotremes have fur, but not whiskers, while the echidnas, in addition to fur, have sharp, defensive spines, which are modified hairs, scattered over their backs and sides.

Monotremes walk in a reptilian manner, like alligators and crocodiles. Like the arms of someone in the middle of doing a pushup, the upper bones of monotreme forelimbs and hindlimbs go straight out from the body, horizontal to the ground, and the lower limb bones go straight down. Other lines of mammal evolution have abandoned this clumsy sort of movement and now carry their entire legs vertically beneath their bodies. Zoologists are not yet sure if the push-up style of legs and walking in monotremes is something left over from their reptilian ancestors or if they are more recent changes to fit their lifestyles.

Another odd monotreme characteristic is that male and female platypus, and male echidnas, have short, sharp, hollow, defensive spurs on the inner sides of the ankles of their rear limbs. The spurs of the male platypus connect with poison glands and are fully functional as stingers.

## GEOGRAPHIC RANGE

Monotremes are found in Australia and New Guinea. Platypus are found in Australia, including the southern island of Tasmania. Echidnas are found in Australia, Tasmania, and New Guinea. Fossil evidence from sixty-three million years ago confirms that monotremes once lived in South America, dating back to a remote time when the continents of Australia, Antarctica, and South America were closer to one another and connected by dry land.

## HABITAT

Platypus live alongside bodies of fresh water, in tropical and temperate (mild) regions of eastern Australia. Echidnas live in most of the wet and dry biomes of Australia, and in the lowland and highland tropical forests of New Guinea.

## DIET

Platypus hunt underwater, snagging and eating various small water creatures. The short-beaked echidna shovels soil and tears up logs for ants and termites, while the long-beaked echidna digs up and eats mainly earthworms.

## BEHAVIOR AND REPRODUCTION

The most well-known feature of monotremes is their method of reproduction. They are the only living mammals in which females lay eggs instead of giving live birth. The length of time the egg remains within the mother is short, only twelve to twenty days. While the egg is still within the mother's oviduct (the tube leading from the ovaries to the cloaca), the tissues of the oviduct secrete a shell onto the egg, as happens in birds and egg-laying reptiles. The monotreme eggshell is soft and leathery, and porous enough to soak up nutrients secreted into the oviduct from the mother's circulatory system.

The embryo begins its development before the egg is laid. When the mother lays her egg, the embryo has already developed to about the same degree as a newborn marsupial. The eggshell is leathery, like a reptile's, spherical, and small, 0.5 to 0.6 inches (13 to 15 millimeters) in diameter, or the size of a grape. After about ten days of the egg's incubation, the young hatches by tearing at the shell by means of a temporary egg tooth on its snout. When the youngster is fully hatched, it nestles close to the mother and feeds on her milk. The young are weaned at four to six months of age.

Female echidnas and platypus may lay up to three eggs at a time, but one is normal, and monotreme females usually bear and raise only one young per year. Females do all the raising of the young. Except during the mating season, individual platypus and echidnas of both sexes lead solitary lives.

A platypus mother incubates her eggs by curling her tail and holding the eggs between the tail and her warm underbelly. She incubates and nurses her young in a "birth chamber" burrow, which she digs and lines with moist leaves and water plants to maintain humidity. Echidna mothers form simple, temporary pouches by constricting special long muscles of their underbellies, and in which they incubate the eggs and later carry the developing young.

The monotremes are unique in yet another way. They are the only mammals to carry a sensory system that detects electricity, along with their usual senses of sight, hearing, etc. The platypus bill contains tiny electroreceptors, specialized sensory nerve endings arranged in rows along the length of the bill, on the upper and lower surfaces. These detect electricity from the muscular systems of underwater animals that the platypus hunts, and even from the electricity created by water as it flows over rocks on the bottom of the lake or river. The electroreceptors are located together with mechanoreceptors that detect underwater turbulence. Together, the two senses allow the platypus to put together a three-dimensional "picture" of its underwater hunting territory.

The bills of echidnas also have electroreceptors, though much fewer than in platypus. Biologists have confirmed the platypus's use of the electrosense, while this has not been found working in echidnas. Most likely the echidnas are gradually losing the electrosense while platypus have developed it into one of nature's most complex sensory systems.

## MONOTREMES AND PEOPLE

The special features of monotremes that set them apart from other mammals make them subjects of fascination and curiosity. Nearly everyone has heard about the platypus and knows that it is an egg-laying mammal. The reptilian features of the living monotremes provide a valuable window back in time to when reptiles were evolving into mammals.

Platypus fur was once a valued commodity because of its softness and fine texture. Hunting of the platypus in the late

1800s and early 1900s nearly drove the animals to extinction. Strict laws within Australia now protect platypus and echidnas, and the animals are fairly abundant today.

Echidnas in New Guinea are sometimes considered pests because they dig up gardens and farmland in their unending search for ants, termites, and earthworms. Habitat loss threatens the long-nosed echidna because it is confined to upland New Guinean forest, a limited habitat. The New Guinean echidnas are also hunted for food.

## CONSERVATION STATUS

Platypus and short-nosed echidnas are protected by law in Australia. Platypus are fairly plentiful in their somewhat limited area. Short-nosed echidnas are plentiful and widespread, because they can live in many different types of biome. Long-nosed echidnas are Endangered, and under serious threat in New Guinea from loss of habitat and being hunted for food with the help of trained dogs.

Probably the most serious problem facing these animals is being hunted, killed, and eaten by carnivorous mammals introduced to Australia and New Guinea by Europeans, such as dogs, cats, rats, and foxes. Native animals prey on the monotremes as well, including some of the larger lizards and the dingo, a breed of dog that the ancestors of the Aborigines brought with them when they colonized Australia thousands of years ago.

## FOUR WORDS

One of the shortest telegrams ever sent was the one that confirmed the fact that platypus and echidnas lay eggs instead of giving live birth. Aboriginals and white settlers had been asserting this for decades, but it seemed so improbable that zoologists insisted on proof. The Scottish zoologist William Hay Caldwell traveled to Australia in 1884 to study platypus and echidnas in the wild. Aboriginals, with their excellent tracking skills, helped by catching the animals in the wilderness and bringing them to Caldwell. When he finally did confirm that echidnas and platypus are egg-layers, he sent the following telegram, on September 2, 1884 to the British Association for the Advancement of Science, which was holding its annual meeting in Montreal: "Monotremes oviparous, ovum meroblastic." The words meant that monotremes lay eggs, and the eggs have large yolks, like birds' eggs.

## FOR MORE INFORMATION

### Books:

Augee, M. L., ed. *Platypus and Echidnas.* Australia: Royal Zoological Society of New South Wales, 1992.

Moyal, Ann. *Platypus: the Extraordinary Story of How a Curious Creature Baffled the World.* Australia: Allen & Unwin Pty Ltd, 2002.

## Periodicals:

Pascual, Rosendo, et al. "First Discovery of Monotremes in South America." *Nature* 356, no. 6371 (April 1992): 704–706.

Krubitzer, L. "What Can Monotremes Tell Us About Brain Evolution?" *Philosophical Transactions of the Royal Society of London, Biological Sciences* 353, no. 1372 (July 1998): 1127–1146.

Pettigrew, J. D., P. R. Manger, and S. L. B. Fine. "The Sensory World of the Platypus." *Philosophical Transactions of the Royal Society of London, Biological Sciences* 353, no. 1372 (July 1998): 1199–1210.

Pettigrew, J. D. "Electroreception in Monotremes." *Journal of Experimental Biology* 202, no. 10 (1999): 1447–1454.

Vergnani, Linda. "On the Trail of Scientific Oddballs (Peggy Rismiller Studies Echidnas)." *The Chronicle of Higher Education* 48, no. 11 (2001): A72.

## Web sites:

Australian Platypus Conservancy. http://www.totalretail.com/platypus (accessed on June 29, 2004).

"Links for Platypus and Echidnas." Department of Anatomy & Physiology, University of Tasmania, Hobart. http://www.healthsci.utas.edu.au/medicine/research/mono/References.html (accessed on June 29, 2004).

Pelican Lagoon Research Centre (for echidnas and other animals). http://www.echidna.edu.au/index.html (accessed on June 29, 2004).

ECHIDNAS
Tachyglossidae

**Class:** Mammalia
**Order:** Monotremata
**Family:** Tachyglossidae
**Number of species:** 2 species

family

CHAPTER

phylum

class

subclass

order

monotypic order

suborder

▲ **family**

## PHYSICAL CHARACTERISTICS

Echidnas (ih-KID-nahz), also called spiny anteaters, are solidly built, short-legged, shuffling mammals that can grow fairly large, up to 14 pounds (6.5 kilograms) for the short-beaked (or short-nosed) echidna and up to 20 pounds (9 kilograms) for the long-beaked (or long-nosed). Head and body length in an adult short-beaked echidna can reach 21 inches (53 centimeters), the stubby tail adding another 3.5 inches (9 centimeters). Head and body length in adult long-beaked echidnas gets as long as 30.5 inches (77.5 centimeters), and the tail, like that of the short-beaked echidna, is a mere stubby shoot. Male echidnas are larger than females. Although echidnas may look overweight, most of the soft tissue mass that might be mistaken for blubber is muscle, lots of it.

The two species look similar but some differences are obvious, especially the snout, which is made of bone, cartilage, and keratin (what claws and fingernails are made of). The snout is shorter and straight or slightly upturned in the short-beaked echidna, but longer, thinner, and downcurving, like the bill of a nectar-sipping bird, in the long-beaked echidna. An echidna's head is small and the neck is not obvious, so that the head seems to flow directly into the body.

Echidnas have full coats of brown or black hair, with scattered, hollow spines, which are really modified hairs, studding the body on the back and sides. The spines are yellow with black tips in some animals, and up to 2.4 inches (6 centimeters) long. In short-beaked echidnas, the spines are longer than the fur, so that the spines are noticeable, but the coat of the long-beaked echidna is just the opposite: the fur is long enough to cover most of the spines.

The four legs are short, with powerful muscles and claws, proper for an animal that frequently digs in the soil and tears open logs and termite mounds. The hind feet point backwards, and are used to push soil away and out when the animal is burrowing.

## GEOGRAPHIC RANGE

The short-beaked echidna lives throughout Australia, Tasmania, and the lowlands of New Guinea. The long-beaked echidna lives only in the New Guinea highlands.

## HABITAT

The short-beaked echidna lives wherever its main food sources, ants and termites, are abundant enough to keep it fed, allowing the species to occupy nearly all habitat types in Australia and New Guinea, from tropical rainforest and grassland to desert. The long-beaked echidna is confined to alpine meadows up to 12,000 feet (3,660 meters) above sea level, and to humid mountain forests in the New Guinea highlands.

## DIET

The short-beaked echidna feeds mainly on ants and termites, but varies its menu with beetles, and grubs, and the like. The animal forages (searches for food) usually by day, or in early morning and evening during very hot weather. It digs up soil, and tears open rotten logs and termite mounds to get at its food. The diet of a long-beaked echidna is almost entirely earthworms, but it varies its diet with insects. The long-beaked echidna feeds at night, poking around in the soil and the blanket of fallen leaves and other litter on the forest floor, sniffing for worms and insects.

## BEHAVIOR AND REPRODUCTION

Echidnas are monotremes, their only living relative being the platypus, and the three species together are the only living, egg-laying mammals. The mother echidna bears a single, small egg with a leathery shell that she tucks into a temporary pouch, where the offspring will hatch and nurse itself on milk excreted through pores (but no nipples) in the mother's skin within the pouch.

## THE ANTEATER SYNDROME

Besides echidnas, several kinds of unrelated mammals that eat mostly ants and termites have evolved in several parts of the world. The others are the anteaters of Central and South America, the aardvark of Africa, the pangolins of Africa and Asia, and the numbat of Australia. Mammals that feast mainly on ants and termites need to be born with certain natural, built-in tools for the job, and all these creatures have them: long, sticky, whiplike tongues that can shoot out of narrow, elongated, tube-shaped snouts; powerful, curved, hooklike claws and heavily muscled limbs for tearing apart termite castles or digging up ant colonies; and powerfully muscled bodies. These animals either have no teeth at all or lose them before they mature (echidnas, New World anteaters, pangolins), lose most of their teeth but keep a few (aardvarks), or seem to be slowly losing their teeth over evolutionary time (numbats).

These ant-eating animals have keen senses of scent and hearing, poor eyesight, and walk clumsily because their long, curved claws slow their gait. They are not diverse. There is only one species of numbat and one of aardvark, two of echidnas, four of New World anteaters, and seven of pangolins. Individual animals of these species lead solitary lives, socialize only to mate, and females nearly always bear and raise one young at a time.

If threatened, an echidna has several options for defense. It can run, climb a tree, or swim. Echidnas do these things quite well. It can wedge itself into a small cranny between rocks, anchoring itself with its paws and spines. If in the open, the echidna can dig itself a hole well within a minute, burying itself, leaving some of the spines on its back poking above the soil as a final barrier.

## ECHIDNAS AND PEOPLE

Echidnas are not as well known as the platypus, but they fascinate naturalists and zoologists for the same reasons: they lay eggs, have a combination of reptilian and mammalian characteristics, and remind us of a time when reptiles were evolving into mammals.

## CONSERVATION STATUS

The short-beaked echidna is still plentiful in Australia, and has no special conservation status listing at present. The long-beaked echidna of New Guinea, on the other hand, is faring poorly. Its forest habitat is being cleared for logging, mining, and agriculture, and people hunt the echidna for food with packs of trained dogs. Because of these threats, the long-beaked echidna is listed as Endangered.

Short-beaked echidna (*Tachyglossus aculeatus*)

## SHORT-BEAKED ECHIDNA
### *Tachyglossus aculeatus*

**Physical characteristics:**   The short-beaked echidna is a compact, heavily muscled, short-legged creature covered with fur and an array of sharp spines. From a distance, it looks and moves something like a porcupine. Up close, it looks less like a porcupine and more like a waddling shrub of grass-like leaves and sharp thorns with a long, probing twig (the snout) at the forward end.

Adult short-beaked echidnas range in head and body length from 14 to 21 inches (35 to 53 centimeters), the stubby tail adding another 3.5 inches (8.9 centimeters). Males weigh about 14 pounds (6 kilograms), while females weigh about 10 pounds (4.5 kilograms).

*The short-beaked echidna can use its spines and claws to stay wedged in a small space for protection. If it cannot hide, the echidna can roll into a ball, leaving its spines exposed. (Illustration by Barbara Duperron. Reproduced by permission.)*

The pelt (fur) varies in color and thickness throughout the species' range, being darker and thicker as one moves south. In northern Australia, echidna pelts are light brown, while in Tasmania they are black.

**Geographic range:**   Australia, Tasmania, and the lowlands of New Guinea.

**Habitat:**   The short-beaked echidna can live in nearly any habitat where it can count on a steady food supply of ants and termites. This adaptability has allowed the species to occupy nearly all habitat types in Australia and New Guinea, from tropical rainforest and grassland to desert.

**Diet:**   Short-beaked echidnas are ground foragers that feed by wandering across fields and forest floors, sniffing and lightly poking at the soil with their hard snouts, then gouging out dirt with their powerful legs and claws from an area where the animal has detected ants, termites, worms, or other soil-living creatures. Or, an echidna may tear open a rotten log to get at ants, or a termite mound for termites. Once an echidna has exposed the insects or worms, it shoots out its long, ropy, sticky tongue, laps up the insects, then reels in the tongue, loaded along its length with up to twenty insects at a time.

**Behavior and reproduction:**   Short-beaked echidnas have one annual breeding season, July through August. Courtship behavior in echidnas is a sight not soon forgotten, since several males will follow single file in an "echidna train" behind a female for one to six weeks. Sooner or later, the female halts and the males encircle her continuously, gouging out a circle of dirt around her. The female at last selects one male from the gang and mates with him, after which the two part and go separate ways. Fathers do not help with raising the young.

About twenty-four days after mating, the female lays her egg. When the mother senses that the egg is ready to emerge, she lays on her back and guides it as it slowly rolls down and over her underbelly and into the pouch, which closes to hold and shelter the egg.

A newly hatched echidna is the size of a jellybean. The mother carries the hatchling in her pouch for fifty to fifty-five days. She then removes the youngster and hides it in a burrow or cave, returning every five days to nurse the infant. The youngster is able to move about and forage but continues to nurse until it is six months old, and becomes independent at one year of age.

To protect itself, a short-beaked echidna may wedge itself into small spaces in burrows, rocks, or tree roots, where it can secure itself by using its claws and spines to wedge its body within the space. If caught in the open, the echidna can roll itself into a ball, head and legs tucked underneath and the protective spines pointing outward. It can also burrow and bury itself in the soil within a minute, leaving only its topmost spines visible as a final defense.

**Short-beaked echidnas and people:**   Most people in Australia are either fond of echidnas or indifferent toward them. They are not considered pest animals.

**Conservation status:**   Short-beaked echidnas are protected by law in Australia, and are plentiful there, since they can adapt to a wide range of habitats. Despite their high population, their numbers are declining. Research on short-beaked echidnas is ongoing at Pelican Lagoon Research Center on Kangaroo Island, Australia.  ■

## FOR MORE INFORMATION

### Books:

Kennedy, Michael, compiler. *Australasian Marsupials and Monotremes: An Action Plan for Their Conservation.* Gland, Switzerland: IUCN, Species Survival Commission, Australasian Marsupial and Monotreme Specialist Group, 1992.

Rismiller, Peggy. *The Echidna: Australia's Enigma.* Westport, CT: Hugh Lauter Levin Associates, 1999.

Stodart, Eleanor. *The Australian Echidna.* Boston: Houghton Mifflin Company, 1991.

**Periodicals:**

Griffiths, M., B. Green, R. M. C. Leckie, M. Messer, and K.W. Newgrain. "Constituents of Platypus and Echidna Milk." *Australian Journal of Biological Science* no. 37 (1984): 323–329.

Vergnani, Linda. "On the Trail of Scientific Oddballs. (Peggy Rismiller studies echidnas)." *The Chronicle of Higher Education* 48, no. 11 (Nov 9, 2001): A72(1).

**Web sites:**

*Echidna Central.* http://www.isidore-of-seville.com/echidnas (accessed on June 29, 2004)

Pelican Lagoon Research Centre, Australia. http://www.echidna.edu.au/ (accessed on June 29, 2004).

## DUCK-BILLED PLATYPUS
### Ornithorhynchidae

**Class:** Mammalia

**Order:** Monotremata

**Family:** Ornithorhynchidae

**One species:** Duck-billed platypus (*Ornithorynchus anatinus*)

## PHYSICAL CHARACTERISTICS

A platypus, at first glance, resembles an otter with a duck's bill on its face and a beaver's tail in back. An adult platypus, about the size of a house cat, weighs from 3 to 5 pounds (1.5 to 2.5 kilograms), its adult head and body length runs 12 to 18 inches (30 to 45 centimeters), and the tail adds another 4 to 6 inches (10 to 15 centimeters). Males are larger than females.

The snout, despite its duckbill shape, is soft, moist, and rubbery in texture, not hard like a bird's beak. The bill has an upper and lower section, like that of a mammal or bird, and the jaw hinging and motions are like those of mammals. The nostrils are set close together on the top of the upper bill.

The word "platypus" means "flat feet," referring to the animal's webbed, somewhat ducklike feet. The scientific name, *Ornithorhynchus anatinus*, means, in Latin, "bird-snout, resembling a duck." The plural is "platypuses" or just "platypus."

Most of the body is covered with fine, soft fur. The pelt color varies from dark amber to very dark brown on the platypus's back and sides, and from grayish white to yellowish brown on the underbelly. Platypus fur is fine, soft, and dense, with up to 900 hairs per square inch of skin. The fur has two layers, an undercoat with a woolly texture and an overcoat of coarser hair. As the platypus dives, the two fur layers trap a layer of air next to the skin, thus keeping the body dry and helping to insulate it against cold while the platypus swims, often throughout the night, and sometimes in temperatures close to freezing.

The body is somewhat flattened and streamlined. The limbs are short and muscular. As in other monotremes, the limbs of

phylum

class

subclass

order

monotypic order

suborder

▲ **family**

the platypus are set in a permanent push-up position, the upper limb bones extending out from the sides of the body, horizontal to the ground, the lower limb bones going straight down. Although an excellent swimmer, the platypus is clumsy when trying to walk on land, and seldom does so anyway, except within its tunnels, since it burns up twice as much body energy moving about on land as it does swimming underwater.

All four feet have five claws apiece and are webbed, but the webbing of the front feet extends in a flat flange beyond the toes when the platypus swims. Back on land or in its burrow, the animal folds the extra webbing under its forefeet and walks on its knuckles. The platypus uses the forelimbs and forefeet for swimming and digging, while using the hind feet and claws as combs to keep the fur clean and waterproof.

The eyes are small and the external ears are mere holes in the skull, although the internal structure of the ears is like that of other mammals. There are two long grooves for protecting the eyes and ears, a single groove surrounding both the eye and ear on each side. These grooves are closed underwater, shutting both eyes and ears, when the platypus dives to hunt for food. Out of water, the senses of sight and hearing are sharp.

Both hind limbs of the male bear hollow, pointed, poison spurs mounted on the insides of the ankles, just above the heels. There are venom glands, one in each thigh, called the "crural glands" because they are controlled by the crural nerves, which are major motor nerves of the hindlimbs. The glands secrete venom that is passed through ducts to the sharp spurs, which the platypus can erect like jacknife blades and stab into other animals.

Both sexes have the spurs when they are young. At four months of age, male spurs are protected by a covering of whitish, chalky material that sloughs off completely by the end of the first year of age. Females bear smaller, useless spurs, without venom, that they shed by ten months of age.

The platypus's flat, beaverlike tail is used as a swimming rudder, a shovel, for fat storage, and by the mother for keeping eggs and young warm. The tail can store up to fifty percent of a platypus's total load of body fat. Female platypus use the tail to carry leaves to the nesting chamber, and both sexes use it to sweep loosened soil out of the way when digging. The tail has no fine fur, only coarse, bristly hair on its upper surface to aid in carrying or sweeping.

## GEOGRAPHIC RANGE

Platypus are found only in mainland Australia and the southern island of Tasmania. Platypus are distributed along Australia's east coast, to about 500 miles (800 kilometers) inland, from Cooktown, Queensland to Melbourne, Victoria, and into Tasmania.

## HABITAT

All platypus live on the edges of freshwater bodies like lakes, ponds, rivers, and streams, in tropical and temperate regions.

## DIET

The platypus eats small freshwater animals, which it hunts at night, underwater, with its eyes and ears closed. It finds and catches underwater creatures that are swimming or sunken in the bottom mud by tracking them down with its sensitive bill, which can detect electricity and motion.

Diet is varied, including adult and larval water insects, crayfish (called "yabbies" in Australia), fish, frogs, tadpoles, snails, spiders, freshwater mussels, worms, fish eggs, and unlucky insects that fall into the water from overhanging trees. Occasionally, platypus probe for food at the edge of the water, grubbing under rocks or among roots of plants. A platypus must eat one third to one half of its body weight in food every day.

## BEHAVIOR AND REPRODUCTION

Platypus are either solitary, or a male and female may live together, sharing a burrow. Platypus build two types of burrows along the banks of creeks and ponds. One is a "camping burrows," an all-purpose shelter for male and female; the other is the "nesting burrow," built only by the female, and containing a breeding chamber, or room, for birthing and raising the young. Both sorts of burrows keep their entrances at, slightly above, or below water level, the entrance tunnel climbing at an angle a few feet above water level to prevent flooding of the burrow. The openings can be difficult to spot, since platypus prefer to build them as hidden as possible in sturdy, concave banks with reeds and other aquatic plants at the water's edge, and overhanging sod and tree roots.

A burrow's entrance tunnel is barely wide enough to allow the platypus to pass, so that when the animal emerges from water and forces itself through the entrance tunnel, water on the pelt is squeezed and sponged off, and the platypus's fur is dry when it enters the main tunnel. A platypus may have up to a dozen camping burrows strung along the banks of its territory, providing numerous nearby, safe havens. The animal rotates the burrows for shelter, staying at each a few days, probably to keep down its population of parasites.

A nesting burrow can be as long as 90 feet (30 meters), with two or more branching tunnels that circle about and eventually lead to the central nesting chamber.

Platypus normally hunt and feed at night, but have been seen doing so in the daytime. In the water, a platypus propels itself with powerful strokes of its forelimbs, the extended webbing adding extra push to the motions. It uses the hindlimbs and tail only for steering. As it swims, the platypus swings its head from side to side, allowing a full scan of its surroundings with its sensitive bill. The platypus feeds by snagging swimming creatures with its bill and by rousting them out of stream bottom mud and gravel, shoveling it up with its bill to put buried creatures to flight, then catching them as they try to escape.

Since the platypus must breathe air, it combines underwater hunting with trips to the surface to exhale and inhale. It will usually stay submerged for about a minute at a time, although it can stay submerged for up to five minutes. Platypus blood is especially rich in red cells and hemoglobin, the substance in blood that carries oxygen. The platypus can also ration its blood oxygen supply by reducing its heartbeat from two hundred beats per minute to ten beats per minute.

When not out hunting, a platypus rests in its burrow for up to seventeen hours a day. Platypus are active throughout the year, even in cooler southern Australia and Tasmania, where water temperature drops nearly to the freezing point. Individuals have been known to go into periods of torpor, or sluggishness and reduced activity with a lowering of body temperature, during the coldest months. Such a period, which can last up to six days, is not true hibernation but allows the animal to conserve energy in cold times.

Platypus are for the most part silent. Some naturalists have heard threatened platypus make soft, growling sounds that are only audible at close range. Lifespans for platypus in captivity and in the wild can reach sixteen years.

Platypus mate from August to October. Following an elaborate courtship ritual that includes the male holding on to the female's tail, and the pair swimming in slow circles, the two copulate in the water. Then the female tends to the nesting burrow

## SEEING ELECTRICITY AND PRESSURE?

The monotremes, the echidnas and platypus, are the only living mammals that are known to have an ability to sense electricity. The platypus bill is something unique in nature, so sophisticated and advanced that no one can call the platypus "primitive." The skin surface of the bill contains 40,000 tiny electroreceptors, or specialized sensory nerve endings, arranged in rows along the length of the bill. These detect tiny, underwater bursts of electricity from the muscles of swimming creatures that the platypus hunts. The electroreceptors are intermingled with 60,000 mechanoreceptors, nerves ending at the skin in tiny "push rods" that respond to small pressure changes and detect the movements of prey animals underwater and on the bottoms of streams and ponds. Together, the two senses allow the platypus to home in on prey.

In addition to detecting bursts of electricity from prey animals, the electroreceptors in a platypus's bill can probably detect the tiny electric currents made by water flowing over and around rocks and sunken logs, thus producing a three-dimensional map of a river or lake bottom within the platypus brain. In the platypus, the combined abilities of electroreception and mechanoreception are so sensitive and detailed that they have become something like vision, providing a three-dimensional "view" of the platypus's underwater world, and enabling the platypus to pinpoint, in all three dimensions, the exact locations of its prey.

and chamber, carrying wet leaves and moss with her folded tail for lining the chamber, to prevent the eggs from drying out. The female lays one to three eggs in the chamber two to four weeks after mating. A typical egg is slightly oval, about half an inch in diameter (13 millimeters), with a soft, leathery shell like a reptile's.

The mother incubates the eggs by holding them against her belly fur with her tail, maintaining a constant temperature of 90°F (31.5°C). The young hatch in about ten days, each tearing through the eggshell with a temporary egg tooth. The newly hatched, inch-long young are fragile and translucent, blind and furless, and at about the same stage of development as a newly born marsupial young.

The mother, having no nipples, nurses the young with milk that comes directly from her belly skin. In about four months,

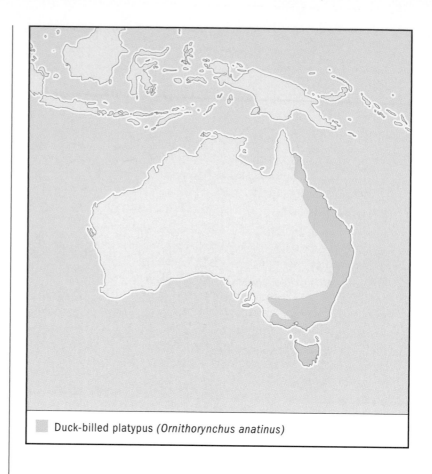

Duck-billed platypus (*Ornithorynchus anatinus*)

the young emerge for the first time from the burrow, each about a foot long and with a full coat of fur.

Predators of platypus, other than humans, include birds of prey such as hawks, eagles, and owls; Murray cod, a freshwater fish; and crocodiles. Carpet pythons, goanna lizards and rakali, or Australian water-rats, prey on young platypus in burrows. Carnivorous mammal species introduced by European settlers, including foxes, dogs, and cats, prey on platypus, although some of these predators are dealt painful ends by the poison spurs of male platypus.

## PLATYPUS AND PEOPLE

The platypus, almost as much as the kangaroo, has become a national symbol of Australia and of the odd, weird, and outright bizarre creatures native to that continent and country. The platypus is a symbol, as well, for the unique, the quirky,

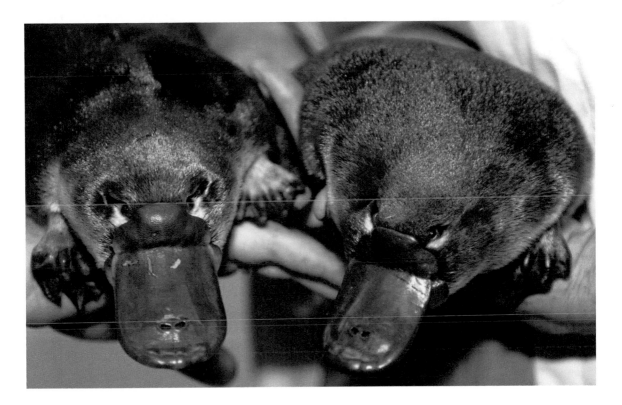

and the unexpected in nature, which makes the animal and its behavior a subject of curiosity and science education.

Platypus were nearly wiped out by hunting, into the early twentieth century, for their fine, soft, waterproof fur. Nevertheless, humans, out of carelessness and ignorance, continue to make life miserable for the platypus. The animals become entangled in fishing hooks and lines, and in fishing nets; such encounters end in drowning or in the scarring of the bill. Tasmania's platypuses are being impacted by infection from an introduced fungus and by chemical pollutants.

Well-meaning people may try to rescue a platypus that is wandering and seems to be lost, a move that often proves harmful to people and platypus. A wild platypus captured by humans will probably die of shock. The rescuers may end up with days of pain and misery from a platypus sting. Wildlife education in Australia stresses leaving lost animals alone and calling a local office of the Australian Government Department of the Environment and Heritage so that someone can professionally capture and care for a lost platypus.

*The world's first platypus twin puggles (baby platypus) born in captivity are shown together for the first time in 2003. (AFP PHOTO/Torsten BLACKWOOD. Reproduced by permission.)*

Recently, platypus have started invading human-made urban waterways in Melbourne, Victoria, while disappearing from some wild areas, for reasons still not understood. The urban platypus most likely have been forced into artificial waterways due to destruction of their habitat by development, and there is enough live platypus food in the waterways to feed a platypus population. The Australian Platypus Conservancy and the Melbourne Water Department together have surveyed and taken counts of the urban platypus populations. They found that platypus in the waterways were as healthy and well-fed as those in the wild, while some individual platypus from the waterways have migrated and re-colonized river banks with improved habitat.

## CONSERVATION STATUS

Platypus are considered "common but vulnerable" by the government of Australia. It is plentiful in some areas, but is considered vulnerable due to habitat destruction from dams, irrigation projects, being caught in fish nets and lines, and water pollution.

Platypus are strictly protected by law and harsh penalties in Australia, which is agreeable with most, if not all, Australians, since the animals are not pests and are now national emblems. The Australian government and private groups like the Australian Platypus Conservancy keep close eyes on platypus populations and have proposed relocating some of the urban platypus to suitable natural areas where they have been driven from by development in the past.

## FOR MORE INFORMATION

### Books:

Augie, M. L. *Platypus and Echidnas.* Mosman, Australia: The Royal Zoological Society of New South Wales, 1992.

Moyal, Ann Mozley. *Platypus: The Extraordinary Story of How a Curious Creature Baffled the World.* Washington, D.C.: Smithsonian Institution Press, 2001.

Short, Joan. *Platypus.* New York: Mondo Publishing, 1997.

### Periodicals:

Hughes, R.L. and L. S. Hall. "Early Development and Embryology of the Platypus." *Philosophical Transactions of the Royal Society of London* 347 (1998): 1101–1114.

Musser, A. M. "Evolution, Biogeography and Paleontology of the Ornithorhynchidae." *Australian Mammalogy* 20 (1998): 147–162.

Pettigrew, J.D., P. R. Manger, and S. L. B. Fine. "The Sensory World of the Platypus." *Philosophical Transactions of the Royal Society of London* 347 (1998): 1199–1210.

Siegel, J. M., P. R. Manger, R. Nienhuis, H. M. Fahringer, and J. D. Pettigrew. "Monotremes and the Evolution of Rapid Eye Movement Sleep." *Philosophical Transactions of the Royal Society of London* 347 (1998): 1147–1157.

Strahan, R. and D. E. Thomas. "Courtship of the Platypus, *Ornithorhynchus anatinus*." *Australian Zoologist* 18, 165–178. 1975.

**Web sites:**

*What is A Platypus? and Other Quandries: Platypus Online Resource Guide.* http://www.platypuscomputing.com/rglinks.html (accessed on June 29, 2004).

Australian Platypus Conservancy. http://www.totalretail.com/platypus (accessed on June 29, 2004).

# monotypic order
## CHAPTER

## PHYSICAL CHARACTERISTICS

The word "opossum," commonly used to refer to all species within the family Didelphidae, is derived from an Algonquian Indian word for the Virginia opossum, the only living marsupial species north of the U.S.-Mexico border. "Possum," without the first "O," refers to certain Old World marsupials in Australia and New Guinea.

Didelphidae are tiny to medium-sized animals, most tending toward the smaller end of the size spectrum. Males are larger than females. In most species, the tail is about the same length as the combined head-and-body length, or longer, scaly and only lightly furred, and is prehensile (able to grasp) to varying degrees among species. In the smallest species, adult head and body length runs 3.3 to 7.2 inches (8.5 to 18.5 centimeters) and tail length is 3.5 to 10 inches (9 to 25 centimeters). In the largest species, adult head and body length runs 13 to 19.5 inches (32.5 to 50 centimeters) and tail length is 10 to 21 inches (25.5 to 53.5 centimeters). Adult weight in the larger species is usually between 4.5 and 12 pounds (2 and 5.5 kilograms).

The limbs of Didelphidae are short, except for the yapok (or water opossum), whose hind legs are a little longer than the forelegs. All four feet bear five digits and the hallux (HAL-lux; big toe) is opposable. All digits are clawed, except for some species in which the hallux lacks a claw. The muzzle (mouth area) is long and pointed, and the ears are prominent. The canine teeth are long and large.

The fur may be fine and velvety, thick and woolly, or somewhat coarse and stiff. Pelt colors, combinations, and patterns vary widely among genera (JEN-uh-rah) and species. The brown four-eyed opossum and the gray four-eyed opossum owe their common names to a colored spot of fur above each eye. In some species, there are dark brown or black patches around the eyes.

In most Didelphidae species, the back and sides of the body are dark, the underparts lighter. Upperparts may be gray, dark brown or reddish brown, the underparts white or yellowish. The thick-tailed opossum has an elaborate coloration that varies among individuals. The upper body fur may be yellow, yellow-brown, or dark brown, while the underparts are reddish-brown, light brown, or dark brown. The fur may have an unusual purple tinge. The face may show vague markings. The body shape of this species is also unusual, tending toward a long, low-slung, weasel-like form, with short but strong legs.

## GEOGRAPHIC RANGE

In a very general sense, the Didelphidae can be said to inhabit both New World continents, from southeastern Canada to southern South America, but the common or Virginia opossum is the only marsupial making its home in the continental U.S. and Canada. All other species of Didelphidae range across Mexico, Central, and South America, from northern Mexico to southern Patagonia in South America, and on some of the Lesser Antilles Islands.

## HABITAT

The Virginia opossum inhabits the widest range of habitats of any New World opossum, being found over most of the continental United States and southeastern Canada, in forest, grassland, and desert. The other species variously inhabit tropical and subtropical forests, and a few, like the Patagonian opossum, inhabit temperate grasslands in South America. The dryland mouse opossum prefers desert-like conditions in Central America.

## DIET

Diet among Didelphidae is omnivorous, with some variation among species. Food sources include insects, small reptiles, small mammals, especially rodents, birds' eggs, fruits, seeds, snails, freshwater crustaceans, earthworms, and carrion. One species is skilled at subduing scorpions. The yapok, or water

## "NEW WORLD" MARSUPIALS?

When you hear or read the word "marsupial," you probably think of kangaroos, koalas, and Australia. Maybe you think of New Guinea, the big tropical island just north of Australia, and its hordes of tree kangaroos and other marsupial types, or the Virginia opossum, the only wild marsupial in North America north of Mexico. South and Central America might not even come to mind, but an extraordinary seventy-five species of marsupial mammals live today on those landmasses, from the deserts of northern Mexico through the forests of Central and South America, and across the grasslands of Patagonia, almost to the southern tip of South America. How did they get there, on the other side of the Pacific Ocean from Australia?

Eighty million years ago, small, early mammals, including marsupials, were flourishing. Today's southern continents were united in a supercontinent called Gondwana, which split from the northern supercontinent, Laurasia, made up of the present-day northern continents, around 160 million years ago. The two giant continents continued to split apart into the continents of the present day. The southern continents of Australia, Antarctica, and South America remained joined into a great landmass that allowed early animals to wander freely back and forth across the landmass. Ninety million years ago, Antarctica separated from South America, isolating South America (which had lost its connection with Laurasia 160 million years ago), and isolating the ancestors of the Australian marsupials and monotremes in what would become the present-day island continent of Australia and its large satellite island, New Guinea. South America, like Australasia (Australia and nearby islands), became a continent-sized refuge for early marsupial types, although these would be sharing the continent with placental mammals. By forty million years ago, marsupials had become extinct in North America, Africa, Asia, and Antarctica but flourished in Australasia and South America, where they continued to evolve and diversify.

opossum, hunts and eats freshwater fish. Some species store fat in the bases of their tails to carry them through the lean months.

## BEHAVIOR AND REPRODUCTION

New World opossums are marsupials, mammals that give birth to tiny, only partly developed young that crawl into the mother's pouch, latch their jaws tightly onto a milk nipple, and finish their development. Most mammals are placental, meaning that they carry their young in the womb for longer periods before birthing them, and these are born in a more completely developed state. "Marsupial" comes from "marsupium," the Latin word for pouch or bag, and names that special feature of marsupials.

Not all species have females with complete, functional pouches. In species without pouches, newborn young just cling with their jaws onto the mother's nipples and grasp her fur, remaining so until weaning, or stopping breastfeeding, and clinging to the mother wherever she goes. Some of the non-pouched opossums have partial pouches that cover only the rows of nipples on either side, and run the length of the underbelly. Females may have from five to as many as twenty-five nipples. In the common large opossum species, a typical female has a functional, snug, fur-lined pouch and thirteen nipples inside, arranged in a circle, with one nipple in the center, although the number of nipples may vary among species and even among individual females within a species.

American opossums may have definite mating seasons in more temperate regions, or may breed anytime of the year in the tropics. Litter sizes generally run between four and nine young. As many as sixteen young, or a record fifty-two for the Virginia opossum, may be born in a single litter. In such large litters, some of the young are likely to die before weaning, depending on the number of nipples the mother has. The gestation period is short, about two weeks, followed by up to ten weeks of pouch life. When leaving the pouch, the young may still nurse and ride on their mother's back for another month before striking off on their own. Individuals reach reproductive age at four months to one year. Lifespans among Didelphidae species are short, only one to five years.

For shelter, some American opossum species build nests of twigs and leaves, or of grasses; others dig their own burrows or use burrows abandoned by other animals, abandoned birds' nests, or shelter in hollow logs and among rocks.

All but a few species are nocturnal (nighttime) foragers, and as far as anyone knows, all are solitary, breaking that rule only during mating times. Outside of the mating season, same-sex individuals of a species, upon meeting, ignore or threaten each other. During the breeding season, a male and female may stay together for several days. Some species are mainly arboreal (spending most of their time in trees), others forage on the ground, and some do both. The Patagonian opossum is an excellent swimmer in freshwater, where it hunts for fish, even though it is not as specialized as the water opossum.

## NEW WORLD OPOSSUMS AND PEOPLE

As a whole, the Didelphidae are no threat or bother to humans. People hunt and eat some species and use their fur for clothing and parts of clothing. The gray short-tailed opossum frequents houses in South America, where it is welcome because it hunts and eats rodents and insects infesting the houses.

Brown four-eyed opossums, gray four-eyed opossums, woolly opossums, and common mouse opossums occasionally raid fruit and corn crops. The southern opossum, and the white-eared opossum sometimes kill poultry.

## CONSERVATION STATUS

Out of all the Didelphidae species, the IUCN lists three as Critically Endangered (facing an extremely high risk of extinction), three as Endangered (facing a very high risk of extinction), fifteen as Vulnerable (facing a high risk of extinction), and eighteen as Near Threatened (close to becoming threatened with extinction).

Virginia opossum *(Didelphis virginiana)*

## VIRGINIA OPOSSUM
### *Didelphis virginiana*

**Physical characteristics:** The Virginia opossum is one marsupial that a majority of Americans have surely seen, if only as roadkill. These opossums have low-slung, vaguely rat-shaped bodies that in adults can weigh up to 14 pounds (6.4 kilograms). Males are larger than females. Adult head and body length can reach 20 inches (50 centimeters), and the tail length can reach 18 inches (47 centimeters). The body fur is light to dark grayish, due to a coat of white fur with black tips under a longer coat of pale guard hairs. The head is white and elongated, and studded with long whiskers. In some individuals, the gray coat may extend in a stripe across the crown, tapering to an end between the eyes. The eyes are black and shiny. The long, strong tail is scaly, colored whitish or pinkish, and nearly hairless, much like a rat's, and is prehensile, able to grasp tree branches

Virginia opossums can eat poisonous snakes. They are immune to the venom of these snakes, including copperheads, water moccasins, and rattlesnakes. (Illustration by Jonathan Higgins. Reproduced by permission.)

and carry nesting materials. The ears, nostrils, forepaws, and hindpaws are pinkish and only sparsely furred. Each paw has five digits, and the hallux (HAL-lux; big toe) is opposable, allowing the opossum to grasp branches.

**Geographic range:**   The Virginia opossum is one of the few marsupials, in Australasia or the Americas, that is at home in temperate regions with cold winters. Its range extends as far north as Ontario, Canada, and as far south as Costa Rica in Central America. Virginia opossums are found in North America, from Central America and Mexico in the south, through the United States east of the Rocky Mountains and north into southwestern Ontario. Opossums are also found along the west coast of the United States.

**Habitat:**   Virginia opossums prefer living in forest, farmland, and suburbia with possible denning sites and a water source close at hand, but this adaptable species can survive and thrive almost anywhere, including grassland and near-desert conditions. These opossums are nomadic, seldom staying in one foraging area for more than a year. Individuals may sleep during the  day in whatever temporary shelters they find, or build nests, lined with leaves. Refuges include woodpiles, thickets, rock crevices, and in various human-made structures such as under porches and raised houses, and in barns, drainpipes, and sheds.

**Diet:**   The Virginia opossum is truly omnivorous, eating almost anything that can be considered food. A partial list of dietary preferences includes rats, mice, moles, slugs, snails, shrews, worms, beetles, ants, grasshoppers, crickets, frogs, garbage, fruit, corn, berries, and carrion.

An even more unusual source of food is poisonous snakes, to whose venoms the opossums are immune. This includes copperheads, water moccasins, and rattlesnakes.

**Behavior and reproduction:** Like most opossums, Virginia opossums live and forage, search for food, solitarily. They forage mostly at night, but sometimes during the day. If male individuals meet, they avoid each other or sound off with threat displays, with hissings, growlings, and screechings, often going on to one-on-one combat. Males fight one another ferociously during mating seasons. On the other hand, if a male and female meet during the breeding season, they will mate and then stay together for several days.

Mating seasons vary according to how far north individual opossums live. Virginia opossums begin mating in December in the southern states, in March in the northernmost states and Canada, and in January and February for areas between. In Canada and in the north and central states, females usually bear only one litter per year. Two or even three litters are common in the southern states and further south.

Young are born thirteen days after mating. Litters can range in numbers of up to twenty, with a record of fifty-two, but since the mother has only thirteen nipples, only a maximum of thirteen in a litter can survive. Newborns are scarcely bigger than rice grains. The young spend up to 100 days, or slightly over three months, in the pouch. By seventy-five to eighty-five days, the young are weaned and leave the pouch, but remain with the mother for another two or three months before leaving to live on their own. Until they leave, the mother carries the young on her back. Young males reach sexual maturity at eight months, females at six. The longest recorded lifespan in the wild for the Virginia opossum is three years, although captive individuals have lived as long as ten years.

When threatened by a predator, a Virginia opossum may react in any of several ways. Escape is always the optimal choice, and includes climbing trees and swimming. If escape proves impossible, the opossum may use its variation of the basic mammalian threat response, opening its jaws wide, baring its fifty-five teeth, and hissing at its foe. It may also discharge a foul-smelling, greenish fluid from anal glands. Or, the opossum may use its "drooling" display, building up its saliva content, drooling from its mouth and blowing froth and bubbles from its nostrils, in hopes of convincing a predator that the opossum is seriously diseased and therefore dangerous to eat.

The opossum's final defensive recourse is either fighting back or performing its most famous behavior, "playing possum." The animal collapses, the eyes glaze, the jaws open, the tongue lolls, the teeth are partly bared, and the stinky anal fluid release adds the final carrion touch. The deathlike state is a form of catatonia, in which the animal lies limp, does not react to touch or prodding, and cannot be roused by any method. The muscles become limp, basic functions slow. Predators of opossums, among them coyotes, dogs, bobcats, and birds of prey, will reject the seemingly dead opossum and leave it untouched. From one minute to six hours after the predator has left the scene, the opossum rouses itself and moves off.

Throughout its range in Canada and in parts of the United States that have long, cold winters, Virginia opossums feed to build up extra body fat in the fall in preparation for the lean winter months. The species doesn't hibernate, but in especially cold weather, individuals may stay quietly in their shelters for a few days. Otherwise, they're outside and hiking across the snow to forage.

**Virginia opossums and people:**  Virginia opossums sometimes help themselves to human garbage, but cause far less mess and destruction than do raccoons. Virginia opossums, like most mammals, can carry and transmit rabies. Virginia opossums have been, and still are, hunted for food and for their pelts.

Their ability to eat almost anything organic puts Virginia opossums in the front ranks of living nature's cleaning crews. They eat pest insects like cockroaches, garden pests like snails and slugs, pest mammals like roof rats and mice, and they eat all varieties of carrion.

**Conservation status:**  Virginia opossums have adapted to humans successfully, are in no danger of extinction, and have even extended their ranges in some areas.  ■

Water opossum *(Chironectes minimus)*

## WATER OPOSSUM
### *Chironectes mlnimus*

**Physical characteristics:** Unlike most of the New World opossums, the yapok, or water opossum, is specialized for an aquatic lifestyle. It is the only living aquatic marsupial species. In general terms, the yapok can be thought of as a sort of marsupial otter. The name "yapok" is derived from the Oyapock River in northern South America.

Adult head and body length runs 10.5 to 16 inches (27 to 40 centimeters); tail length, 12 to 17 inches (31 to 43 centimeters); and adult body weight, 1.3 to 1.7 pounds (0.6 to 0.8 kilograms). The animal is covered with short, dense, water-repellent fur, unique among the Didelphidae. The sides and upper body are black, with three pairs of

*The water opossum is the only marsupial that lives in the water. It has water-repellent fur and webbed hind feet. (Illustration by Jonathan Higgins. Reproduced by permission.)*

prominent, grayish bands that run vertically from the light gray underbelly almost to the spine. The head is blunter and wider than is common among Didelphidae species. The upper part of the head, including the eye area, is black. A dark gay bar runs the length of the snout from the nostrils to the crown. The lower part of the head is grayish. A prominent white stripe runs from above each eye to the ear. The eyes are large and black. The prominent, nearly furless ears are oval in shape. Conspicuous tufts of long, white or gray whiskers are mounted on each side of the head near the nostrils and over the eyes.

The hindfeet are webbed and the yapok uses them as its main propulsion organs when swimming. The hallux (first toe), usually shorter than the other toes in mammals, is elongated in the yapok, making the foot shape symmetrical and thus able to push more efficiently against the water. The forefeet are not webbed, and have elongated, furless fingers with reduced claws, which are furnished with a well-developed tactile sense.

Among the yapok's many peculiarities is that both females and males carry well-developed pouches that open toward the rear. The female uses a muscle to close her pouch when carrying young, which can survive without oxygen for several-minute intervals. The male uses his pouch to hold and protect the scrotum, drawing it up and into the pouch when he swims.

**Geographic range:** Yapoks are found in Central and South America, from southern Mexico and Belize through all of Central America, and into Colombia, Venezuela, the Guianas, Ecuador, Peru, Paraguay, Brazil, and northern Argentina.

**Habitat:** Yapoks live along streams, rivers, and lakes in tropical and subtropical rainforests of Central and South America, from sea level to 6,000 feet (1,830 meters) or more above sea level.

**Diet:** The yapok eats crayfish, shrimp, fish, and some water plants.

**Behavior and reproduction:** Females are polyestrous, meaning that they come into heat and become receptive to mating more than once a year. A breeding pair stays together for several days, the male following and circling the female until actual mating. A typical litter contains one to five young.

Yapok young have the fastest rate of development among all the Didelphidae species. After about forty days in the pouch, the young have grown body fur, pigmentation and the various markings, and opened their eyes. At about fifty days, the young begin to let go of the nipples and leave the pouch, but continue to suckle and stay with the mother, sometimes riding on her back.

Individual water opossums are solitary and hostile toward others of their species, except during mating times. An individual hunts and forages in freshwater streams, between rest periods, throughout the night. During the day, the animal rests in a temporary ground nest that it constructs from leaves and grass in a shady area. Close by is a more permanent underground burrow, which the yapok excavates in the stream bank, with its entrance a few inches above the water line. The entrance tunnel is about 2 feet (0.6 meters) long, and leads to a den lined with leaves or grasses. Individuals use their prehensile tails to carry nesting materials.

A yapok fishes and forages underwater, propelling itself with alternate strokes of its powerful hind legs and webbed feet. The animal shuts its eyes and ears and depends partly on its whiskers to detect motion, while its fingers, acutely sensitive to touch, are used to contact, check the texture of, and grasp prey.

The longest known lifespan for a captive yapok is three years.

**Water opossums and people:**   Water opossums, confined to forests and riversides by their specialized lifestyles, are no threat or bother to humanity. Humans hunt them for their waterproof pelts, to be made into garments and accessories.

**Conservation status:**   The yapok is listed as Near Threatened, not currently threatened, by the IUCN.  ■

## FOR MORE INFORMATION

### Books:

Nowak, Ronald. M. *Walker's Mammals of the World.* Baltimore: Johns Hopkins University Press, 1995.

Szalay, Frederick. *Evolutionary History of the Marsupials and an Analysis of Osteological Characters.* Oxford, U.K.: Cambridge University Press. 1994.

### Periodicals:

Cifelli, R. L., and Brian M. Davis. "Marsupial Origins (Paleontology)." *Science* 302, no. 5652 (December 12, 2003): 1934.

de Muizon, C., and R. L. Cifelli. "A New Basal Didelphoid (Marsupialia, Mammalia) from the Early Paleocene of Tiupampa (Bolivia)." *Journal of Vertebrate Paleontology* 21, no. 1 (2001): 8–97.

de Muizon, C., R. L. Cifelli, and R. C. Paz. "The Origin of the Dog-like Borhyaenoid Marsupials of South America." *Nature* 389, no. 6650 (Oct 2, 1997): 486–489.

Goin, F. J., et al. "New Discoveries of 'Opossum-like' Marsupials from Antarctica (Seymour Island, Medial Eocene)." *Journal of Mammalian Evolution* 6, no. 4 (1999): 335–365.

Hamrick, M. W. "Morphological Diversity in Digital Skin Microstructure of Didelphid Marsupials." *Journal of Anatomy* 198 (2001): 683–688.

## PHYSICAL CHARACTERISTICS

The New World marsupial order Paucituberculata contains only one surviving family, the Caenolestidae, or shrew opossums (the true shrews, family Soricidae, are not marsupial but placental mammals). Shrew opossums are mouse-sized marsupial mammals with dense, dark gray or brown fur. Also called mouse opossums and rat opossums, their appearance is more suggestive of shrews. Shrew opossums have long, conical, pointed snouts and tiny, beady eyes. There are three genera (JEN uh-rah; plural of genus, JEE-nus) and five species: the living members of order Paucituberculata and family Caenolestidae are relicts, little-changed survivors of a once far more diverse assemblage of genera and species. Information about them is spotty, since the animals are nocturnal and secretive, and live for the most part in remote, difficult terrain.

Head and body length across species runs from 3.5 to 5.5 inches (9 to 14 centimeters), and tail length is 3.5 to 5.5 inches (9 to 14 centimeters), the tail length being about the same as the head and body. Males are larger than females, males weighing from 1 to 1.5 ounces (25 to 41 grams), females from 0.5 to 1 ounce (16.5 to 25.5 grams). A shrew opossum has five digits on each foot, the two small outer toes of the forefeet with blunt nails, the remaining three equipped with curved, sharp, strong claws. The hind feet have strong, curved claws on all toes except the so-called great toe, which is small and carries a small nail.

The fur of shrew opossums is thick and soft, covering the entire body and less dense on the tail. The coat has a disorderly

phylum

class

subclass

order

● **monotypic order**

suborder

family

look because different areas of the coat have different textures. The fur may be dark on the dorsal (upper) parts of the body, with lighter-colored under parts, or dark all over the body. Dark colors vary from gray-brown, black-brown, to near-black. The ears are shaped much like those of typical mice, and large enough to protrude well above the thick fur. Hearing is acute, as is the tactile (touch) sense of the long whiskers.

The upper lips bear small flaps of skin on both sides, a feature found only in the Caenolestidae. The Chilean opossum has these and similar flaps on its lower lips. Their function is, so far, unknown. They may be barriers to prevent blood, pieces of flesh, and dirt from collecting on the sides of the jaws. The tail is about as long as the combined head and body. The tail fur, sparser than on the body, is the same color as the upper pelt, but may include a white tip in some individuals. The tail is not prehensile, meaning it is not able to curl around and grasp objects. The tail of the Chilean shrew opossum swells up with stored fat for the southern winter months. Females do not have pouches and have four nipples, except for females of the Chilean shrew opossum, which have seven nipples, the seventh located on the midline of the underbelly.

The rostrum, or the front part of the skull including the jaws, is long and tapering. Each of the lower incisors has only one cusp, or protruding bump on its crown, unlike most mammal teeth, hence the order name, Paucituberculata, meaning, in Latin, "few bumps," since this feature is found in all species, living and extinct, in the order.

## GEOGRAPHIC RANGE

The gray-bellied shrew opossum, the blackish shrew opossum, and the silky shrew opossum are found in isolated, separated populations in the mountains of the Western Andes, from Colombia and Venezuela in the north and southwards through Ecuador, Peru, and Argentina. The Incan shrew opossum inhabits southern Peru, while the Chilean shrew opossum lives along the south-central coast of Chile and on the close offshore Chilean island of Chiloé, plus another population in Argentina.

## HABITAT

The gray-bellied shrew opossum, the blackish shrew opossum, the silky shrew opossum, and the Incan shrew opossum live in dense vegetation in cool, rainy mountain forests and

## DYNASTY IN EXILE

Like the few poor refugees of a downfallen, once mighty civilization, the five living shrew opossum species, lurking in the undergrowth of temperate forests in South America, are but a pale afterglow of their former splendor. From seventeen to twenty-four million years ago, the order Paucituberculata included four other families besides Caenolestidae, while the caenolestids were the most abundant marsupials in terms of species during that era. The extinct Paucituberculata species had teeth specialized in unique ways, and lived in both temperate and tropical biomes throughout most of the South American continent.

The extinct families of Paucituberculata are Paleothentidae, Abderitidae, Polydolopidae, and Argyrolagidae. Species of Paleothentinae had developed an enlarged forward lower molar with a shearing crest. Abderitinae species took that molar further and equipped it with a forward-facing, sharp, high, serrated blade. The species of Polydolopidae carried a number of enlarged, forward-directed lower incisors and a pair of large shearing teeth of uncertain origin. The Polydolopidae were small marsupials, the largest no bigger than a rabbit, that behaved and were equipped much like rodents. The rodent-like Argyrolagidae resembled small kangaroos, with strong, two-toed hind feet and a long, well-muscled tail. They moved about by hopping and leaping, much like kangaroos. Family Paleothentidae evolved an impressive nine genera and nineteen species.

meadows, from 4,500 to 12,000 feet (1,500 to 4,000 meters) above sea level. The Chilean shrew opossum inhabits rainy lowland temperate rainforest along the Chilean coast from sea level to 2,270 feet (1,135 meters), preferring dense forest with mossy trees and logs, and soaking wet forest floors.

## DIET

Shrew opossums forage nocturnally, at night, on the ground, and are carnivorous (meat-eaters) with some herbivory (plant-eating). They eat insects, earthworms, small vertebrates, fruits, other plant food, and fungi, in forest floor growth and in alpine meadows, traveling among feeding areas by means of trails through ground vegetation that they maintain by constant use. A shrew opossum uses its lower canines to stab and skewer prey, then uses its sharp premolars to slice the prey into pieces.

## BEHAVIOR AND REPRODUCTION

Little is known about the particulars of breeding among shrew opossum species. Field researchers have found lactating (producing milk for young) females of the Chilean shrew opossum in February, March, May, October, November, and December, suggesting a breeding season from December through May, and no breeding from June through September, the coldest months in the Southern Hemisphere. Breeding season for the silky shrew opossum, which lives in a less stressful climate, is thought to begin in July.

Since shrew opossums are marsupials, the unborn young remain in the females' uterus (YOO-ter-us; womb) only a few days, then are born in an incomplete state, to be suckled by the mother until they complete development. Suckling shrew opossums cling to their mother as she moves about. Litters probably number up to four individuals.

If alarmed, a shrew opossum will hop forward repeatedly on all fours, a mode of locomotion unique to the Caenolestidae. Shrew opossums have also been observed climbing trees, though not foraging in trees. The animals rest during the day in hollow logs and burrows. Despite their fattened tails, Chilean shrew opossums have been observed running across packed snow in midwinter.

## SHREW OPOSSUMS AND PEOPLE

Tiny, secretive, and living in remote regions, shrew opossums have very little interaction with humanity and pose no threats.

## CONSERVATION STATUS

The World Conservation Union (IUCN) lists the Chilean shrew opossum as Vulnerable (facing a high risk of extinction), due to deforestation (removing trees) from logging.

Silky shrew opossum (*Caenolestes fuliginosus*)

| | |
|---|---|
| **SILKY SHREW OPOSSUM**<br>*Caenolestes fuliginosus* | **SPECIES<br>ACCOUNT** |

**Physical characteristics:** The silky shrew opossum is probably the best known of the shrew opossum species. Its head and body length ranges from 3.7 to 5.3 inches (9.3 to 13.5 centimeters), the tail 3.7 to 5 inches (9.3 to 12.7 centimeters). The fur on the dorsal (back) body is soft and thick, and colored a dark brown gradually giving way to lighter brown on the lower body and underbelly.

**Geographic range:** The silky shrew opossum inhabits the western Andes of northern and western Colombia, extreme western Venezuela, and Ecuador.

*Silky shrew opossums look for food on the ground at night. During the day, the animals stay in hollow logs and burrows. (Illustration by Brian Cressman. Reproduced by permission.)*

**Habitat:** This shrew opossum is nocturnal and terrestrial, preferring cool, wet areas with heavy vegetation. The species is found in alpine scrub forests and meadow zones of the Andes, at altitudes from 4,500 to 12,000 feet (1,500 to 4,000 meters).

**Diet:** Silky shrew opossums eat mostly caterpillars, centipedes, and spiders, varied with fruit.

**Behavior and reproduction:** The breeding season is believed to be July, because animals caught in August were suckling (nursing, or feeding breast milk) their young.

Silky shrew opossums run by bounding, front feet and rear feet working as units and alternating. If threatened, an individual will open its jaws wide and hiss. The tail is not prehensile (able to grab or hold things), but the animal will use it as a sort of third leg when sitting upright.

**Silky shrew opossums and people:** There is little to no interaction between silky shrew opossums and humans.

**Conservation status:** The silky shrew opossum has no special conservation status. ■

### FOR MORE INFORMATION

**Books:**

Lee, Anthony K., and Andrew Cockburn. *Evolutionary Ecology of Marsupials.* New York: Cambridge University Press, 1985.

Nowak, Ronald M. *Walker's Mammals of the World,* 6th ed. Baltimore: Johns Hopkins University Press, 1999.

Simpson, George Gaylord. *Splendid Isolation: The Curious History of South American Mammals.* New Haven, CT: Yale University Press, 1980.

Szalay, Frederick S. *Evolutionary History of the Marsupials and an Analysis of Osteological Characters.* New York: Cambridge University Press, 1995.

**Periodicals:**

Bown, T. M., and J. G. Fleagle. "New Colhuehuapian and Santacrucian Microbiotheriidae and Caenolestidae From Patagonian Argentina." *Journal of Vertebrate Paleontology* 14, no. 3 (1994): 18.

Cifelli, Richard L., and Brian M. Davis. "Marsupial Origins." (Paleontology). *Science* 302, no. 5652 (2003): 1899–1900.

Flynn, J. J., and A. R. Wyss. "New Marsupials From the Eocene-Oligocene Transition of the Andean Main Range, Chile." *Journal of Vertebrate Paleontology* 19, no. 3 (1999): 533–549.

Marshall, L. G. "Systematics of the South American Marsupial Family Caenolestidae." *Fieldiana Geology* (1980): 145.

Meserve, P. L., , B. K. Lang, and B. D. Patterson. "Trophic Relations of Small Mammals in a Chilean Temperate Rainforest." *Journal of Mammalogy* 69 (1988): 721–730.

Patterson, B. D. "Dominance of South American Marsupials (Scientific Correspondence)." *Nature* 337, no. 6204 (1989): 215.

Patterson, B. D., and M. H. Gallardo. *"Rhyncholestes raphanurus."* *Mammalian Species* 286 (1987): 1–5.

Sanchez-Villagra, M. R. "The Phylogenetic Relationships of Argyrolagid Marsupials." *Zoological Journal of the Linnean Society* 131, no. 4 (2001): 48–496.

# monotypic order
### C H A P T E R

## PHYSICAL CHARACTERISTICS

The common name monito del monte is Spanish for "little monkey of the mountain." The "monkey" aspect of the common name derives from the animal's nearly furless, somewhat monkey-like hands and feet. Another local common name for the species is colocolo. The scientific name of this species has recently been changed to *Dromiciops gliroides*, and the species may be referred to as *Dromiciops australis* even in recent writing.

As with the other living New World marsupial orders, the single living species of Microbiotheria is a remnant with a more diverse past. The fossil record has revealed an extinct genus, *Microbiotherium,* with six known species, that thrived during the Oligocene and Miocene Epochs (thirty-four million years ago to five million years ago, for a period of thirty-nine million years). Today, *D. gliroides* represents an order with only a single living species.

An adult monito del monte's size is between a rat's and a squirrel's. The head-and-body length runs 3.3 to 5 inches (8.3 to 13 centimeters). The tail length is about the same, running 3.5 to 5 inches (9 to 13.2 centimeters), The adult body weight runs about a half ounce to just over one ounce (16.7 to 31.4 grams). The animal's coat of fur is fine, short and thick. The upper body pelt is brown, with several light gray patches or spots on the shoulders and rump. The face fur is gray, the large eyes encircled with prominent black rings. The belly fur is pale tan.

The tail is completely furred, except for a furless area, about an inch long (2.5 to 3 centimeters), on the underside, at the

## MONITOS AND MISTLETOES

The thousand-or-so species of mistletoe are distributed over most of the world, including the moist temperate forests of southern South America. Mistletoes are hemiparasites, meaning partly parasitic. Although they have green leaves for photosynthesis, they live on tree branches and trunks, anchoring themselves and tapping into the wood to steal nutrients and water from the host tree. In most species of mistletoe, the seeds are spread by birds, which eat the seeds and defecate (DEF-uh-kate) them later while roosting. If they void the seeds while roosting on a tree branch, the seeds, covered with a gluey substance called viscin (VIS-in), are likely to stick to the branch and grow up to be mistletoes.

In an exception to the habit of birds being the main vectors, or transporters, for mistletoe species, the monito del monte feeds and disperses seeds of the mistletoe species *Tristerix corymbosus*. In fact, the little marsupial, as far as anyone knows, is the only disperser of the seeds of this mistletoe species. This was discovered by Guillermo Amico and Marcelo Aizen of the National University of Comahue, Argentina. During field studies, they came across numerous strings of mistletoe seeds sticking to the trunks of host trees. They were seeds of *T. corymbosus*, the fruits of which are green when ripe. Normally, green color in fruits indicates that they are not yet edible, so that fruit-eating birds will pass them up. The large number of *T. corymbosus* strings glued to tree trunks was also unusual, since birds defecate mistletoe species' seeds while roosting on tree branches. Only some of the seeds end up on branches and grow, and birds have no special ability to aim for tree trunks.

On the other hand, some mammal species consume ripe green fruit. That known fact and the sight of lots of mistletoe seeds on tree trunks indicated an arboreal, or tree-living, mammal as the seed-eater and disperser. Further searching and observing revealed that mammal to be the monito del monte. The species gorges on the mistletoe fruit. The animals peel the rinds off the fruit with their front paws, swallow the innards whole, seeds and all. Soon after a meal of mistletoefruits, the marsupial defecates almost all the seeds, undamaged by the animal's digestive system, in and on its foraging territory, which includes tree trunks and branches.

tip. The one-third of the tail closest to the body has the same sort of dense, woolly fur as the body, while the rest of the tail has straight, dark brown fur. The female's well-developed pouch is comfortably lined with light brown fur and has four nipples. The ears are moderately furred.

*Young monitos del monte first live in their mother's pouch, then in the nest, and finally ride on her back while she looks for food. (Illustration by Michelle Meneghini. Reproduced by permission.)*

As in many small marsupials, the snout is conical, cone-shaped, and tapering, but shorter than is usual among marsupials.

### GEOGRAPHIC RANGE

The monito del monte has a limited range in South America, in southern Chile, overlapping into Argentina, from Concepción, Chile, southward to and including the Chilean island of Chiloé, and inland to the Andes and just over the border into Argentina.

### HABITAT

Monitos del monte live in dense, cool, temperate rainforests, in the lowlands and the Andes mountains, from sea level to 6,000 feet (1,850 meters) above sea level. They most often live in thickets of Chilean bamboo (*Chusquea* species), especially *Chusquea valdiviensis*, the most common ground plant in these forests.

The forest type where the monito del monte makes its home is as unique as the animal itself. Called Valdivian temperate forest, it is located in a limited range in southern South America between the Andes and the Pacific Ocean, most of it in Chile with some extending into Argentina. The Valdivian forest biome is isolated from the rest of the world by deserts, mountains, and oceans. The forest is a treasure house of ancient plants and animals, some of which date back, little changed, from the time when the southern continents were all attached together, forming the ancient supercontinent of Gondwana. The Valdivian forests have been in their present isolated condition for thirty million years. A full 90 percent of the seven hundred flowering plant species there are endemic, meaning they are found no where else in the world. One third of the woody plants (trees, shrubs, woody vines) have living relatives in Australia, New Zealand, New Caledonia (an island northeast of Australia), and Tasmania, all linking to an ancient common landmass. The monito del monte is a living fossil whose relationship with other marsupials shows the same sort of geographic split as do the Valdivian plants.

Monito del monte (*Dromiciops gliroides*)

## DIET

The monito del monte is mostly insectivorous, meaning that it forages for and eats insect larvae (LAR-vee) and pupae (PYOO-pee). They also eat some plant material. They do most of their foraging at night, in the trees and on the ground. In the Southern Hemisphere in autumn, the animals gorge, doubling their body weights in a week, most of the extra weight being fat packed into the base of the tail.

## BEHAVIOR AND REPRODUCTION

Colocolos are solitary, nocturnal foragers, both in trees and on the ground. They build and shelter in globe-shaped nests of sticks and water-repelling *Chusquea* bamboo leaves, lined with moss and grass, in protected areas, and often concealed by a final overlay of gray moss. The nests are about 8 inches (20 centimeters) in diameter. Nest locations may be rock clefts, hollows of trees, or in dense ground shrubbery. The nests are snug and comfortable, but in the coldest months, monitos del monte hibernate, living off fat reserves in the base and first third of the tail.

Since monitos del monte are marsupials, birth and nurturing of the young follow the standard marsupial model: the young are born at an incomplete stage of embryonic development, crawl from the birth canal over the mother's belly fur to the pouch, and there latch onto nipples and remain so, nourished by milk, until they complete their development.

Colocolos mate in the Southern Hemisphere spring and early summer—October through December. A female has a single litter of one to four young annually. Litters of five young have been seen, but since the mother has only four nipples, the fifth cannot survive. On leaving the pouch, the young first reside in the nest, then ride on the mother's back, clinging to her fur as she forages, before beginning to forage on their own. The offspring live solitary lives but continue to associate, off and on, with the mother. The young of both sexes reach sexual maturity in two years. Males remain with females only during the breeding season. The maximum lifespan of this species is probably three to four years.

Colocolos hibernate, intermittently, in their nests, during the cool and cold months, depending on temperature and food availability. Torpor, the low state of body activity in hibernation, is triggered by absence of food over time or by outside temperature. A torpor bout, or period of lowered body functions, may last a few hours to several days (five days is the longest known bout period). Hibernating colocolos rouse themselves spontaneously, probably cued by a temperature increase in their surroundings or a signal from some internal clock. These periods of hibernation, along with the stored tail fat, enable the colocolo to conserve body energy while waiting out periods of low food availability and cold.

## MONITOS DEL MONTE AND PEOPLE

There is little interaction between these small, secretive animals and humans. In the Lake Region of Chile, a superstition holds that seeing a monito del monte in the home brings bad luck, and that the only cure is burning down the house. One the other hand, the animal's consumption of insects serves as a local control on insect populations.

Scientific value of the monito del monte is immense, because of its ancient origins and relationships.

## CONSERVATION STATUS

Monitos del monte are listed as Vulnerable, facing a high risk of extinction in the wild, on the Red List of the World Conservation Union (IUCN). The main problem facing the species is ongoing deforestation.

## FOR MORE INFORMATION

### Books:

Aplin, K. P., and M. Archer. "Recent Advances in Marsupial Systematics With a New Syncretic Classification." In *Possums and Opossums: Studies in Evolution.* Vol. I. Chipping Norton, U.K.: Surrey Beatty and Sons PTY Limited, 1987.

Feldhamer, G. A., L. C. Drickamer, S. H. Vessey, and J. F. Merritt. *Mammalogy: Adaptation, Diversity, and Ecology.* Boston: WCB McGraw-Hill, 1999.

Szalay, F. "A New Appraisal of Marsupial Phylogeny and Classification." In *Carnivorous Marsupials.* Sydney, Australia: Royal Zoological Society of New South Wales, 1982.

Vaughan, T. A., J. M. Ryan, and N. J. Czaplewski. *Mammalogy,* 4th ed. Philadelphia: Saunders College Publishing, 2000.

### Periodicals:

Amico, G., and M. A. Aizen. "Mistletoe Seed Dispersal by a Marsupial." *Nature* no. 408 (2000): 929–930.

Bozinovic, Francisco, G. Ruiz, and M. Rosenmann. "Energetics and Torpor of a South American "Living Fossil," the Microbiotheriid *Dromiciops gliroides.*" *Journal of Comparative Physiology* B 174 (2004): 93–297.

Hershkovitz, P. "Ankle Bones: The Chilean Opossum *Dromiciops gliroides* Thomas, and Marsupial Phylogeny." *Bonner Zoologische Beiträge* no. 43 (1992): 181–213.

Hershkovitz, P. "*Dromiciops gliroides* Thomas, 1894, Last of the Microbiotheria (Marsupialia), With a Review of the Family Microbiotheriidae." *Fieldiana Zoology (New Series)* 93, no. 1502 (2004).

Kirsch, J. A. W., A. W. Dickerman, O. A. Reig, and M. S. Springer. "DNA Hybridisation Evidence for the Australian Affinity of the American Marsupial *Dromiciops australis.*" *Proceedings of the National Academy of Science, USA* no. 88 (1991): 10465–10469.

Marshall, L. G. "*Dromiciops australis.*" *Mammalian Species* 99 (1978): 1–5.

Pridmore, P. A. "Locomotion in *Dromiciops australis* (Microbiotheriidae)." *Australian Journal of Zoology* no. 42 (1994): 679–699.

Westerman, M., and D. Edwards. "The Relationship of *Dromiciops australis* to Other Marsupials: Data From DNA-DNA Hybridisation Studies." *Australian Journal of Zoology* no. 39 (1991): 123–130.

Horovitz, Inez, and M. R. Sánchez-Villagra. "A Morphological Analysis of Marsupial Mammal Higher-Level Phylogenetic Relationships." *Cladistics*19, no. 3 (June 2003): 181–212.

**Web sites:**

Terrestrial Ecoregions—Valdivian temperate forests (NT0404). http://www.worldwildlife.org/wildworld/profiles/terrestrial/nt/nt0404_full.html (accessed on June 29, 2004).

Animal Diversity Web, University of Michigan. http://animaldiversity.ummz.umich.edu/site/index.html (accessed June 29, 2004).

AUSTRALASIAN CARNIVOROUS
MARSUPIALS

**Dasyuromorphia**

**Class:** Mammalia

**Order:** Dasyuromorphia

**Number of families:** 3 families

order

CHAPTER

## PHYSICAL CHARACTERISTICS

Most familiar mammals such as cats, dogs, and horses are called eutherian (yoo-THEER-ee-an) mammals. These mammals have a placenta, an organ that grows in the mother's uterus (womb) and lets the mother and developing offspring share food and oxygen. Marsupials do not have a developed placenta. Because of this, they give birth to young that are physically immature and undeveloped. The young are not able to survive on their own. Instead, they are carried around for several months in their mother's pouch, or they are attached to the mother's teats, or nipples, outside the pouch, and carried until they have grown and matured enough to fend for themselves. The Australasian (living in Australia and nearby islands) carnivorous marsupials are made up of three families of marsupial mammals with a total of about seventy-one species.

Australasian carnivorous marsupials vary widely in weight, from less than one ounce (28 grams) to more that 65 pounds (30 kilograms). The combined length of their head and body ranges from less than 2 inches (5 centimeters) to 51 inches (130 centimeters). The largest Australasian carnivorous marsupial, the Tasmanian wolf, became extinct in the early 1900s. The largest living member of the Dasyuromorphia order is the Tasmanian devil.

Australasian carnivorous marsupials are all four-footed, with four toes on each of the two front feet and either four or five toes on each of the two back feet. On each back foot is a toe called a hallux (HAL-lux) that does not have a claw. Species that

phylum

class

subclass

● **order**

monotypic order

suborder

family

live mainly in trees tend to have wider feet than ground-dwelling species and use their hallux to help them grip branches. The tails of Australasian carnivorous marsupials vary in length. Some species have tails nearly as long as their bodies. All of these animals have pointed snouts and a combination of sharp pointed teeth and grinding teeth to help them eat meat.

The fur of carnivorous marsupials ranges from grayish or reddish brown to sand colored, depending on the habitat in which they live. A few have black fur, and some species have underbellies that differ slightly in color from the rest of their fur. The fur on the bodies and heads is usually short, but the fur on the tail can be either very short or very bushy. Some of the animals in this order have distinct markings, such as the numbat's stripes, but most do not.

## GEOGRAPHIC RANGE

Animals in this order live in Australia, Tasmania, and New Guinea, and also inhabit some of the nearby Pacific islands.

## HABITAT

Australasian carnivorous marsupials live in many different habitats, from the tropical rainforest to the desert. Each species has adaptations that allow it to live in its own particular environment. For example, the numbat has claws that are good for scratching at the dirt and digging out termites in the forest where it lives. The spotted-tail quoll has special ridges on the bottoms of its paws and sharp claws that help it climb large trees.

Many of the Australasian carnivorous marsupials live in habitats where it can become very hot or very cold. Different species have different ways of protecting themselves from these extreme temperatures. Some species such as the numbat dig burrows underground that they line with dead leaves and other plant parts for insulation. Other species are able to reduce their body temperatures on purpose. This is called torpor, and it reduces the amount of energy an animal needs to live when it gets too cold or is exposed to other environmental stresses, such as too little food.

## DIET

Australasian carnivorous marsupials eat meat and insects. What each species eats depends on its size, habitat, and what kind of adaptations it has for hunting. Smaller species usually eat insects, and larger species eat other animals, although they sometimes eat insects as well. Many of the larger Australasian carnivorous marsupials can chew and eat whole animals, including the bones and the skin. The numbat lives in the forest and eats termites that it digs out from underground with its sharp claws or finds under the dead branches it pushes away with its pointed snout. The Tasmanian devil eats many different kinds of meat, and has been reported to eat animals as large as wallabies.

## BEHAVIOR AND REPRODUCTION

Most Australasian carnivorous marsupials are nocturnal, meaning that they are only active at night. Some species, however, have shown occasional periods of daytime activity, and a few species such as the numbat are usually active only during the day.

Australasian carnivorous marsupials spend most of their time in the search for food. Each species has different ways of finding prey, from digging for termites, to climbing trees and raiding the nests of possums during the night, to feeding on the bodies of animals that are already dead.

Most Australasian carnivorous marsupials have relatively short life spans. Females usually mate with more than one male, and in many species, offspring born in the same litter have different fathers. Some species in this order only mate once during their lifetime. They usually die soon after reproducing, having used all their energy in a sudden burst of activity required to mate successfully. Antechinus (ant-uh-KINE-us), which are broad-footed marsupial mice, mate in this way. The female lives long enough to raise her young until they can live on their own, but the male often dies before his offspring are mature.

Australasian carnivorous marsupials, like all marsupials, have very short pregnancies, some lasting only days. They give birth to immature young that are usually blind and hairless, and always are unable to survive on their own. In most cases, the young make their way into the mother's pouch, which contains milk teats, and are carried with her wherever she goes. Some species have young that crawl to external teats, or nipples, of the mother. They cling there and are carried wherever the mother goes, protected only by the hairs on her underbelly. Many do not survive to maturity.

The amount of time the young spend growing outside of the mother's womb, or uterus, depends on the species. It can be as

short as a few weeks or as long as many months. In most species, once the young have grown enough to fend for themselves, they spend a short amount of time in the mother's nest or den, wandering further each day to find food, until at last they leave the nest for good.

## AUSTRALASIAN CARNIVOROUS MARSUPIALS AND PEOPLE

Farmers consider many Australasian carnivorous marsupials pests because they prey on livestock such as sheep and chickens. Some animals have been collected for zoos, but none of the animals in this order have been significantly hunted for their fur. In times past, some may have been hunted for food by aboriginal peoples.

## CONSERVATION STATUS

Many Australasian carnivorous marsupials have not been studied by scientists. There are no good estimates of how many are left in the wild and how things such as deforestation (clearing the land of trees) are affecting them. One family in this order, Tasmanian wolves, has already gone extinct. The last time a Tasmanian wolf was confirmed to exist in the wild was in 1930. The last remaining animal was in captivity in a zoo and died shortly thereafter in 1936.

Many Australasian carnivorous marsupials such as the southern dibbler and the sandhill dunnart are considered to be Endangered, or facing a very high risk of becoming extinct in the wild. Many others are considered Vulnerable, which means they face a high risk of extinction in the wild.

There are many reasons that Australasian carnivorous marsupials are facing the threat of extinction. The cutting down of forest areas to clear land for agriculture affects many species, as does the changing pattern of fires set to clear grassland areas. Many species are Vulnerable or Endangered in Australia and surrounding areas because of the introduction of the red fox, which is not native to the region. In areas where the red fox is found, populations of Australasian carnivorous mammals have substantially decreased.

# FOR MORE INFORMATION

## Books:

Fenton, Julie A. *Kangaroos and Other Marsupials.* Chicago: World Book, 2000.

Hoare, Ben, ed. *International Wildlife Encyclopedia,* 3rd ed. Tarrytown, NY: Marshall Cavendish, 2002.

Nowak, Ronald M., ed. *Walker's Mammals of the World,* 5th ed. Baltimore and London: Johns Hopkins University Press, 1991.

Woods, Samuel G. *Sorting Out Mammals: Everything You Want to Know About Marsupials, Carnivores, Herbivores, and More!* Woodbridge, CT. Blackbirch Marketing, 1999.

## Periodicals:

Hecht, Jeff. "The Sun Warmed Up Evolution For Us All." *New Scientist* (August 31, 2002): 17.

## Other sources:

"The Amazing Marsupials." *Australian Ark Documentary Series.* Columbia Tristar, 1994.

**MARSUPIAL MICE AND CATS, TASMANIAN DEVIL**

**Dasyuridae**

**Class:** Mammalia

**Order:** Dasyuormorphia

**Family:** Dasyuridae

**Number of species:** 69 species

CHAPTER

phylum

class

subclass

order

monotypic order

suborder

▲ **family**

## PHYSICAL CHARACTERISTICS

Members of the family Dasyuridae include marsupial mice and cats and the Tasmanian devil. Marsupials are animals that do not have a very well developed placenta. A placenta is an organ that grows in the mother's uterus (womb) that allows the developing offspring to share the mother's food and oxygen. Because of this, pregnancy in marsupials is short and the young are born undeveloped and unable to fend for themselves. After birth, the young move to the mother's pouch and attach to her milk teats (nipples) until they have finished developing enough to live on their own.

None of the members of the family Dasyuridae are very large. This order includes some of the world's smallest marsupials, members of the genus (JEE-nus) *Planigale*, some of which are less than 4 inches (10 centimeters) long and weigh less than 0.2 ounces (5 grams). Other members of this family vary in size up to the Tasmanian devil, which is the largest species. The Tasmanian devil can be up to 25 inches (62 centimeters) long and weigh up to 29 pounds (13 kilograms).

Marsupial mice and cats, as well as the Tasmanian devil, have four legs. They have four toes on each of their two front feet and either four or five toes on their two back feet. When they have five toes on their back feet, the fifth toe is a hallux (HAL-lux). A hallux is a toe that does not have a claw. The species in this family usually have pointed snouts and long tails.

The fur of animals in this family is mostly gray or brownish, and sometimes is black. Fur color often depends on the habitat in which the species lives, and the kind of fur that best camouflages them helps them avoid predators, animals that hunt them for food. Some of the species have other markings. The northern quoll has white spots on its otherwise brown body. The teeth of members of this family vary depending on the preferred diet, but most have some sharp teeth for slicing and biting and other wider, flatter teeth for grinding. This combination of teeth is helpful for catching and eating other animals and insects.

### GEOGRAPHIC RANGE

Members of Dasyuridae live in Australia, New Guinea, and Tasmania, and can also be found on some small islands in that area of the Pacific.

### HABITAT

Members of the family Dasyuridae live all over Australia, Tasmania, and New Guinea, and occupy all types of habitats. Some species live in trees, but most species are ground dwelling; some species prefer open grassland, and others prefer forests. Animals that have different habitats have different ways of finding or making dens and different ways of finding food.

### DIET

What the members of this family eat depends on their size. The species that have smaller bodies, such as the marsupial mice, usually eat insects and sometimes catch and eat small animals such as lizards. These smaller animals will eat large animals only if they are already dead, in which case they will feed from the carcass. Larger species in this family eat mainly other vertebrates, or animals that have backbones, such as wallabies and birds. Species that eat mainly vertebrates will occasionally eat some insects and other invertebrates, animals without backbones, as well. Some species will even supplement their diet with food that does not come from other animals, such as flowers and fruit. All species in this family are scavengers when they get the chance. They will eat animals that are already dead, if they are available. Members of this family are usually nocturnal and hunt and are active mainly at night.

**TAZ**

Tasmanian devils have a reputation around the world for being vicious destroyers of property thanks to a Warner Brothers cartoon character named Taz. Taz, a Tasmanian devil, spins like a tornado destroying everything in his path. He stands on his hind legs and has teeth that can crush through anything. Although Tasmanian devils do have sharp teeth and very strong jaw muscles, they do not stand on their back legs alone. Tasmanian devils can be vicious when they feel threatened, but do not spin and certainly cannot destroy entire forests!

## BEHAVIOR AND REPRODUCTION

Like all marsupials, species in this family give birth to young that are often blind and hairless, and are not able to survive on their own. This means that pregnancy for these species is usually very short. When the young are born, they either move into the mother's pouch or to her underbelly where they attach themselves to her teats. When attached in this way, the developing young travel with their mother for weeks or months as they continue to grow and develop. Once the young are able to survive on their own, they are weaned from their mother and detach from her nipples. After this, there is usually a period during which the young stay close to home and hunt away from their mother for increasingly long periods before going off on their own. The males of these species usually travel farther from the mother's nest to find territories of their own than the females do.

Some species in this family mate only one time before they die. The males of these species often die soon after mating, although the females live long enough to raise their young and sometimes to have a second litter. Scientists think that the reason that males of some species only mate once and then die is because it takes so much energy for the males to mate, especially in years when there is not much food available. Scientists think that these animals use up so much energy mating that they no longer have enough energy to stay healthy.

## MARSUPIAL MICE, CATS, TASMANIAN DEVIL, AND PEOPLE

Members of this family usually do not have much direct interaction with people. Some species, however, have been thought to kill livestock and because of this have been hunted by farmers.

## CONSERVATION STATUS

No species in this family are known to be extinct, but many, such as the Kangaroo Island dunnart, are Endangered. Animals that are considered Endangered face a very high risk of becoming extinct in the wild. Many other members of this family are Vulnerable, facing a high risk of extinction in the wild. There are some species in this family that scientists do not yet have enough information about to know if they are endangered or not.

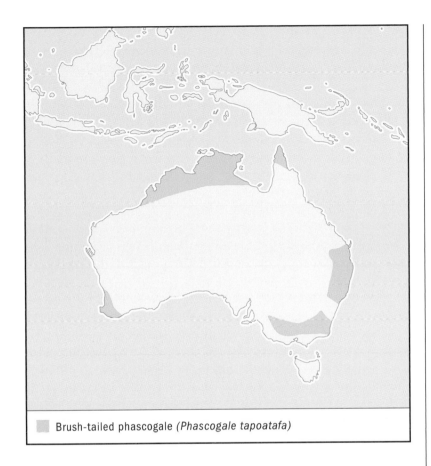

Brush-tailed phascogale *(Phascogale tapoatafa)*

## BRUSH-TAILED PHASCOGALE
### *Phascogale tapoatafa*

**Physical characteristics:** The brush-tailed phascogale has gray colored fur on its back and white or creamy fur on the underside of its body. Its brush tail is black with long, 2-inch (5.5-centimeter) hairs. Its body is 5.8 to 10.3 inches (14.8 to 26.1 centimeters).

**Geographic range:** Brush-tailed phascogales live in coastal areas of Australia.

**Habitat:** These animals live in dry eucalyptus forests and woodlands with an open understory—not a lot of smaller plants growing under the tallest trees—in temperate and tropical areas of Australia.

*Brush-tailed phascogales prefer Australia's eucalyptus forests for foraging and nesting sites. (Michael Morcombe/Bruce Coleman Inc. Reproduced by permission.)*

**Diet:** Brush-tailed phascogales feed on nectar (sweet liquid produced by plant flowers), large insects, spiders, and small vertebrates, animals with a backbone. They tear the bark off of trees to look for food.

**Behavior and reproduction:** This animal spends much of its time up in trees, and is nocturnal, or active at night. Brush-tailed phascogales make their nests in tree holes or forks, and also mate there. Females give birth to about eight young, who are attached to her nipples, feeding, for about forty days. After that, they stay in the nest until they're five months old.

**Brush-tailed phascogales and people:** These animals occasionally eat poultry raised by humans, but they also eat mice and insects, which humans may appreciate.

**Conservation status:** The brush-tailed phascogale is not currently threatened. ■

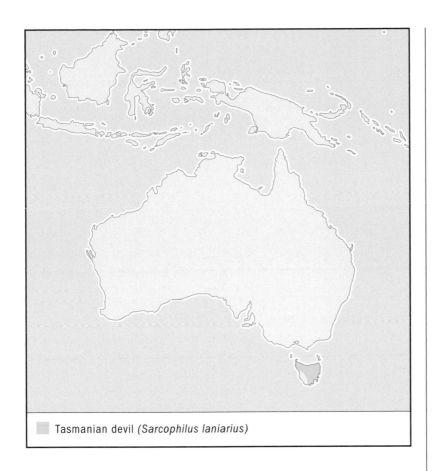

Tasmanian devil (*Sarcophilus laniarius*)

## TASMANIAN DEVIL
### *Sarcophilus laniarius*

**Physical characteristics:** The Tasmanian devil is a four-footed mar-supial with four toes on its two front feet as well as four on its back feet. It does not have a hallux. It has black fur with some white mark-ings, usually on the chest, shoulder, and rump. The Tasmanian devil has a pointed snout that is pinkish at the tip. Its sharp, pointed teeth are good for cutting and tearing meat. It also has flat grinding teeth for crushing the bones of the animals it eats. The ears of the Tas-manian devil are short and pointed and turn red when the animal is angry. Males of this species usually have a head and body length be-tween 20 and 25 inches (50 to 62 centimeters) and weigh between 17 and 29 pounds (8 to 13 kilograms). Females usually have a head

*The Tasmanian devil's sharp, pointed teeth are good for cutting and tearing meat. Its flat grinding teeth can crush the bones of the animals it eats. (Erwin and Peggy Bauer/Bruce Coleman Inc. Reproduced by permission.)*

and body length between 21 and 22.5 inches (53 to 57 centimeters) and weigh between 10 and 20 pounds (4.5 to 9 kilograms).

**Geographic range:** Tasmanian devils live on Tasmania, a large island off the southeastern Australian coast.

**Habitat:** The Tasmanian devil lives in the forest. It makes dens using leaves and plant material, although it sometimes sleeps in hollow logs or in the dens of other animals.

**Diet:** The Tasmanian devil mainly eats the meat of vertebrate animals. It will even eat poisonous snakes, and also occasionally invertebrates or plants. It is mainly a scavenger, and likes to eat animals that have already been killed by other causes. A scientist who studied the Tasmanian devil found that its favorite foods were wallabies, wombats, sheep, and rabbits. Most of these animals were not hunted by the Tasmanian devil itself, but eaten after other animals, cars, or natural causes killed them. The Tasmanian devil makes use of all the parts of animals that it kills or finds, eating even the bones and fur.

**Behavior and reproduction:** The Tasmanian devil is nocturnal, meaning that it hunts and is active mainly at night. When Tasmanian devils feel threatened or are fighting, they can be very loud. They begin by growling softly, but become increasingly louder and can even make horrible screeching noises. Most mating occurs in February or March. Females are pregnant for about one month and then give birth to young that move into the mother's pouch and attach to her nipples. Female Tasmanian devils have four nipples, which means that four is the most young that can be supported while they develop. Tasmanian devils normally have two or four babies at a time.

**Tasmanian devils and people:** Most contact between humans and the Tasmanian devil has occurred because the Tasmanian devil may eat animals that farmers keep as livestock. The Tasmanian devil will eat chickens if the coops are not well protected, and also sheep and lambs. Farmers sometimes kill Tasmanian devils to keep them away from their livestock.

**Conservation status:** The Tasmanian devil used to live all over Australia, but now lives only in Tasmania. Scientists believe that this species disappeared from the Australian mainland because it had to compete with the dingo, a wild dog that is introduced, not a native species. There is no information on how many Tasmanian devils are left in the wild in Tasmania, but it is likely that they are being affected by the clearing of land for agriculture. ■

## FOR MORE INFORMATION

### Books:

Fenton, Julie A. *Kangaroos and Other Marsupials.* Chicago: World Book, 2000.

Hoare, Ben, ed. *International Wildlife Encyclopedia,* 3rd ed. Tarrytown, NY: Marshall Cavendish, 2002.

Nowak, Ronald M., ed. *Walker's Mammals of the World,* 5th ed. Baltimore and London: Johns Hopkins University Press, 1991.

Woods, Samuel G. *Sorting Out Mammals: Everything You Want to Know About Marsupials, Carnivores, Herbivores, and More!* Woodbridge, CT: Blackbirch Marketing, 1999.

### Web sites:

Tasmanian Department of Primary Industries, Water & Environment. *Tasmanian Devil.* http://www.dpiwe.tas.gov.au/inter.nsf/WebPages/BHAN -5358KH?open (accessed on June 30, 2004).

### Other sources:

"The Amazing Marsupials." *Australian Ark Documentary Series.* Columbia Tristar, 1994.

## NUMBAT
### Myrmecobiidae

**Class:** Mammalia

**Order:** Dasyuromorphia

**Family:** Myrmecobiidae

**One species:** Numbat (*Myrmecobius fasciatus*)

family

CHAPTER

phylum

class

subclass

order

monotypic order

suborder

▲ **family**

## PHYSICAL CHARACTERISTICS

Numbats, sometimes called banded anteaters, are small marsupial mammals that live in the southwestern region of Western Australia. Considered to be one of the most beautiful and distinctively marked marsupials, numbats are the only species of the Myrmecobiidae family.

Numbats are small, four-legged animals that are a little larger than rats. Weighing about 1 pound (0.45 kilograms), they range in total length from 12 to 19 inches (30 to 47 centimeters). Their tails can be 5 to 8 inches (13 to 20 centimeters) long. Their front feet have five toes and their back feet have four toes. All of the toes have strong claws to help them dig quickly for termites, their preferred food. They also have an extraordinarily long tongue that they use to gather the termites from underground and from holes in rotting trees. Unlike other marsupials, the female numbat does not have a pouch to carry her young, but she does have four nipples on her underside. The young cling to the nipples on her belly while they develop.

The numbat has coarse, short fur that varies in color from grayish brown to reddish brown. The numbat is distinctively marked with a series of five to seven white stripes that run across its rump and lower back. A black band bordered by two white bands runs on each side of the head from the snout through the eye and to the base of the ear. Their underside has paler fur and the fur on their tail is long.

## GEOGRAPHIC RANGE

In the late eighteenth and early nineteenth century, when Europeans began to settle in Australia, numbats occupied a much larger area than they do today. At that time, numbats lived in the southern half of central and western Australia. They lived as far east as New South Wales and as far north as the Northern Territory. Today, numbats inhabit nine wild and two free-range areas across the southern region of Western Australia.

## HABITAT

Numbats once lived in a variety of habitats from open forests to grasslands. Today they prefer areas with plenty of ground-level cover in order to protect them from the weather and predators such as hawks and red foxes. Numbats also use hollow logs and thickets to protect themselves from predators, animals that hunt them for food.

## DIET

Numbats mainly eat termites—their pointed snouts allow them to sniff out the insects underground. They then use their sharp claws to dig small holes and retrieve the termites from underground tunnels using their long, slender tongues. The numbat's tongue can extend as much as 4 inches (10 centimeters) from its mouth. Saliva on the tongue makes the termites stick to it, so that the numbat can quickly pull its tongue back into its mouth with the termites attached. The numbat's salivary glands are large to provide enough saliva for this kind of eating. Another way that numbats find termites is by turning over fallen branches and sticks using their snout and front paws. A numbat that was studied in captivity ate between 10,000 and 20,000 termites per day. In the course of eating termites, ants and other insects sometimes also are consumed. Numbats do not chew their food, even though they have more teeth (between forty-eight and fifty-two of them) than any other marsupial.

## BEHAVIOR AND REPRODUCTION

The numbat is a solitary animal and is the only Australian mammal that is active only during the day (diurnal). During

### THE DANGER OF INTRODUCING A FOREIGN SPECIES

Whenever an new animal is introduced into an environment, there can be unexpected consequences. The red fox was introduced when Europeans arrived in Australia. For numbats and several other Australian species, the introduction of this animal was disastrous. Numbats had not evolved ways to protect themselves against this new, non-native predator. As a result, foxes killed thousands of numbats and numbat populations substantially decreased. Only by starting programs to lessen the number of red foxes could the numbats be saved.

A numbat's tongue can be as long as 4 inches (10 centimeters) from the opening of the mouth. The numbat uses it to gather temites from underground or from holes in rotting trees. (Frans Lanting/Minden Pictures. Reproduced by permission.)

most of the year, numbats are active from mid-morning until late afternoon, when the temperatures are warmest. However, during the hottest part of the year they avoid activity around noon and prefer to forage in the early morning and late afternoon.

When numbats reproduce, they do not form pairs, so the female is left to raise her young alone. After only a fourteen-day pregnancy, the female gives birth to an average of four young, which she continues to carry without a pouch. Marsupial mammals like the numbat do not form a placenta when their young are in their mother's womb. Instead, they are born under-developed and spend time developing outside attached to their mother's milk teats. Unlike other marsupials, the numbat does not have a pouch. When the young are born, they are hairless and their eyes are still sealed shut. They crawl toward their mother's nipples, which are on her belly, and attach themselves there. They remain on the mother's belly and are carried with her for six to seven months while they grow hair and continue to develop. The young then spend several more months in the

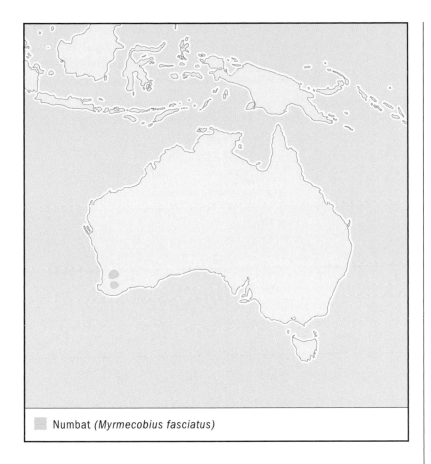
Numbat (*Myrmecobius fasciatus*)

mother's nest. While in the nest, their eyes open and they begin to explore. By early the following year, numbat young venture out on their own.

## NUMBATS AND PEOPLE

The numbat was known to central Australian aboriginal (native) people as "walpurti." At one time they were hunted for food. Aboriginal people would track individual numbats to their burrows and then dig them up. Today they have no known economic value, although scientists and ecotourists are interested in observing them. As many as two hundred numbats have been collected as museum specimens.

## CONSERVATION STATUS

Numbats are a conservation success story. By 1985, so many numbats had disappeared that only two numbat populations remained. At that time they were considered Endangered and likely to become extinct. An effort to increase numbat populations was undertaken that involved the poison baiting of red foxes, a major predator of the numbat. Numbat populations were also moved into other habitats, and numbats that had been raised in captivity were introduced into the wild. These programs have been successful, because there are now nine wild numbat populations and two that live on fenced reserves. In 1994, numbats were upgraded from Endangered to a conservation status of Vulnerable. Although they are still at risk, they are unlikely to become extinct in the immediate future.

## FOR MORE INFORMATION

### Books:

Swan, Erin Pembrey, and Jose Gonzales. *Meat-Eating Marsupials (Animals in Order).* New York: Franklin Watts, 2002.

Nowak, Ronald M., ed. *Walker's Mammals of the World,* 5th ed. Baltimore and London: Johns Hopkins University Press, 1991.

Woods, Samuel G. *Sorting Out Mammals: Everything You Want to Know About Marsupials, Carnivores, Herbivores, and More!* Woodbridge, CT: Blackbirch Marketing, 1999.

### Periodicals:

McCreery, Susan. "Fenced in and Free." *Australian Geographic* (January–March 2003): 31.

### Web sites:

Tasmanian Department of Primary Industries, Water & Environment. *Numbats.* http://www.dpiwe.tas.gov.au (accessed on June 30, 2004).

**TASMANIAN WOLF**

**Thylacinidae**

**Class:** Mammalia

**Order:** Dasyuromorphia

**Family:** Thylacinidae

**One species:** Tasmanian wolf
(*Thylacinidae
cynocephalus*)

phylum

class

subclass

order

monotypic order

suborder

▲ **family**

## PHYSICAL CHARACTERISTICS

Although Tasmanian wolves, sometimes called Tasmanian tigers, are extinct, or no longer living today, scientists have learned much about them from fossils and earlier written records. These wolves looked like dogs, and they walked on all four legs, although their legs were shorter than most dogs. They had a long narrow snout, ears that stood up, and a straight tail. Tasmanian wolves had short sandy-brown hair with a distinctive set of stripes that ran across their back. The stripes were dark brown and ran from the shoulders to the base of the tail.

Female Tasmanian wolves were smaller than males, with some males growing to twice the weight of females. While females may have averaged 33 pounds (15 kilograms), males could grow to be more than 60 pounds (27 kilograms). Tasmanian wolves had sharp teeth with four incisors in the top of their mouth and three in the bottom. This allowed them to tear their preferred food, meat.

Like all native Australian and Tasmanian mammals, Tasmanian wolves were marsupials. They lacked a placenta, an organ that grows in the mother's uterus and lets the mother and developing baby share food and oxygen. Because of this, they gave birth to young that were physically immature and unable to survive on their own. After a short pregnancy, the young were carried for several months in a pouch that opened under the mother's tail and faced backward. The young attached to milk teats, or nipples, in the pouch and fed until they grew large enough to survive on their own.

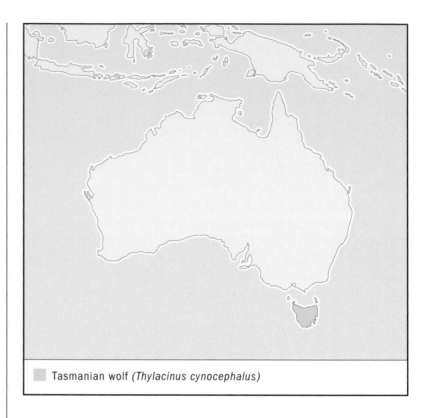

Tasmanian wolf (*Thylacinus cynocephalus*)

## GEOGRAPHIC RANGE

When Tasmanian wolves were still alive, they were thought to have lived on the entire island of Tasmania. By the 1800s, Tasmanian wolves were rare in the southwest and western regions of the island, except in coastal areas. Scientists have learned this by reading the diaries of early settlers and examining the bounty payment records of people who lived during that time. Early settlers in Tasmania thought of Tasmanian wolves as pests to be eliminated, and bounty money was paid to hunters who killed them.

## HABITAT

Tasmanian wolves lived in a great variety of habitats, although most often they were found in open areas. These included grassy woodlands, open forests, and coastal regions. They avoided dense forests and wetlands and liked to live in areas that Tasmanian devils, another animal in this order, live in today. The Tasmanian wolves hid in rock outcroppings and dense vegetation during the day and probably built dens there, but they would hunt at night in open grasslands.

## DIET

Since Tasmanian wolves are no longer living today, no one knows for sure what they ate. When they were alive, people were more interested in classifying them and studying how they were related to other animals than in learning about how they lived or what they ate. Scientists can make some guesses about their diet, however, by comparing Tasmanian wolves to animals that live today.

Tasmanian wolves were carnivores, or meat eaters. It is believed that they ate many different kinds of animals including birds, small mammals, and even some larger mammals such as wombats, bandicoots, possums, and kangaroos, although it is likely that these larger animals were eaten less often. By looking at the size of their leg bones, scientists believe that Tasmanian wolves did not run very fast, and captured their prey by sneaking up on it or ambushing it rather than running it down.

*W. Baker © 2003*

*Most of what is known about Tasmanian wolves comes from what people wrote about them before they became extinct in the 1930s. Scientists can study related animals to try to figure out what they might have eaten and how they lived. (Illustration by Wendy Baker. Reproduced by permission.)*

## BEHAVIOR AND REPRODUCTION

Not much is known about the behavior and reproduction of Tasmanian wolves. These animals were bred in captivity only once, although females with live young in their pouches were caught and kept in zoos. Scientists think that reproduction was timed so that young Tasmanian wolves left their mothers during the warmer months, as this was when food was more available, giving the young a better chance of survival. They believe that pregnancy lasted only one month. The poorly developed young then moved into the mother's pouch where they nursed until they were developed enough to survive on their own and eat solid food. Beyond this, little is known about their reproductive systems, how long the young would stay in their mother's pouch, or even how many young were in an average litter.

## TASMANIAN WOLVES AND PEOPLE

People have had unfriendly relationships with Tasmanian wolves. Native peoples on the island of Tasmania and in Australia killed and ate Tasmanian wolves for food. It is thought that although many groups did use the Tasmanian wolves for food, some would build special shelters to worship the head and skin of the animal afterwards.

## FARMING AND WILD ANIMALS

When people begin to farm in areas that were once wild, they often interact with new animals. Farmers who raise sheep, cattle, or other livestock find that wild animals will feed on their flocks. This was probably true of the Tasmanian wolves, although most scientists believe that wild dogs were responsible for killing more sheep and cattle than Tasmanian wolves. Even so, farmers hunted Tasmanian wolves and hired bounty hunters to help them. This drove the Tasmanian wolves to extinction, despite the fact that they may not have been responsible for all the farmers' losses.

Once European settlers and farmers came to the region, hunting of the wolves increased dramatically. Sheep farmers were losing sheep and assumed that the Tasmanian wolves were responsible. It is likely that the wolves did kill some sheep, but wild dogs probably killed more sheep that the wolves. Even so, farmers and bounty hunters continued to hunt the Tasmanian wolves. By the early 1900s, most were gone, and by 1912 bounty hunting of Tasmanian wolves was halted. This was not early enough to save them from extinction. The last time a Tasmanian wolf was confirmed to exist in the wild was in 1930. Despite the official protection that began on July 14, 1936, the last Tasmanian wolf died that September.

## CONSERVATION STATUS

Tasmanian wolves are extinct. They were killed off mostly by farmers and bounty hunters during the 1800s. Tasmanian wolves were thought of as pests and killers of livestock, much the way the coyote was thought of during the settlement of the American West.

## FOR MORE INFORMATION

**Books:**

Fenton, Julie A. *Kangaroos and Other Marsupials.* Chicago: World Book, 2000.

Hoare, Ben, ed. *International Wildlife Encyclopedia,* 3rd ed. Tarrytown, NY: Marshall Cavendish, 2002.

Nowak, Ronald M., ed. *Walker's Mammals of the World,* 5th ed. Baltimore and London: Johns Hopkins University Press, 1991.

Swan, Erin Pembrey, and Jose Gonzales. *Meat-Eating Marsupials (Animals in Order).* New York: Franklin Watts, 2002.

Woods, Samuel G. *Sorting Out Mammals: Everything You Want to Know About Marsupials, Carnivores, Herbivores, and More!* Woodbridge, CT: Blackbirch Marketing, 1999.

**Web sites:**

Tasmanian Department of Primary Industries, Water Environment. "Tasmanian Tiger." http://www.dpiwe.tas.gov.au/inter.nsf/WebPages/BHAN-53777B?open (accessed on June 30, 2004).

**Other sources:**

"The Amazing Marsupials." *Australian Ark Documentary Series.* Columbia Tristar, 1994.

**Class:** Mammalia

**Order:** Peramelemorphia

**Number of families:** 2 families

order

## PHYSICAL CHARACTERISTICS

Peramelemorphia is an order of small ground-dwelling marsupials known as bandicoots and bilbies. All species in this order live either in Australia, New Guinea, or a few nearby Indonesian islands. Although some of the species in this order have been classified differently in the past, current genetic evidence has led scientists to divide this order into two families, the Peramelidae and the Peroryctidae. The Peramelidae include the true bandicoots of Australia and the bilbies. The Peroryctidae are made up of the spiny bandicoots of the New Guinea rainforest.

Bandicoots and bilbies look like a cross between a rabbit and a rat. They range in size from 6.5 to 23 inches (17 to 60 centimeters), excluding tail length, and weigh from 0.3 to 10.5 pounds (0.1 to 4.8 kilograms). Their tails are usually short in proportion to their bodies.

Bandicoots and bilbies have small pointed snouts and ears that are usually short and rounded. One exception is the greater bilby which has long rabbit-like ears. Most species have thin, rat-like tails, and their fur is usually solid earth tone colors. The fur of the rainforest bandicoots is harsh and spiny.

The front legs of most species in this order are adapted for digging. The front feet have strong claws on toes two, three, and four. Toes one and five are either absent or very small and clawless. The hind limbs are strong and muscular, allowing these animals to leap and hop like a rabbit. However, they are also able to run at a fast gallop. On the hind legs, the bones of the second and third toe are fused, joined into one, but still have separate claws. This pattern of fused toes suggests that these animals may have evolved from the Diprotodonta family.

Bandicoots and bilbies are omnivores, meaning they eat both plants and animals. Members of this order have teeth that are adapted to this diet. Their tooth pattern suggests that they may have evolved from the Dasyuromorphia order (Australasian carnivorous marsupials). Because of the conflicting physical evidence, scientists remain unsure exactly which other marsupial families are their closest relatives.

## GEOGRAPHIC RANGE

Species in this order are found only in limited parts of Australia, New Guinea, and the Indonesian island of Seram. In the past, these animals were abundant. They were found in about 70 percent of Australia, throughout New Guinea, and on several other Indonesian islands. Since the beginning of the twentieth century, their range has been drastically reduced by human activities.

## HABITAT

The two families in this order live in different habitats. Peramelidae, or true bandicoots and bilbies, live in dry, desert areas, dry grassland, shrubby grassland, open forest, and suburban gardens. Peroryctidae, or spiny bandicoots, live in the tropical rainforests of New Guinea. Several species live in isolated areas at elevations up to 13,000 feet (4,000 meters).

## DIET

Bandicoots and bilbies are omnivores, eating both plants and animals, and insects such as ants and termites usually make up most of their diet. They also eat earthworms, insect larvae, insects such as centipedes, and plant parts, such as seeds, bulbs, and fallen fruit. Occasionally larger species eat lizards and mice. They are opportunistic feeders, tending to eat whatever food is available.

Bandicoots and bilbies find food by smell and hearing. Their eyesight is poor. When they locate food underground, they dig cone-shaped holes up to 5 inches (13 centimeters) deep and remove the food with their long tongues. Because so much of their food is dug out of the ground, they also accidentally eat a lot of dirt. Studies have found that between 20 and 90 percent of their waste is earth that was swallowed with the food, then passed through their digestive system. Some species that live in desert areas do not need to drink water. They can get all the moisture they need from their food.

## BEHAVIOR AND REPRODUCTION

Most species in this order are nocturnal, active only at night. The exception is the southern brown bandicoot, which is active mainly during the day. All members of this order live alone, coming together only for a short time to mate. Females will mate with more than one male. Many species mate year round. Both males and females are territorial. Males have larger territories than females. Some species mark their territory with scent from a special gland. Males become aggressive when another male enters their territory. Males kept together in captivity will fight.

Most familiar mammals such as dogs, rabbits, and horses, are called eutherian (yoo-THEER-ee-an) mammals. These mammals have a placenta, an organ that grows into the mother's uterus (womb) and lets the mother and developing offspring share food and oxygen until the organs of the developing young mature. Marsupial mammals do not have this type of developed placenta. Most marsupials have what is called a yolk-sac placenta, where there is no sharing of the mother's food and oxygen.

Bandicoots and bilbies are different from other marsupials, because they have a second placenta in addition to the yolk-sac placenta. This placenta resembles the placenta in eutherian mammals, but does not function as well, because it does not attach as closely to the wall of the mother's uterus. As a result, members of the order Peramelemorphia have very short pregnancies, and, like other marsupials, the young are physically immature and undeveloped when they are born. At birth they crawl to their mother's backward-opening pouch where they attach to the mother's teats, or nipples. They are carried inside the pouch until they are mature enough to survive independently.

## BANDICOOTS, BILBIES, AND PEOPLE

Aboriginal (native) people hunted bandicoots and bilbies for meat and fur, however these animals were abundant, and hunting did not cause a major decrease in their populations. The coming of European colonists to Australia and New Guinea began the decline of many species of bandicoots and bilbies. Europeans changed the ecology of Australia. They introduced non-native species such as the red fox and the domestic cat, both of which prey on bandicoots and bilbies. They also introduced rabbits that compete with them for food. In addition, Europeans introduced cattle and sheep ranching to Australia. This reduced the habitat suitable for many species of bandicoots and bilbies. Finally, native people regularly burned the grassland, and the plants that grew after the burn provide a good habitat for bandicoots and bilbies. This practice changed after large scale livestock ranching began, creating less diverse habitats that did not support these native species well.

The number of bandicoots and bilbies has decreased dramatically since the beginning of the twentieth century. Three species have gone extinct. Conservation organizations are tying to provide safe habitat for these animals by fencing preserves and controlling predators, animals that hunt them for food. However, people living in suburban areas still tend to think of bandicoots and bilbies as pests, because they dig up lawns and gardens when hunting for food.

**YOU DIRTY BANDICOOT**

Bandicoots reminded European settlers in Australia of rats. They had a very low opinion of the animal. Today in Australia the word "bandicoot" when applied to a person is considered a mild term of abuse and disrespect.

## CONSERVATION STATUS

Since the coming of European colonists in 1770, three species have gone extinct: the pig-footed bandicoot, the desert bandicoot, and the lesser bilby. The number of animals in four other species has dropped to dangerously low levels and they are considered Endangered, facing a very high risk of extinction in the wild, or Vulnerable, facing a high risk of extinction in the wild. So little is known about most of the species in the Peroryctidae family that their conservation status cannot be accurately evaluated.

Since the 1980s captive breeding and conservation programs have succeeded in increasing the number of bilbies. The Australian Bilby Appreciation Society has developed public relations programs to increase awareness of the need to protect these animals. They have also raised money for a fenced preserve, because bilbies cannot thrive in the wild without predator control. Other species have been the focus of less conservation awareness and continue to decline.

## FOR MORE INFORMATION

**Books:**

Finney, Tim F. *Mammals of New Guinea,* 2nd ed. Ithaca, NY: Cornell University Press, 1995.

Menkhorst, Frank. *A Field Guide to the Mammals of Australia,* 2nd ed. Oxford, U.K.: Oxford University Press, 2001.

Nowak, Ronald. M. *Walker's Mammals of the World.* Baltimore: Johns Hopkins University Press, 1995.

**Periodicals:**

Smyth, Chris. "Bilbies' Call of the Wild." *Habitat Australia* (October 1998): 13.

**Web sites:**

"Nature Conservation" Queensland Government Environmental Protection Agency/Queensland Parks and Wildlife Service. http://www.epa.qld.gov.au/nature_conservation (accessed on May 14, 2004).

University of Michigan Museum of Zoology. "Order Peramelemorphia." *Animal Diversity Web.* http://animaldiversity.ummz.umich.edu/site/accounts/information/Peramelemorphia.html (accessed on June 30, 2004).

**Other sources:**

Australian Bilby Appreciation Society. P. O. Box 2002, Rangview, Victoria 3132 Australia. E-mail: bilbies@optusnet.no.SPAM.com.au Web site: http://members.oze-mail.com.au/bilbies.

**BANDICOOTS AND BILBIES**
**Peramelidae**

**Class:** Mammalia

**Order:** Peramelemorphia

**Family:** Peramelidae

**Number of species:** 10 species

family

CHAPTER

## PHYSICAL CHARACTERISTICS

Peramelidae are Australian bandicoots and bilbies. This family is sometimes referred to as the true bandicoots to distinguish it from the Peroryctidae, or rainforest bandicoots of New Guinea. True bandicoots are small marsupials with long, pointed snouts. They range in size from 6.5 inches (17 centimeters) and 5 ounces (140 grams), or about the size of a mouse, to 23 inches (60 centimeters) and 10.5 pounds (4.8 kilograms), or about the size of a cat.

Bandicoots live and feed on the ground. They have claws to dig for food, and in the case of bilbies, digging burrows. Their front feet have five toes. The middle three toes have strong claws. Toes one and five are either small or absent. On the hind feet, the bones of the second and third toes are joined, but each toe has a separate claw. Bandicoots look something like a cross between a rat and a rabbit. Their hind legs are longer than their front legs and are strong and well developed for hopping and leaping. They are also able to gallop.

Most bandicoots have short rounded ears and a thin, short tail. However, the extinct pig-footed bandicoot had both long ears and a long tail, and the bilby's ears are very large. All bandicoots have good hearing and a good sense of smell, but poor eyesight. They are nocturnal, or active at night, when their sense of smell and hearing are important in helping them locate food.

True bandicoots live mainly in dry areas. Their fur ranges from dark brown to gray and they are normally darker on their back than on their belly, allowing them to blend into the deserts

phylum

class

subclass

order

monotypic order

suborder

▲ **family**

and dry grasslands where they live. Most bandicoots are solid colored, although a few, such as the eastern barred bandicoot, are striped. The fur of true bandicoots is soft when compared to the harsh, spiky fur of the rainforest bandicoots.

## GEOGRAPHIC RANGE

Before the arrival of European colonists in 1770, bandicoots and bilbies were found in about 70 percent of Australia and on several nearby islands. Today they are found in many fewer places in Australia and the island of Tasmania. The bilby, especially, can be found only in isolated pockets mainly on protected park land or in captive breeding areas.

## HABITAT

Bandicoots and bilbies prefer dry areas. Before European colonization, up to five species could be found in the Australian inland deserts. Today only one species lives there. Other species live in dry grasslands and open forests. Three species have adapted to human activity and live in suburban neighborhoods and parks.

## DIET

True bandicoots are omnivores. They eat both plants and animals. Included in their diet are ants, termites, insect larvae (LAR-vee), earthworms, spiders, centipedes, bulbs, seeds, and bird eggs. Larger species will occasionally eat lizards and mice. Although bandicoots eat a variety of food, each colony seems to prefer one or two particular foods, probably because these are more easily available. Bandicoots dig for food with their strong claws. They make holes up to 5 inches (13 centimeters) deep and scoop out the food with their long tongues. Some species that live in desert areas do not need to drink water. They can get all the moisture they need from their food.

## BEHAVIOR AND REPRODUCTION

True bandicoots are nocturnal. The exception is the southern brown bandicoot, which is active mainly during the day. Bandicoots are solitary animals, living alone and coming together only to mate.

Bandicoots are territorial animals. The males defend larger territories than the females. They challenge any other male that comes into this area, and will fight if the intruder does not leave. Although females spend all night feeding, males spend part of the night patrolling their territories and marking them with scent to scare off other males.

Female bandicoots can reproduce at about four months of age. A female may mate with several different males. Pregnancy is one of the shortest of all animals—from twelve days to a few weeks.

Like all marsupials, bandicoots do not have a well-developed placenta. A placenta is an organ that grows in the mother's uterus (YOO-ter-us; womb) that allows the developing offspring share the mother's food and oxygen. Most marsupials have what is called a yolk-sac placenta, where there is no sharing of the mother's food and oxygen. Bandicoots and bilbies are different from other marsupials, because they have a second placenta in addition to the yolk-sac placenta. This placenta resembles the placenta in eutherian (yoo-THEER-ee-an) mammals, such as dogs, rabbits, and humans, but does not function as well, because it does not attach as closely to the wall of the mother's uterus.

Young bandicoots, called joeys, are born hairless, blind, and poorly developed. They are about 0.4 inches (1 centimeter) long. They use their front legs to pull themselves into their mother's pouch. There they attach to her teats, or nipples, where they remain for at least several weeks until they are able to survive on their own. After that they may remain in the nest and be fed by the mother for another week or two before becoming completely independent. Rarely do bandicoots have more than four young in a litter, and one or two offspring are more common. The death rate of newborn bandicoots is high. Those that live to adulthood have a lifespan of two to three years. Predators of the bandicoot include red foxes, dingoes (wild dogs), and feral cats (domestic cats that have been turned loose and become wild). Rabbits are their main competitors for food.

## BANDICOOTS, BILBIES, AND PEOPLE

Australian aboriginal (native) people considered the bandicoot one of the creators of life. According to their legends, Karora, a giant bandicoot, awoke from under the earth and gave birth to humans out of his armpit. Aborginal people also hunted bandicoots for food.

European colonists thought bandicoots looked like rats and tended to treat them as pests. Many were killed when colonists tried to rid Australia of rabbits that were introduced and soon overran the country, because they had no natural predators.

## THE EASTER BILBY

Starting in the 1990s, the Foundation for Rabbit-Free Australia and the Save the Bilby Fund began a public relations campaign to replace the Easter rabbit with the Easter bilby. The fund teamed up with candy makers to make chocolate bilbies for children's Easter baskets. Part of the sales price of each candy bilby went to bilby conservation and restoration programs. By 2004, several hundred thousand dollars had been raised through candy bilby sales.

Legal protection of bandicoots did not occur until the middle of the twentieth century, after several species were already extinct. Today conservation groups are trying to save bandicoots and bilbies, but many suburban residents still consider them pests, because they dig up gardens when hunting for food. They also carry ticks, lice, and fleas.

### CONSERVATION STATUS

Three species of bandicoot are extinct: the pig-footed bandicoot, the desert bandicoot, and the lesser bilby. All the extinct species lived in the dry inland area of Australia. The western barred bandicoot is considered Endangered, facing a very high risk of extinction. Four other species are considered Vulnerable, facing a high risk of extinction. Captive breeding projects have been started to save the greater bilby and the western barred bandicoot. These projects have had some success, but it is unlikely that populations of bandicoots in the wild will increase without control of their predators (animals that hunt them for food).

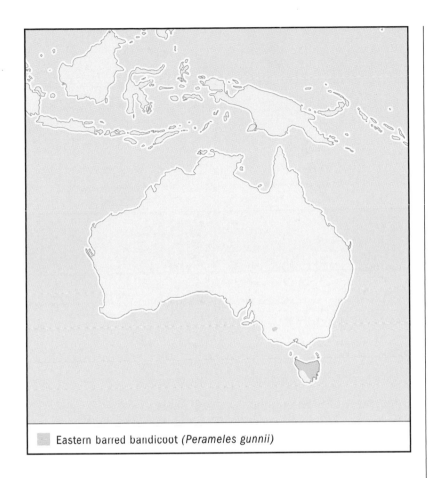

Eastern barred bandicoot (*Perameles gunnii*)

## EASTERN BARRED BANDICOOT
### *Perameles gunnii*

**Physical characteristics:** The eastern barred bandicoot, also called the barred bandicoot, the Tasmanian barred bandicoot, the striped bandicoot, or Gunn's bandicoot, measures 10.5 to 14 inches (27 to 35 centimeters) not including the tail and weighs 26.5 to 35 ounces (0.75 to 1 kilogram). It has grayish brown fur with pale bars on its hindquarters. It has large ears, a thin, pointed snout, and its tail is relatively short.

**Geographic range:** Eastern barred bandicoots are found in the Australian state of Victoria and on the island of Tasmania. At one time it was also found in the state of South Australia, but it is now extinct there.

**Habitat:** This species lives in grasslands, open grassy woodlands, and suburban yards and parks.

**Diet:** Eastern barred bandicoots eat mainly insects, insect larvae, earthworms, bulbs, seeds, and fallen fruit.

**Behavior and reproduction:** Eastern barred bandicoots have the shortest pregnancy of any mammal—around twelve days. The young, usually only two or three, are carried in the mother's pouch another fifty-five days and become completely independent about three weeks later. This species becomes fully mature and capable of reproducing at about four months of age and has a lifespan of two to three years.

**Eastern barred bandicoots and people:** Aboriginal peoples hunted the eastern barred bandicoot for food. Suburban residents find it a pest because it digs up lawns when hunting for food.

**Conservation status:** As of 2003, the eastern barred bandicoot was considered Vulnerable to extinction. At one point it was considered Critically Endangered. In 1991, only 109 animals were known to exist on mainland Australia.

Serious conservation efforts are underway in Victoria. These include habitat protection, predator control, community education, captive breeding, and reintroduction of captive-bred bandicoots to the wild. By 1993, the population had grown to over seven hundred animals. The main threats to this species are predators such as the red fox and cats, and being hit and killed by automobiles.

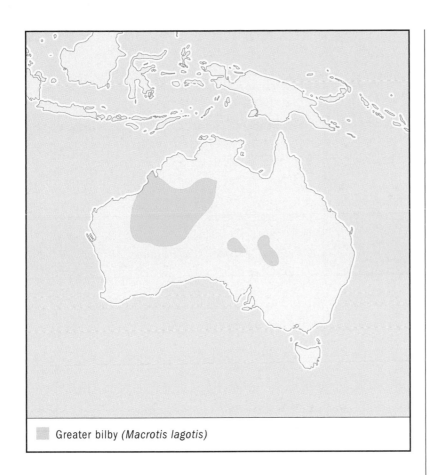

Greater bilby (*Macrotis lagotis*)

## GREATER BILBY
### *Macrotis lagotis*

**Physical characteristics:** The greater bilby, also called the rabbit-eared bandicoot, is a small bilby about the size of a rabbit. It measures 9 to 10 inches (23 to 26 centimeters). Males weigh from 2 to 5.5 pounds (1 to 2.5 kilograms). Females are smaller, weighing from 1.8 to 2.5 pounds (0.8 to 1.1 kilograms). Bilbies have soft, silky blue-gray fur on their back and white bellies. They have a long, thin snout and a long black tail with a white tip. The lesser bilby, a relative of the greater bilby, became extinct in 1931, so the greater bilby is usually referred to simply as the bilby.

*Bilbies are the only bandicoots that dig burrows. They stay in their burrows during the day to keep cool. (Howard Hughes/Nature Focus. Reproduced by permission.)*

**Geographic range:** Bilbies are found in the Northern Territory, Western Australia, and Queensland, but their populations are isolated from each other.

**Habitat:** Bilbies prefer hot, dry grassland, and will occasionally live in dry, shrubby, open woodlands.

**Diet:** Bilbies feed at night. They are omnivores, and like other bandicoots eat insects, insect larvae, earthworms, bulbs, and seeds.

**Behavior and reproduction:** Bilbies are the only bandicoots that dig burrows. They are excellent diggers, and these burrows can be up to 6 feet (2 meters) deep. They stay in the burrows during the day for protection against the heat.

Like all bandicoots, bilbies live alone, coming together only to mate. They mate throughout the year and give birth only fourteen days after mating. The young are then carried in the mother's pouch for eighty days. After they leave the pouch, they live in the burrow with their mother who feeds them for another two weeks.

**Greater bilbies and people:** Bilbies were very common until the beginning of the twentieth century and were an important source of food for native peoples. However, their numbers rapidly decreased with the introduction of non-native predators such as the red fox and the cat. Today, the bilby has become a symbol of Australia's efforts to save its native species.

**Conservation status:** As of 2003, the bilby was considered Vulnerable to extinction. Their numbers decreased because of non-native predators, competition for food by rabbits, and changes in habitat brought about by livestock ranching and farming. The bilby has been the focus of an intensive public awareness and recovery program. The Save the Bilby Appeal was begun in 1999 and has been quite successful. Sales of chocolate Easter bilbies have helped to finance captive breeding programs and reintroduction of bilbies to the wild. Most recently, the Save the Bilby Appeal has started a campaign to fence a large area where bilbies released into the wild will be protected from predators. ■

# FOR MORE INFORMATION

## Books:

Menkhorst, Frank. *A Field Guide to the Mammals of Australia,* 2nd ed. Oxford, U.K.: Oxford University Press, 2001.

Nowak, Ronald M. *Walker's Mammals of the World.* Baltimore: Johns Hopkins University Press, 1995.

## Periodicals:

Clark, Tim W., Richard P. Reading, and Gary Backhouse. "Prototyping for Successful Conservation: The Eastern Barred Bandicoot Program." *Endangered Species Update* (July–August 2002): 125.

Smyth, Chris. "Bilbies' Call of the Wild." *Habitat Australia* (October 1998): 13.

## Web sites:

Queensland Government Environmental Protection Agency/Queensland Parks and Wildlife Service. *Nature Conservation.* http://www.epa. qld.gov.au/nature_conservation (accessed on June 22, 2004).

University of Michigan Museum of Zoology. "Family Peramelidae." *Animal Diversity Web.* http://animaldiversity.ummz.umich.edu (accessed on June 22, 2004).

## Other sources:

Australian Bilby Appreciation Society. P.O. Box 2002, Rangview, Victoria 3132 Australia. E-mail: bilbies@optusnet.no.SPAM.com.au Web site: http://members.oze-mail.com.au/bilbies

family

CHAPTER

phylum

class

subclass

order

monotypic order

suborder

▲ **family**

## PHYSICAL CHARACTERISTICS

Peroryctidae are spiny bandicoots. They look like a cross between a rabbit and a rat. In many ways they are similar to the bandicoots in the Peramelidae family. Spiny bandicoots range in size from about 6.5 to 22 inches (17.5 to 56 centimeters), not including the tail. They vary in weight from 14 ounces to 10 pounds (0.4 to 4.7 kilograms). The giant bandicoot of southeastern New Guinea is the largest species. The mouse bandicoot is the smallest.

Spiny bandicoots have rough, spiky fur that is usually blackish or brown on the back and white or tan on the belly. Most species are a solid color, but the striped bandicoot has darker stripes on its rump and around its eyes. Like the true bandicoots, spiny bandicoots have claws that are adapted to digging for food. Their front feet have five toes. The middle three toes have strong claws. Toes one and five are either small or absent. On the hind feet, the bones of the second and third toes are joined, but each toe has a separate claw. The hind legs are longer than the front legs and are strong and well developed for hopping and leaping. They are also able to move with a running gait.

Spiny bandicoots differ from true bandicoots mainly in the shape of their skulls, the habitats they prefer, and the roughness of their fur. Recent studies show that they also are genetically different from true bandicoots.

## GEOGRAPHIC RANGE

Spiny bandicoots live mainly on the island of New Guinea and a few small neighboring islands. One species is found in

Australia only on the northernmost tip of Queensland, the part of Australia closest to New Guinea.

## HABITAT

Spiny bandicoots prefer damp, humid habitats. They live in tropical rainforests and mountain rainforests at elevations from zero to 14,800 feet (zero to 4,500 meters). Species living in the same area tend to live at different elevations.

## DIET

Like all bandicoots, spiny bandicoots are omnivores, meaning they eat both animals and plants. Most of their diet consists of insects, insect larvae, earthworms, spiders, centipedes, bulbs, seeds, and fallen fruit. Spiny bandicoots appear to eat more vegetable material, especially fruit, than true bandicoots. This may be because fruit is more available in the damp habitats they prefer than in the dry habitats preferred by true bandicoots. They either lick their food off the ground or dig for it with their strong claws. They can dig holes up to 5 inches (13 centimeters) deep and scoop out the food with their long tongues.

## BEHAVIOR AND REPRODUCTION

Spiny bandicoots are nocturnal, feeding during the night and resting during the day in nests of leaves, hollow logs, or shallow burrows. They live alone, coming together only briefly to mate. They are territorial animals, protecting an area against other members of their species and becoming aggressive if their area is invaded.

Little is known about spiny bandicoots. They are difficult to observe, because they live in remote or mountainous areas and are active only at night. Bandicoots are marsupial mammals. Most marsupials have what is called a yolk-sac placenta. A placenta is an organ that grows in the mother's uterus (womb). In eutherian (yoo-THEER-ee-an) mammals, such as dogs, cows, and humans, the placenta allows the developing offspring share the mother's food and oxygen. In animals with a yolk-sac placenta, there is no sharing of the mother's food and oxygen.

### THE TINIEST BANDICOOT

The mouse bandicoot measures only 6 inches (15 centimeters) long. It is extremely difficult to observe, and was not discovered until 1932. It lives in moss forests at altitudes of 6,300 to 8,200 feet (1,900 to 2,500 meters), and is active only at night. By 1977 only four specimens of this species had been collected for study.

Bandicoots differ from other marsupials, because they have a second placenta in addition to the yolk-sac placenta. This placenta resembles the placenta of eutherian mammals, but does not function as well, because it does not attach as closely to the wall of the mother's uterus. As a result, spiny bandicoots have short pregnancies, and the young are born nearly helpless. They drag themselves into their mother's pouch where they attach to her teats, or nipples and are carried until they have matured. Spiny bandicoots normally have only one or two young at a time, but little is known about how long they are carried in their mother's pouch, when they become old enough to reproduce, or how long they live in the wild.

## SPINY BANDICOOTS AND PEOPLE

In New Guinea, spiny bandicoots are hunted and are an important food source for native peoples. Otherwise, these animals are of interest mainly to scientists and conservationists.

## CONSERVATION STATUS

Very little is known about the size of spiny bandicoot populations in the wild. In fact, so little is know about them that they are not given a conservation rating, although they probably are under pressure from human activities such as logging.

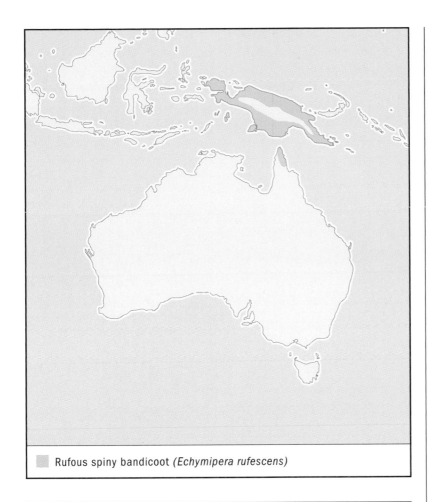

Rufous spiny bandicoot *(Echymipera rufescens)*

## RUFOUS SPINY BANDICOOT
### *Echymipera rufescens*

**Physical characteristics:** Rufous spiny bandicoots have a total head and body length of about 12 to 16 inches (30 to 41 centimeters) and weigh between 1.1 and 4.4 pounds (0.5 to 2.0 kilograms). The short black tail is almost hairless. The fur on their back is coarse, spiky, and reddish brown. The fur on their belly is white. The rufous spiny bandicoot sometimes is called the long-nosed echymipera, the spiny bandicoot, or the rufescent bandicoot.

**Geographic range:** The rufous spiny bandicoot is the only member of the Peroryctidae family that lives in Australia. There it lives only

Rufous spiny bandicoots' favorite food is insects. They dig insects out of the ground with their claws and lap them up with long, thin tongues. (Illustration by Gillian Harris. Reproduced by permission.)

on the Cape York Peninsula of Queensland. This animal also lives in western and southeastern New Guinea and the neighboring islands of Kei and Aru.

**Habitat:** Rufous spiny bandicoots prefer lowland tropical rainforests below an elevation of 3,900 feet (1,200 meters). They occasionally are can be found in open costal woodlands or disturbed grasslands.

**Diet:** Rufous spiny bandicoots are omnivores, meaning they can eat both plants and animals, but their preferred food is insects. They feed on the ground, digging out insects with their claws and lapping them up with long, thin tongues.

**Behavior and reproduction:** This bandicoot lives and feeds on the ground and is strictly nocturnal. It digs shallow burrows to rest in during the day. Rufous spiny bandicoots live alone and appear to be territorial.

Very little is known about this animal's reproductive cycle. Some scientists believe that this species breeds year round in New Guinea and seasonally in Australia, but not enough animals have been studied to form firm conclusions. Litters usually consist of from one to three young that are carried in the mother's pouch until they mature.

**Rufous spiny bandicoots and people:** Native peoples of New Guinea hunt these bandicoots for food.

**Conservation status:** The rufous spiny bandicoot appears to be common to abundant within its very limited range, especially in Australia. However, the small number of places in which this species is found has become cause for concern among conservationists. ■

## FOR MORE INFORMATION

### Books:

Finney, Tim F. *Mammals of New Guinea,* 2nd ed. Ithaca, NY: Cornell University Press, 1995.

Menkhorst, Frank. *A Field Guide to the Mammals of Australia,* 2nd ed. Oxford, U.K.: Oxford University Press, 2001.

Nowak, Ronald M. *Walker's Mammals of the World.* Baltimore: Johns Hopkins University Press, 1995. http://www.press.jhu.edu/books/walkers_mammals of_the_world/marsupialia/marsupialia. peramelidae.echymipera.html (accessed on June 30, 2004).

### Web sites:

University of Michigan Museum of Zoology. "Family Peroryctidae."*Animal Diversity Web* http://animaldiversity.ummz.umich.edu (accessed on June 30, 2004).

monotypic order
CHAPTER

## PHYSICAL CHARACTERISTICS

Marsupial moles, also called blind sand burrowers, are unusual and rarely seen animals found in Australia. Marsupial moles are about 4 to 6 inches (10 to 15 centimeters) long and weigh only 1 to 2.5 ounces (40 to 70 grams). They have fine golden fur, and are shaped like flattened cylinders.

The body of the marsupial mole shows many adaptations that allow it to live almost its entire life underground. These moles have five toes on each foot. On the front feet, toes three and four are enlarged and have triangular, spade-like claws that are used for digging. The animals have no functional eyes. Only a dark spot marks where the remains of an eye can be found under the skin. In addition, marsupial moles have no external ears, although they do have ear openings under the fur, and it is believed that they can hear. Five of the animal's seven neck vertebrae, neck bones, are fused, or joined together, probably to strengthen the head so that it can push through sand.

A horny shield somewhat like a thick fingernail protects the nose. The nose openings or nostrils are small slits, probably to prevent them from filling with sand as the animal digs. Female marsupial moles also have a backward-opening pouch in which they carry their young. Again, this is probably an adaptation so that the pouch does not fill with sand as they move forward. The tail is short, less than 1 inch (2.5 centimeters), hairless, and covered with a leathery skin and ends in a hard, horny knob.

Genetic studies show that marsupial moles are not closely related to any other Australian marsupial. In 1987 a fossil marsupial mole was found at Riversleigh, an area that was known to be a rainforest habitat millions of years ago. Scientists think that this fossil mole used its broad claws to burrow through leaves and moss on the forest floor. When the climate changed and Australia became drier, these claws allow it to adapt to living in sand.

## GEOGRAPHIC RANGE

Marsupial moles live in the deserts of Western Australia, South Australia, the Northern Territory and southwestern corner of Queensland.

## HABITAT

These moles live in sandy desert regions and seem to prefer sand plains near seasonal rivers or sand ridges where spinifex grass grows.

## DIET

Marsupial moles hunt and feed underground, digging their food out of the sand. They are insectivores, eating mainly ants, termites, and insect larvae (LAR-vee). They have also been known to eat seeds and small lizards. Marsupial moles kept in captivity and fed on the surface take their food underground to eat it.

## BEHAVIOR AND REPRODUCTION

Marsupial moles are active under the ground both day and night. They "swim" or burrow through sand rapidly. They normally tunnel about 4 to 8 inches (10 to 20 centimeters) under the surface. However, they occasionally dig down to depths of more than 8 feet (2.5 meters). When moving through sand, the mole uses its wide front claws to shovel soil backward under its belly. Then the hind feet push together to propel the body forward. These moles do not leave the burrows. The sand fills in the area behind them as they move.

Marsupial moles seem to appear on the surface more often after a heavy rain, although some scientists question if they actually appear more often or if their tracks are simply more noticeable in damp sand. On the surface, they move slowly with a shuffling side-to-side gait and drag their tail, leaving a distinctive pattern of parallel lines. They move only short distances before re-entering the sand. The speed with which they dig allows them to avoid most predators, animals that hunt them for food.

## BRRR—IT'S COLD

Marsupial moles are used to living where it is hot. They begin to shiver when the temperature drops to 59°F (15°C) and die of hypothermia, a condition where core body temperature decreases, soon afterwards. Most marsupial moles kept in captivity have died because people did not understand that they need to be kept at temperatures of 73 to 81°F (23 to 27°C) to survive.

Almost nothing is known about marsupial mole reproduction. Females have two teats, nipples, in a backward-opening pouch.

## MARSUPIAL MOLES AND PEOPLE

Aboriginal (native) people call the southern species of marsupial mole Arra-jarra-ja or Kakarratul and the northern species Itjari-itjari. These people probably ate moles when they could catch them, but because of the difficulty in hunting them, they were not a major food source. Today marsupial moles are of interest to scientists and the public mainly because of their rarity and interesting adaptations to life underground.

## CONSERVATION STATUS

Although the distribution and population size of marsupial moles is not known, both species, the northern marsupial mole and the southern marsupial mole, are considered Endangered, facing a very high risk of extinction in the wild in the near future. Marsupial moles receive legal protection from the Australian government. In an effort to learn more about the marsupial mole population, the University of Western Australia supports a program for the public to report sightings of these animals.

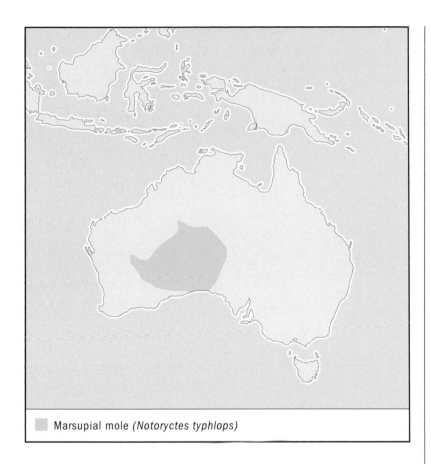

Marsupial mole *(Notoryctes typhlops)*

## SOUTHERN MARSUPIAL MOLE
### *Notoryctes typhlops*

**Physical characteristics:** The southern marsupial mole, sometimes called the greater marsupial mole or just the marsupial mole, has a total head and body length of 3.5 to 7 inches (9 to 18 centimeters) and a 1-inch (2-centimeter) tail. It weighs about 1.2 to 2.5 ounces (35 to 70 grams).

Southern marsupial moles have short legs, spade-like claws on the front feet, and flat nose shields. They also lack eyes and external ears.

**Geographic range:** Southern marsupial moles are found in Western Australia, the southern Northern Territory, and northwestern South Australia. The northern part of its range may overlap with the range of the northern marsupial mole.

*Because marsupial moles live most of their lives underground, it is difficult for scientists to study them. Their behavior, and even how many there are, are not well known. (B. G. Thomson. Reproduced by permission.)*

**Habitat:** Southern marsupial moles live underground in sandy plains and sand ridges.

**Diet:** This species eats mostly insects and insect larvae.

**Behavior and reproduction:** Marsupial moles "swim" rapidly through sand, living most of their lives underground. They appear to live alone. Almost nothing is known about their reproductive pattern.

**Southern marsupial moles and people:** Southern marsupial moles have little practical value to humans, but they are a symbol of the rare and unusual animals of Australia. Their bodies are an excellent example of adaptation to their environment.

**Conservation status:** These moles have been listed as Endangered, facing a very high risk of extinction, even though little is known about their abundance. It appears, however, as if their numbers are declining. One reason may be compacting of the soil they live in by vehicles or livestock. ∎

## FOR MORE INFORMATION

### Books:

Menkhorst, Frank. *A Field Guide to the Mammals of Australia,* 2nd ed. Oxford, U.K.: Oxford University Press, 2001.

Nowak, Ronald M. *Walker's Mammals of the World.* Baltimore: Johns Hopkins University Press, 1995.

### Web sites:

Withers, Philip, and Graham Thompson. "Marsupial Moles (*Notoryctes*)." University of Western Australia Zoology Department. http://www .zoology.uwa.edu.au/staff/pwithers/marsupialmole/Default.htm (accessed on June 30, 2004).

University of Michigan Museum of Zoology. "Order Notoryctemorphia." Animal Diversity Web http://animaldiversity.ummz.umich.edu/site/ accounts/information/Notoryctemorphia.html (accessed on June 30, 2004).

KOALA, WOMBATS, POSSUMS,
WALLABIES, AND KANGAROOS
Diprotodontia

Class: Mammalia
Order: Diprotodontia
Number of families: 10 families

order

CHAPTER

## PHYSICAL CHARACTERISTICS

Diprotodonts are an order of about 131 species of marsupial mammals that live in Australia, New Guinea, and parts of Indonesia. The order also contains a family of giant diprotodonts that are now extinct. Within this order are some of Australia's best known marsupials, including the kangaroos, koalas, and wombats, as well as some of the least known species such as cuscus and potoroos.

Diprotodonts have evolved to fill almost every terrestrial (land) ecological niche, and as a result, they have evolved special physical features that allow them to live most efficiently in their chosen environment. For example, some tree-dwelling (arboreal) gliding possums have evolved a skin membrane that stretches from wrist to ankle and acts as a parasail, allowing them to stay away from predators, animals that hunt them for food, and conserve energy by "flying" from tree to tree. Wombats have evolved strong claws and short, stocky bodies well suited for digging. Kangaroos have strong hind limbs that allow them to race across open grassland at speeds up to 35 miles (55 kilometers) per hour and to leap distances of up to 30 feet (9 meters). Possums and cuscus have evolved tails that can curve around and grasp a branch (prehensile tails).

As a result of this diversification, the species in this order look very different from one another. However they all share at least two physical characteristics that include them as diprotodonts. All members of this order have two large incisor

phylum

class

subclass

● **order**

monotypic order

suborder

family

teeth on the lower jaw. Incisors are front teeth that are modified for cutting. These teeth are also noticeable in more familiar rodents such as beavers and rabbits. Most members of this order also have three pairs of incisors on the upper jaw, and a few species have a second small pair on the lower jaw as well. In addition, members of this order have no canine teeth. Canine teeth are sharp, pointed teeth used for tearing food, and are located between the incisors in the front and the molars (grinding teeth) in the back. Diprotodontia have an empty space where canine teeth usually are located. This pattern of teeth has evolved because most members of this order are herbivores, or plant eaters. They need sharp front teeth to clip off the tough grasses and other plants that make up most of their diet, and they need molars to grind the plants, but they do not need canines to tear their food apart the way carnivores (meat-eaters) do. A few species in this order now eat insects, invertebrates, or flower nectar, but their tooth pattern suggests that at one time during their evolution, they also ate plants.

Besides sharing a common pattern of teeth, all diprotodonts have a condition in their hind limbs called syndactyly (sin-DACK-tuh-lee). Syndactyly means "fused toes." In members of this order, bones of the second and third toe on the hind feet have grown together into a single bone as far down as the claw. However, this fused bone has two separate claws—this twin claw is used for grooming. In many species in this order, the fourth hind toe is enlarged, and the fifth toe is either very small or absent.

On the front limbs of many species, the first two fingers oppose the other three. This means that these fingers, like the thumb on a human hand, can reach across and touch the tip of the other three fingers (unlike, for example, a dog paw or human foot where none of the toes can bend to touch each other). This adaptation is found mainly in species that live in trees, as it helps them grasp branches and climb.

Diprotodonts are marsupials, and like all marsupials they give birth to very poorly developed young after a short pregnancy. The young then attach to teats (nipples) in the mother's pouch and are carried for weeks or months until they mature enough to live independently. All diprotodonts have forward-opening pouches (like the kangaroo) except for wombats and koalas. Wombats are burrowing animals. A backward opening pouch is an advantage when digging, because it will not fill up with dirt. The backward opening pouch of the koala, which lives in trees, may be left over from a time when its ancestors lived on the ground and dug like the wombat.

Diprotodonts have soft fur, and many species have been hunted for their skins. Most species are earth tone colors, grays and browns, but some have quite eye-catching coloration, such as the yellow-footed rock wallaby, whose patches of red, yellow, and white contrast with its gray fur. Diprotodonts range in size from the red kangaroo, which weighs up to 187 pounds (85 kilograms) to the little pygmy possum, which weighs only about a quarter of an ounce (7 grams). In the past, the fossil record shows that there were much larger diprotodonts living in Australia. These animals became extinct about 50,000 years ago when humans first appeared in Australia.

## GEOGRAPHIC RANGE

Diprotodonts are native only in Australia, New Guinea, and a few islands of Indonesia. The brush-tailed possum was introduced to New Zealand, where it is considered a pest.

## HABITAT

Diprotodontia have evolved to take advantage of almost every terrestrial habitat. This expansion into different habitats is called radiation. Kangaroos graze on grasslands, cuscus and tree kangaroos live in tropical rainforest trees. Some pygmy possums live in the mountains where it snows six months out of the year. Despite the variety of habitats where members of this order can be found, some individual species live in very restricted areas, because they have evolved to use a very specific set of resources.

## DIET

For the most part, diprotodonts are herbivores. Those species that do not eat leaves, fruits, and roots now, probably had ancestors that did. Many species have developed extra large or extra long digestive tracts that allow them to eat leaves and grass with low nutritional value. In addition, they have evolved behaviors that reduce their need for energy. For example, koalas sleep about twenty hours per day to conserve energy.

Some species, such as the mountain pygmy possum, feed heavily on insects. Others species eat insects, worms, and even occasionally a lizard, in addition to a mainly vegetarian diet. The honey possum has developed a long snout that allows it to feed exclusively on plant pollen and nectar.

## BEHAVIOR AND REPRODUCTION

Diprotodonts are mainly active at twilight and night. The only species that is active exclusively during the day is the musky rat-kangaroo, although some diprotodonts that live in the forest tend to be active during both day and night. The mountain pygmy possum is the only diprotodont, and in fact the only marsupial, to hibernate or become inactive in cold months.

Many diprotodonts live alone, coming together only to mate, but there are exceptions. Kangaroos tend to associate in loose groups, called mobs, but there is no definite leader and no co-operation among members as there is in a structured group like a wolf pack. Common wombats visit each other's burrows and are not aggressive toward each other, but they do not live together in social groups. Likewise, koalas live near each other, but have their own personal space. On the other hand, hairy-nosed wombats may live in large groups of up to fifty animals, sharing a series of interconnected burrows. Small possums, such as the honey possum and feather-tailed possum, may huddle together for warmth, but larger species of possum live alone. Diprotodonts can be very noisy. They use barking, sneezing, hissing, grunting, gurgling, and growling to mark their territories and communicate their moods to other members of their own species.

In terms of reproduction, diprotodonts, like all marsupials, have short (two weeks to one month) pregnancies. At birth, the newborn is tiny (in some species, as small as a jelly bean). The young are carried in the mother's pouch for weeks or months until they can survive in the outside world. Many species continue to nurse their young after they leave the pouch. Wombats and possums carry their young on their back after they outgrow the pouch. In many species the young may remain with the mother outside the pouch for up to several months before becoming completely independent.

## DIPROTODONTS AND PEOPLE

Two members of this order, the kangaroo and the koala, and are national symbols of Australia, and are used heavily in tourist promotions. Kangaroos have been hunted since the first humans arrived in Australia. Today there is a market for kangaroo meat, both for use in pet food and for humans, and leather made of kangaroo skins. The common brush-tail possum has adapted to suburban environments, and is considered a nuisance. Introduced into New Zealand in 1840, the brush-tailed possum is an invasive alien (introduced, non-native species) that damages native plants and animal habitats. Many farmers also see the wombat as a pest, since its burrows allow rabbits (invasive aliens in Australia) to cross under fences intended to keep them out of grasslands. Kangaroos, however, have benefited from the colonization of Australia by Europeans. Europeans cleared the land for grazing livestock. This increased the amount of grassland habitat favorable to kangaroos and allowed their populations to increase.

## CONSERVATION STATUS

The arrival of Europeans and the animals they introduced (rabbits, red foxes, cats, sheep, cattle) significantly changed the habitats of some diprotodonts and put others in direct competition with these introduced animals for food. Hunting, clearing the land for farming, changing patterns of burning grassland, and economic development have put pressure on these animals, often forcing them into marginal habitats, reducing their range or fragmenting them into isolated populations.

About 25 percent of the species in this order are considered threatened or potentially in danger of extinction. Six species have gone extinct in recent years. However, three other species thought to be extinct have been found to be still alive, although considered Critically Endangered, facing an extremely high risk of extinction. The northern hairy-nosed wombat is also Critically Endangered, with possibly fewer than 100 individuals left in the wild. Its cousin, the southern hairy-nosed wombat, is Endangered, facing a very high risk of extinction, because of its limited range. On the other hand, the koala, once threatened with extinction in 1920, has been the target of successful conservation (though in some areas, koalas are dying or being relocated because of overcrowding).

### MODERN DISCOVERIES

One might think that with our ability to go to every corner of the planet, all the marsupials in Australia and New Guinea would have been discovered. Imagine scientists' surprise and excitement in the 1980s when two new species of diprotodonts were discovered in Australia. Then, in the 1990s, four new diprotodonts were found in New Guinea. It is possible that in the twenty-first century, other adventurous scientists will find still more new species from this order.

## FOR MORE INFORMATION

### Books:

Finney, Tim F. *Mammals of New Guinea,* 2nd ed. Ithaca, NY: Cornell University Press, 1995.

Menkhorst, Frank. *A Field Guide to the Mammals of Australia,* 2nd ed. Oxford, U.K.: Oxford University Press, 2001.

Nowak, Ronald M. *Walker's Mammals of the World.* Baltimore: Johns Hopkins University Press, 1995.

### Web sites:

Australian National Parks and Wildlife Service. http://www.nationalparks.nsw.gov.au/ (accessed on June 30, 2004).

Marsupial Society of Australia. "Fact Sheets." http://www.marsupialsociety.org (accessed on June 30, 2004).

Parks and Wildlife Service Tasmania. http://www.parks.tas.gov.au (accessed on June 30, 2004).

Queensland Government Environmental Protection Agency/Queensland Parks and Wildlife Service. "Nature Conservation." http://www.epa.qld.gov.au/nature_conservation (accessed on June 30, 2004).

**KOALA**

**Phascolarctidae**

**Class:** Mammalia

**Order:** Diprotodontia

**Family:** Phascolarctidae

**One species:** Koala (*Phascolarctos cinereus*)

phylum

class

subclass

order

monotypic order

suborder

▲ **family**

## PHYSICAL CHARACTERISTICS

Koalas are known worldwide as one of the symbols of Australia. Their gray and white fur, broad head, small eyes, large furry ears, and round belly make them appear cuddly like a teddy bear.

Koalas range in size from 24 to 33 inches (60 to 85 centimeters) and in weight from 8.8 to 33 pounds (4 to 15 kilograms). This is an unusually large size range. Koalas living in the northern (warmer) part of their range are on average 45 percent smaller than those in the southern (colder) areas. In addition, males can be up to 50 percent larger than females.

Koalas are arboreal, meaning they live in trees. They have strong arms and legs with five toes that end in sharp curved claws to help them climb. The first two toes on the front legs are opposable. This means that these toes, like the thumb on a human hand, can reach across and touch the tip of the other three toes (unlike, for example, a dog paw or human foot, where none of the toes can bend to touch each other). This adaptation helps koalas to grasp branches and climb. The first toe of the hind food is short, broad, and clawless. It is also helpful in gripping branches. As in all members of the order Diprotodontia, the bones of the second and third toes of the hind foot are fused. This condition is called syndactyly (sin-DACK-tuh-lee). The single fused bone, however, has two separate claws. This twin claw is used in grooming.

Koalas do not build nests or live in dens. Their fur protects them from the weather. As a result, the fur of animals living in the colder regions of the range is thicker than that of animals living where it is warmer. In the past, many koalas were killed

## KOALA BEARS?

Because of their teddy bear look, koalas are sometimes called koala bears. They are not, of course bears. They are not even closely related to bears. In fact, their closest living relative is the wombat, a stocky, burrowing marsupial.

for their fur. Males have a gland on their chest that produces scent used for marking trees to warn off other males and establish their own individual territory. Females have a backward-opening pouch in which they carry their young. Koalas also have a tiny brain. It is only 0.2 percent of their body weight.

## GEOGRAPHIC RANGE

Koalas are found in isolated patches along the eastern coast of Australia from Queensland to Victoria.

## HABITAT

Koalas eat only eucalyptus (yoo-kah-LIP-tus) leaves. Therefore, they are limited to areas where eucalypts grow. This can range from wet tropical forests to dry open woodlands.

## DIET

Koalas have strong food preferences. They eat the leaves of about 30 of the 650 species of eucalyptus trees that grow in Australia. Eucalyptus leaves are not an ideal food. They are low in nutrients, hard to digest, and contain toxins (poisons).

In order to digest these leaves, koalas have evolved certain adaptations. They avoid the most poisonous species of eucalypts, and their liver is capable of detoxifying, or making harmless, some of the harmful chemicals in the leaves. They have strong grinding teeth (molars and pre-molars) that grind the tough leaves into a paste. Finally, they have an enormously long cecum (SEE-kum) in which the leaves are digested. The cecum is part of the digestive system. It is a type of sac located where the large and small intestine meet. In the koala, the cecum can be more than 75 inches (2 meters) long. The cecum contains bacteria that help break down the eucalyptus leaves. Koalas get most of the water they need from their diet. However, when fresh water is available, they will drink.

## BEHAVIOR AND REPRODUCTION

One reason that koalas can exist on low-nutrient food is that they have developed a lifestyle that allows them to conserve

Koalas come out of their mother's pouch when they're about six months old, and cling to her belly or back until they are one year old. (© Kenneth W. Fink/Photo Researchers, Inc. Reproduced by permission.)

energy. They sleep for up to twenty hours each day, and also spend part of the time that they are awake resting. They are nocturnal animals, feeding mainly at night.

Koalas live alone. Males use the scent gland on their chest to mark certain trees as their own territory. They will fight with other male koalas that come into their home trees. The male's home territory often overlaps with that of several females.

Koala (*Phascolarctos cinereus*)

The size of the territory depends on how plentiful the food supply is.

Koalas mate during the cool season in Australia. A dominant male will mate with as many females as he can find. Once mating is complete, the animals go their separate ways, and the male has nothing to do with raising the offspring. Koalas are capable of mating when they are two years old, but generally do not begin to reproduce until they are four or five. Their lifespan is about ten years in the wild, and almost double that in captivity.

A single baby is born after a thirty-five–day pregnancy. The baby is tiny, measuring less than an inch (2 centimeters) and weighing less than 0.02 ounces (0.5 grams). The newborn crawls to its mother's pouch where it stays for five to seven months. When it is about half a year old, it comes out of the pouch and clings to its mother's belly or back. During this time, it still nurses, but it also eats vegetable material that has passed through the mother's digestive system. Scientists believe that in this way the bacteria in the cecum that is needed to digest eucalpytus leaves is passed on from mother to child. The young koala stays with its mother until it is about a year old. By age two it begins looking for its own territory.

## KOALAS AND PEOPLE

Aboriginal peoples of Australia hunted koalas for food, as did Europeans when they arrived in Australia. Today koalas are symbols of Australia recognized throughout the world. Their image attracts many tourists, and their image can be found on all types of souvenirs. Very few koalas are sent to zoos outside Australia because of the difficulty in keeping them supplied with fresh eucalyptus leaves.

## CONSERVATION STATUS

By the end of the 1920s millions of kolas had been hunted for their fur, and these animals had become extinct in parts of their original range. Intense conservation programs, including protecting habitat, breeding programs, and relocation of some animals, has resulted in a substantial increase in the koala population. There are even some areas where overcrowding is occurring today, leaving the koalas vulnerable to disease and starvation. Today, although there are plenty of koalas, conservationists are concerned about their loss of habitat. The areas in which koalas live are some of the most rapidly developing places in Australia. The Australian Koala Foundation has been a leader in mapping koala habitat and lobbying for its protection.

## FOR MORE INFORMATION

**Books:**

Menkhorst, Frank. *A Field Guide to the Mammals of Australia,* 2nd ed. Oxford, U.K.: Oxford University Press, 2001.

Nowak, Ronald M. *Walker's Mammals of the World.* Baltimore: Johns Hopkins University Press, 1995. Online at http://www.press.jhu.edu/books/walkers_mammals_of_the_world (accessed on May 8, 2004).

Wexo, John B. *Koalas and other Australian Animals.* Poway, CA: Zoobooks/Wildlife Education, 1997.

**Web sites:**

Australian National Parks and Wildlife Service. "Koala." http://www.nationalparks.nsw.gov.au/npws.nsf/Content/The+koala (accessed on June 30, 2004).

**Other sources:**

The Australian Koala Foundation. G. P. O. 2659, Brisbane, Queensland 4001 Australia. Phone: 61 (07) 3229 7233. Fax: 61 (07) 3221 0337. E-mail: akf@savethekoala.com Web site: http://www.savethekoala.com/.

**WOMBATS**
**Vombatidae**

**Class:** Mammalia
**Order:** Diprotodontia
**Family:** Vombatidae
**Number of species:** 3 species

## PHYSICAL CHARACTERISTICS

Wombats are stout, stocky burrowing marsupials with powerful forearms and sharp claws for digging. A marsupial is a mammal that does not have a well-developed placenta and gives birth to immature and underdeveloped young, which it then continues to nurture, often in a pouch, until the young are able to fend for themselves. Wombats are about 3.3 feet (1 meter) long and weigh from about 55 to 88 pounds (25 to 40 kilograms). Their fur varies from gray to brown.

All three species of wombat look similar. They have large heads, small ears and eyes, and short, strong necks. They have front teeth, incisors, that continue to grow throughout their life and must be worn down by the food they eat. The main physical difference among the three species is the presence or absence of hair on their nose. Male and female wombats look similar. The female has a backward-opening pouch in which she carries her young. In the past, fossils show that there were as many as nine species of wombat, including one that weighed 440 pounds (200 kilograms). Today the closest living relative of the wombat is the koala.

## GEOGRAPHIC RANGE

Wombats live in southeastern Australia. The common wombat is fairly widespread and can be found in parts of New South Wales, Victoria, South Australia, and Tasmania. The northern hairy-nosed wombat lives only in one place in Queensland, and the southern hairy-nosed wombat lives in a small area along the south central coast of Australia.

phylum
class
subclass
order
monotypic order
suborder
▲ **family**

## THE WOMBAT BOY

In 1960 Peter "PJ" Nicholson was a fifteen year old student at Timbertops, a rural Australian boarding school. PJ became fascinated with wombats. For a year, he sneaked out at night and crawled down wombat burrows. He was patient, visiting often and letting the wombats become comfortable with him. Eventually he traveled 70 feet (21 meters) inside the tunnels to the wombat nests. The measurements and maps that he made of the tunnels were published, and his information is still used by scientists. PJ Nicholson later earned a degree in economics, although he never lost his interest in wildlife.

## HABITAT

Wombats live under the ground in open grassland, open woodlands, and dry, shrubby, forested areas. They prefer areas where the ground is soft enough to dig extensive burrows.

## DIET

Wombats are herbivores, and eat only plants. They mainly eat native grasses, but will also eat roots, bark, and moss. They graze above ground at night and may travel up to 1.8 miles (3 kilometers) each night looking for food. Because the food they eat is high in fiber and hard to digest, it is held in their digestive system for up to seventy hours in order to break down the fiber and release the nutrients.

## BEHAVIOR AND REPRODUCTION

Wombats are nocturnal, active at night. During the day they rest in their burrows, which can be 100 feet (30 meters) long and 6 to 7 feet (1.8 to 2.1 meters) deep. The burrows usually have several entrances and side branches and are large enough for a small adult to fit into them. The southern hairy-nosed wombat builds particularly complex tunnel systems that it may share with other wombats.

Even when they share tunnels, wombats feed alone and are territorial about their feeding grounds. They mark their personal areas with scent and droppings, and act aggressively toward other wombats that move into their territory. Usually, male animals must leave their birth area to find a new territory, but it is the female wombats that are driven out of their birth area and are forced to find new feeding grounds when they mature.

Wombats, like all marsupial mammals, have short pregnancies and give birth to a single tiny, underdeveloped newborn. Pregnancy lasts only about twenty-two days. After birth, the young crawl to the mother's pouch and remain there attached to a teat, nipple, for six to nine months. After leaving the pouch, the young wombat stays with the mother for another year, gradually nursing less and eating more plant material, until it is finally weaned, not nursing, and independent. Wombats become capable of reproducing when they are two years old. They live more than five years in the wild and have lived up to seventeen years in captivity.

## WOMBATS AND PEOPLE

Although wombats have no commercial value, they are considered a symbol of Australia. There are active foster care programs for raising orphaned wombats. However, farmers sometimes see wombats as pests, because their tunnels allow rabbits to pass under rabbit fences and destroy crops. For this reason they are sometimes shot.

## CONSERVATION STATUS

Development in Australia has reduced and fragmented wombat habitat. In addition, dogs, dingoes (wild dogs), and automobiles are the other main threats to wombats. The northern hairy-nosed wombat is Critically Endangered, facing an extremely high risk of extinction in the wild. It lives in only one place, the Epping National Forest in Queensland, where it is off-limits to visitors. As few as 100 individuals may remain in the wild. The other two wombat species are not threatened.

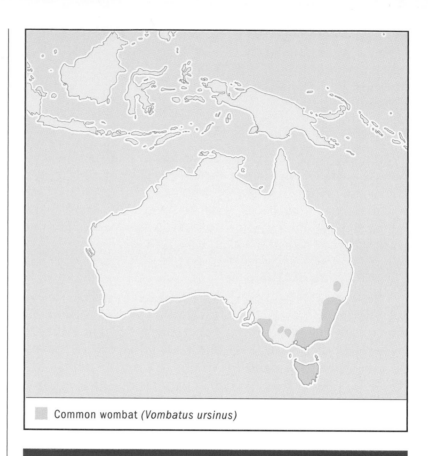

Common wombat (*Vombatus ursinus*)

## COMMON WOMBAT
### *Vombatus ursinus*

**Physical characteristics:** Common wombats have stocky bodies that ranges from 35 to 45 inches (90 to 115 centimeters) and short, stumpy tails only about 1 inch (2.5 centimeters) long. They can weigh anywhere from 48.5 to 86 pounds (22 to 39 kilograms). Their short, coarse fur is black, brown, or gray, and they are distinguished from the hairy-nosed wombats by their bare muzzles.

**Geographic range:** Common wombats are found in southeastern Australia, Tasmania, and Flinders Island.

**Habitat:** Common wombats prefer open forests and woodlands with well-drained soil that is easy to dig.

**Diet:** These animals are herbivores and eat mainly native grasses and roots.

**Behavior and reproduction:** Common wombats live alone and are active at night. They do not often share their burrows with other wombats. They have a home range that usually contains several burrows.

The young can be born at any time of the year. They remain in their mother's pouch for about six months, and continue to stay with the mother outside the pouch for about another twelve months. Males do not help raise their offspring.

**Common wombats and people:** In some areas, this wombat is considered a pest by farmers and is shot or poisoned.

**Conservation status:** These animals are not threatened, even though their habitat has been reduced by development. In many parts of their range, this animal is common. ■

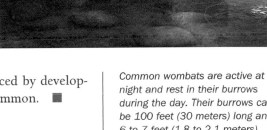

Common wombats are active at night and rest in their burrows during the day. Their burrows can be 100 feet (30 meters) long and 6 to 7 feet (1.8 to 2.1 meters) under the ground. (Norman Owen Tomalin/Bruce Coleman Inc. Reproduced by permission.)

## FOR MORE INFORMATION

### Books:

Cuppy, Will, and Ed Nofzinger. *How to Attract the Wombat.* Boston: David R. Godine, 2002.

Finney, Tim F. *Mammals of New Guinea,* 2nd ed. Ithaca, NY: Cornell University Press, 1995.

Menkhorst, Frank. *A Field Guide to the Mammals of Australia,* 2nd ed. Oxford, U.K.: Oxford University Press, 2001.

Nowak, Ronald M. *Walker's Mammals of the World.* Baltimore: Johns Hopkins University Press, 1995.

Triggs, Barbara. *The Wombat: Common Wombats of Australia,* 2nd ed. Sydney: New South Wales University Press, 1996.

### Web sites:

Marsupial Society of Australia. http://www.marsupialsociety.org (accessed on June 30, 2004).

Marinacci, Peter. *Wombania's Wombat Information Center.* http://www.wombania.com/wombats/index.htm (accessed on June 30, 2004).

"Wombats." Australian National Parks and Wildlife Service. http://www.nationalparks.nsw.gov.au/npws.nsf/Content/Wombats (accessed on June 30, 2004).

# POSSUMS AND CUSCUSES
## Phalangeridae

**Class:** Mammalia
**Order:** Diprotodontia
**Family:** Phalangeridae
**Number of species:** 26 species

## PHYSICAL CHARACTERISTICS

The Phalangeridae family, or phalangers (fah-LAN-jerz), are made up of five groups of species. Three of these groups are cuscuses and two are possums. Phalangers are small- to medium-sized marsupial mammals. Like all marsupial mammals, the females give birth to tiny, underdeveloped young that finish their development in their mother's pouch.

Possums and cuscuses range in size from 24 to 47 inches (60 to 120 centimeters) long, including the tail, and weigh from 2 to 22 pounds (1 to 10 kilograms). The smallest member of this family is the small Sulawesi cuscus, and the largest is the Sulawesi bear cuscus. Both live in Indonesia.

Members of this family have soft, dense fur that hides small ears. Most species are a solid brown or gray, but the Woodlark cuscus and the black spotted cuscus are spectacularly patterned. Many other species have a dark stripe that runs down the top of their back.

All cuscuses and possums are good climbers. Their feet are adapted to life in the trees. Their hind feet have five toes. The first toe (called the hallux, HAL-lux) has no claw, and is opposed to the other four. This means that this toe, like the thumb on a human hand, can reach across and touch the tip of the other toes (unlike, for example, a dog paw or human foot, where none of the toes can bend to touch each other). The first two toes on the front feet are also opposable. This adaptation makes it easier to grip branches when climbing. Possums and cuscuses also have a prehensile, or flexible grasping, tail that they can

wrap around branches to help steady themselves. Usually the tail has no fur on it to improve its grip.

## GEOGRAPHIC RANGE

Phalangers are found in New Guinea, Australia, Tasmania, the Indonesian island of Sulawesi, and a few other small islands. The
common brush-tailed possum was introduced
in New Zealand over a century ago and has
become an alien (non-native) pest species.

## HABITAT

Possums and cuscuses spend their lives in
trees. Most live in rainforests. However, the
common brush-tailed possum has adapted to
life in developed areas. It is often found in
suburban gardens and city parks. Sometimes
it becomes a pest when it makes its home in
buildings by finding openings in the roofline
and nesting between the house ceiling and
the roof.

**ENDANGERED STAMPS**

The common spotted cuscus was
selected to be one of twelve endangered
species featured on a 2001 United Nations
34 cent stamp. Every year since 1993, the
United Nations has released a new series
of stamps in an effort to bring attention
to endangered species and to CITES
(the Convention on International Trade in
Endangered Species), an agreement among
nations to help preserve species by
controlling their exportation and importation
(http://www.cites.org).

## DIET

Possums and cuscuses are herbivores, eating almost exclusively plants. Some eat mainly leaves, while others eat mainly
fruit. The common brush-tailed possum eats a wider variety of
foods than most members of this family, adapting its diet to
what is abundant in any given area.

## BEHAVIOR AND REPRODUCTION

Most members of this family are nocturnal, or active at night,
but the black-spotted cuscus and the Sulawesi bear cuscus feed
during the day. All species are arboreal (tree-dwelling) except
for the ground cuscus—but even though this animal lives in
burrows underground, it is a good climber, and climbs trees to
feed on fruit.

Little is known about the social behavior of members of this
family. Most species appear to live alone, although a few may
form pairs. Males are aggressive toward each other when their
home range overlaps. Females usually produce two litters consisting of one offspring each year. Like all marsupials, the young

are tiny, undeveloped creatures that finish maturing while attached to a teat, or nipple, in the mother's forward-facing pouch. After five to eight months, the young leave the pouch and are carried on their mother's back for a few more weeks or months.

## POSSUMS, CUSCUSES, AND PEOPLE

Cuscuses are hunted for meat and sometimes fur in New Guinea. Some species, such as the common spotted cuscus, are also sold as pets. Cuscuses play a role in religious beliefs in some parts of Indonesia, and in these areas, they are not eaten. The common brush-tailed possum is considered a pest in many areas. The Telefomin cuscus was not discovered until the late 1980s, and so it is of special interest to scientists.

## CONSERVATION STATUS

Two species in this family are considered Endangered and at risk of going extinct in the wild. These are the black-spotted cuscus and the Telefomin cuscus. The population of black-spotted cuscuses is declining because of habitat loss and continued hunting. Little is known about the Telefomin cuscus. Two other species are considered Vulnerable, facing a high risk of extinction, and half a dozen others are of concern to conservationists, but too little is known about them to make an accurate population evaluation.

Ground cuscus (*Phalanger gymnotis*)

## GROUND CUSCUS
### *Phalanger gymnotis*

**Physical characteristics:** The ground cuscus has fur that is light to dark gray with a stripe down its back.

**Geographic range:** This cuscus is found in New Guinea and the Aru Islands.

**Habitat:** This animal lives in the rainforest from sea level to 8,900 feet (2,700 meters).

**Diet:** The ground cuscus eats mostly fruit, but will also eat leaves and sometimes insects and small vertebrates (animals with a backbone).

**Behavior and reproduction:** This is the only cuscus that sleeps in underground burrows and moves along the rainforest floor. Its

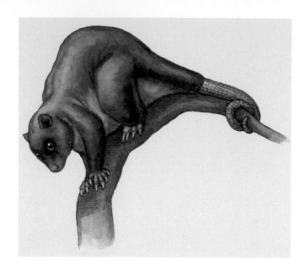

*The ground cuscus is the only cuscus that commonly lives in a burrow in the ground. (Illustration by Bruce Worden. Reproduced by permission.)*

burrows are usually under trees, along streams, or in caves. The ground cuscus is active at night and searches for food on the ground and in trees. The young leave their mother's pouch five to seven months after birth.

**Ground cuscuses and people:** These cuscuses are hunted throughout New Guinea, and are important figures in local folklore in some areas.

**Conservation status:** The ground cuscus is common in many parts of New Guinea, and is probably not threatened. ■

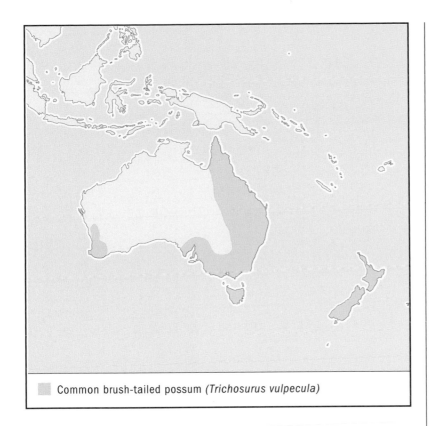

Common brush-tailed possum (*Trichosurus vulpecula*)

## COMMON BRUSH-TAILED POSSUM
### *Trichosurus vulpecula*

**Physical characteristics:** The common brush-tailed possum varies widely in size and color. Its fur can be black, gray, reddish, or brown. In the colder parts of its range, individuals tend to be larger and furrier than those who live in warmer regions. Unlike some members of this family, the common brush-tailed has a patch of bushy fur on its tail.

**Geographic range:** Brush-tailed possums live in eastern and south-western Australia and in New Zealand.

**Habitat:** The brush-tailed possum is adaptable, living in cool, damp forests and dry regions with few trees. It has adjusted successfully to life in city parks and the suburbs.

**Diet:** Common brush-tailed possums are herbivores, eating leaves, buds, flowers, and fruits, garden plants, herbs, and grasses.

**Behavior and reproduction:**   Common brush-tailed possums are active at night and normally live alone. However, if there are many possums and few places to shelter, they may share their sleeping space with another possum. Male common brush-tailed possums try to avoid conflict with other males, although they can be aggressive in defending their home range. They are known for their loud grunts, growls, and screeches that are used to warn away other males during breeding season. Females usually have one offspring each year, born after an eighteen-day pregnancy. The young then live in the mother's pouch for about seven months.

**Common brush-tailed possums and people:**   This animal probably has more contact with people than any other Australian marsupial because it has adapted so well to cities and suburban areas. It is trapped for its fur and is considered a pest in some farming areas and in New Zealand, where it was introduced about 150 years ago.

**Conservation status:** The common brush-tailed possum is common within its range and is not threatened with extinction. ∎

## FOR MORE INFORMATION

### Books:

Finney, Tim F. *Mammals of New Guinea,* 2nd ed. Ithaca, NY: Cornell University Press, 1995.

Menkhorst, Frank. *A Field Guide to the Mammals of Australia,* 2nd ed. Oxford, U.K.: Oxford University Press, 2001.

Nowak, Ronald. M. *Walker's Mammals of the World.* Baltimore: Johns Hopkins University Press, 1995.

### Web sites:

Marsupial Society of Australia. http://www.marsupialsociety.org (accessed May 9, 2004).

Parks and Wildlife Service Tasmania. "Brushtail Possum." http://www.parks.tas.gov.au/wildlife/mammals/btposs.html (accessed on June 30, 2004).

Queensland Government Environmental Protection Agency/Queensland Parks and Wildlife Service. "Nature Conservation." http://www.epa.qld.gov.au/nature_conservation (accessed on June 30, 2004).

family

**CHAPTER**

phylum

class

subclass

order

monotypic order

suborder

▲ **family**

## PHYSICAL CHARACTERISTICS

The musky rat-kangaroo is a small, four legged, marsupial mammal. It is different from most familiar mammals such as cats, dogs, and horses, which are known as placental or eutherian (yoo-THEER-ee-an) mammals. Eutherian mammals have a placenta, an organ that grows in the mother's uterus (womb) and lets the mother and developing offspring share food and oxygen. Marsupials do not have a well-developed placenta. Consequently, they give birth to young that are physically underdeveloped. These young are hairless, blind, and have immature organ systems. They are unable to survive on their own. Instead, after birth they are carried around for several months in their mother's pouch, where they are attached to the mothers teats, or nipples. They are carried and fed this way until they have grown and matured enough to fend for themselves.

Musky rat-kangaroos are fairly small. Their bodies are generally between 6 and 11 inches (15 to 30 centimeters), and they have a total length from nose to tip of the tail of about 11 to 17 inches (30 to 43 centimeters). Musky rat-kangaroos have short brown or reddish fur that is very soft on their backs, while fur on the underside of their belly is slightly paler. Some musky rat-kangaroos have distinctive white markings on their throats that continue in a white line down to their chest.

Musky rat-kangaroos have small heads that are narrow and taper into a pointed snout. Their ears are small and rounded, and their tails are long, thin, and hairless, except for the area where the tail joins the body. The musky rat-kangaroo has four paws with five toes on each of its back feet and four on its front feet. Like other kangaroos, the middle toes have a fused (grown together) bone but separate claws. However, all other living kangaroos have only four toes on their back feet. The fifth toe of the musky rat-kangaroo does not have a claw. It is thought that this extra toe is used to help it climb.

Female musky rat-kangaroos have four nipples inside a forward-opening pouch where the young are carried after birth. Female and male musky rat-kangaroos are about the same size, although females usually weigh a little less than males. The average weight of a musky rat-kangaroo is between 11 and 24 ounces (337 to 680 grams).

### GEOGRAPHIC RANGE

The musky rat-kangaroo lives only in a small area of Australian rainforest in northeastern Queensland.

### HABITAT

Musky rat-kangaroos live on the rainforest floor. They usually prefer places where there are many plants that provide good cover for them. They often live near water, such as streams and lakes, because that is where the vegetation is more dense.

### DIET

Musky rat-kangaroos are omnivores, meaning they eat both plants and animals. They eat small invertebrates such as insects and worms, as well as fruits, nuts, and roots. Musky rat-kangaroos find food by digging with their front paws in the ground and in the dead leaves and other plant material that cover the rainforest floor. When the musky rat-kangaroo eats, it often uses its front paws to hold the food and sits upright on its hind legs.

### BEHAVIOR AND REPRODUCTION

Musky rat-kangaroos are diurnal, which means that they are active during the day. They are the only species in this order that is completely active during the day. At night musky

### SAVING FOOD FOR LATER

Fruits from the rainforest are one of the most important parts of the musky rat-kangaroo's diet. However, these fruits are not easy to find during some parts of the year. The musky rat-kangaroo solves this problem by hiding food when there is an abundance of it, then finding it later when food is scarce. This hiding and finding is called scatterhoarding. Scatterhoarding helps ensure that the musky rat-kangaroo will not go hungry, even when food is scarce.

*Musky rat-kangaroos are active during the day and sleep in their nests at night. Most other marsupials are active at night. (Dave Watts/Naturepl.com. Reproduced by permission.)*

rat-kangaroos sleep in nests. They also may return to their nests to keep cool during the hottest part of the day. To build their nests musky rat-kangaroos use their tails to pick up leaves and other items. They can curl their tails around what they want to hold and carry it back to their nests. This kind of flexible grasping tail is called a prehensile tail. They take the nest materials to clumps of vines or where two tree roots come together and make their nests there.

Instead of hopping on its two hind legs the way many other rat-kangaroos do, the musky rat-kangaroo moves by using all four legs. Consequently, its front and hind legs are more similar in size than in most other rat-kangaroos. Musky rat-kangaroos have been seen climbing trees, but little is known about why they do this.

Musky rat-kangaroos are thought to live and hunt for food primarily alone, although one scientist reported having seen up to three musky rat-kangaroos feeding in the same place. In the wild, they do not appear to be territorial, meaning that they do not defend an area that they consider to be theirs. When musky rat-kangaroos are kept in captivity, male/female relationships must be taken into consideration. Only one male can be kept in a cage at a time, but two females can be kept together. It is also possible for one male to share a space with more than one female. Little research has been done on how musky rat-kangaroos interact with each other.

Musky rat-kangaroos usually mate between February and July. They normally have two offspring at a time, although they sometimes have three. Like all marsupials, the young are born tiny, blind, hairless, and very immature. The young are not able to fend for themselves and must crawl over their mother's fur and into her pouch. In her pouch they attach themselves to a nipple and spend the next twenty-one weeks in the pouch as they grow and develop. After the young leave the pouch they usually spend time in the nest for another few weeks before they begin to leave the nest and follow their mother.

During the period of time in which a young musky rat-kangaroo follows its mother around the outside of the nest, it is known as a "young-at-foot" (sometimes also called a "young-at-heel"). It is not allowed to return to the pouch, although it

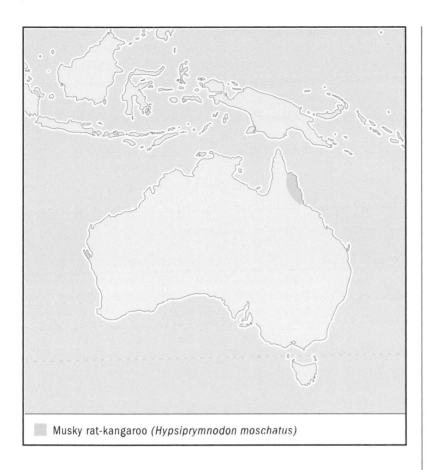

Musky rat-kangaroo *(Hypsiprymnodon moschatus)*

is still allowed to suckle (nurse). The young continue to grow and mature, eventually leaving their mothers to go off on their own.

## MUSKY RAT-KANGAROOS AND PEOPLE

The musky rat-kangaroo does not have any known particular significance to humans, except to the scientists who study them.

## CONSERVATION STATUS

The musky rat-kangaroo not considered threatened in the wild. However, it is of concern to conservationists, because it lives only in a very small area of the rainforest in northeastern Queensland. Its habitat is disappearing because of clear cutting for agriculture. Because the musky rat-kangaroo lives in only one location, any severe loss of its habitat could be devastating to its population.

## FOR MORE INFORMATION

**Books:**

Triggs, Barbara. *Tracks, Scats and Other Traces: A Field Guide to Australian Mammals.* Oxford, U.K.: Oxford University Press, 1996.

Woods, Samuel G. *Sorting Out Mammals: Everything You Want to Know About Marsupials, Carnivores, Herbivores, and More!* Woodbridge, CT: Blackbirch Marketing, 1999.

**Web sites:**

Chambers Wildlife Rainforest Lodges, Tropical North Queensland, Australia. "Musky rat kangaroo." http://rainforest-australia.com/rkangaroo.htm (accessed on June 30, 2004).

**Other sources:**

Berry, Ruth and Mark Chapman. ABC TV Documentaries: *Hypsi: The Forest Gardener.* Aired: 1/16/2001. http://www.abc.net.au/tv/documentaries/stories/s231600.htm (Web site accessed on June 30, 2004).

**Class:** Mammalia
**Order:** Diprotodontia
**Family:** Potoroidae
**Number of species:** 8 species

CHAPTER

## PHYSICAL CHARACTERISTICS

Rat-kangaroos are four-legged marsupial mammals that are smaller than most cats. Marsupial mammals are different from most familiar mammals such as cats, dogs, and horses, which are eutherian (yoo-THEER-ee-an) mammals, meaning they use a placenta in reproduction. A placenta is an organ that grows in the mother's uterus and lets the mother and developing baby share food and oxygen. Marsupial mammals do not use a well-developed placenta. Because of this, they give birth to tiny young that are not physically mature enough to survive on their own. Instead, the young are carried for several months after birth in their mother's pouch, or they are attached to the mother's teats, or nipples, on her underbelly. While they are carried this way, they continue to grow until they have matured enough to fend for themselves.

Rat-kangaroos usually have a head and body length that ranges from about 6 to 16 inches (15 to 42 centimeters). The tails of rat-kangaroos can be nearly as long as their bodies, and range in length from about 5 to 15 inches (12 to 39 centimeters). Rat-kangaroos range in weight from about 0.8 to 8 pounds (0.4 to 3.5 kilograms). Male and female rat-kangaroos are usually about the same size.

Rat-kangaroos have heads that are long and are usually tapered, with small ears that are either round or slightly pointed. Like all kangaroos, their hind legs are longer and stronger than their front legs. This is because rat-kangaroos use their hind legs to move by hopping. Rat-kangaroos have four toes on each

phylum

class

subclass

order

monotypic order

suborder

▲ **family**

## HOW DID THEY GET SUCH BIG FEET?

Rat-kangaroos have back feet that are longer and stronger than their front feet. Scientists think that the ancestors of kangaroos used to jump up quickly and surprise predators. Animals with bigger back feet had an advantage at hopping higher and faster, which might have helped them to survive. Animals with bigger back feet had a better chance of surviving and having offspring, over many generations the genes for big feet got passed on, and the back feet got bigger and bigger, until they are the large back feet that kangaroos have today.

of their back feet, but the second and third toes actually grow together although the claws remain separate. Each of the front feet has five toes, each with a claw. Their second, third, and fourth toes on their front paws are longer than their other front toes, and these longer claws help them dig for food.

The fur of the rat-kangaroo ranges in color from dark brown to gray or light brown. The fur is lighter on the underbelly than on the rest of the body. These animals can use their tails, which usually have fur on them, to curl around objects and hold onto them. This type of tail that can be used to grasp is called a prehensile tail. Female rat-kangaroos have a pouch containing four nipples.

### GEOGRAPHIC RANGE

Rat-kangaroos live on the coasts of Australia, especially the southern and eastern coasts. They also live in Tasmania and on a few nearby islands.

### HABITAT

Rat-kangaroos live mainly in forests where there are many eucalyptus trees. Some types of rat kangaroos, like the burrowing bettong, live in other habitats, such as sandy areas that have dunes.

### DIET

Rat kangaroos are primarily herbivores, meaning that they eat mostly plants rather than animals. They mainly eat the parts of fungi that grow underground. To find this food underground, rat-kangaroos use their well-developed sense of smell to help them know where to dig. They dig using the long, sharp claws on their front paws. Some rat-kangaroos also eat small invertebrates, such as insects. Some also eat grass or fruits.

### BEHAVIOR AND REPRODUCTION

Rat-kangaroos are nocturnal, which means they are awake and do most of their foraging (searching) for food at night. Most of the daylight hours are spent sleeping, most often in a nest. They build nests out of grass, leaves, and other plant material. Many species get the plant material to their nests by curling their prehensile tail around it and holding it against their rump to keep it steady as they carry it to their nest.

Female rat-kangaroos give birth to one baby at a time. The baby is born after around three weeks of pregnancy. When it is born, it is blind, hairless, and not able to live on its own. The newborn crawls into the mother's pouch and attaches it to one of the mother's nipples where it remains until it is mature enough to survive outside the pouch. Once the young animal leaves the pouch, it becomes a "young-at-foot." During this stage, it follows its mother around and still suckles, nurses, but it is not allowed to get back in the mother's pouch. After another period of development, the young rat-kangaroo goes off on its own. Rat-kangaroos do not usually live in groups after the young mature.

On the night that the female gives birth, she mates again. The egg that is fertilized during that mating stops developing until just before the young that is in the mother's pouch is almost old enough to leave the pouch. The same night that the young leaves the pouch, the mother gives birth to a new baby that then crawls into the pouch that just recently been vacated. After this new baby is born, the mother will mate again. This cycle continues, which means that there are often four generations of rat-kangaroos together: a mother, a young-at-foot, a young in the pouch, and a developing baby that has not yet been born.

## RAT-KANGAROOS AND FUNGI: HELPING EACH OTHER

Rat-kangaroos eat the parts of fungi that grow underground and contain the spores. Spores are the reproductive part of the fungi, similar to a tiny seed. Rat-kangaroos eat the fungi for energy. When the fungi are digested, the spores become activated and ready to grow. The spores leave the rat-kangaroo's body in its waste and are ready to grow into new fungi. In this way, the spores are spread to new areas. This type of relationship between two species where both gain something and neither is harmed is called mutualism.

## RAT-KANGAROOS AND PEOPLE

Rat-kangaroos are not known to have any particular significance to people.

## CONSERVATION STATUS

Many species of rat-kangaroo have been threatened by the clearing of land for agriculture, by fires, and by the introduction of predators that are not native to Australia. Some species of rat-kangaroo have already gone extinct. The desert rat-kangaroo has not been seen since 1935. It is thought that the broad-faced potoroo has been extinct since around 1875. Many other species of rat-kangaroos, such as the long-faced potoroo, are Endangered, facing a very high risk of extinction. Conservation efforts to protect rat-kangaroos include controlling the number of introduced predators, establishing breeding colonies, and creating protected zones.

Northern bettong (*Bettongia tropica*)

# NORTHERN BETTONG
## *Bettongia tropica*

**Physical characteristics:** Northern bettongs are about the size of a rabbit, except that their tails are nearly as long as its head and body combined. The length of the head and body is usually about 15 inches (38 centimeters) and the length of the tail is usually about 14 inches (36 centimeters). Northern bettongs weigh about 3 pounds (1.4 kilograms). The back legs are much larger and stronger than the front legs. The head tapers to a pointed snout, and they have small, slightly pointed ears. The fur on the belly is much lighter in color than the rest of the fur. Female northern bettongs have four nipples and a forward-opening pouch.

**Geographic range:** The northern bettong lives on the northeast coast of Australia.

**Habitat:** Northern bettongs usually live in areas of forest that are open and have grass on the forest floor. These areas are often found along the edge of tropical rainforests.

**Diet:** Northern bettongs, like many rat-kangaroos, eat mainly truffles, a type of fungus that grows underground. It also eats cockatoo grass.

**Behavior and reproduction:** The young of the northern bettong are born after twenty-one days and are immature, like the young of all marsupials. The young then move into the pouch where they remain for 106 days (about three and a half months) before they are mature enough to live outside the pouch.

**Northern bettongs and people:** Northern bettongs do not have any known significance to humans, except to the scientists who study them.

*Northern bettongs eat mainly truffles, a type of fungus that grows underground. They use their well-developed sense of smell to find the fungus, and then dig for it using their sharp claws. (Illustration by Bruce Worden. Reproduced by permission.)*

**Conservation status:** Northern bettongs are Endangered, which means that they face a high risk of going extinct in the wild. The main reasons it is endangered are loss of habitat due to clearing of land for agriculture and the destruction of habitat through fires. The red fox, which is not native to Australia, may also prey on the northern bettong, leading to reduced numbers. Conservation measures are being taken through the maintenance of two captive breeding populations of northern bettongs. ∎

## FOR MORE INFORMATION

**Books:**

Triggs, Barbara. *Tracks, Scats and Other Traces: A Field Guide to Australian Mammals.* Oxford, U.K.: Oxford University Press, 1996.

Woods, Samuel G. *Sorting Out Mammals: Everything You Want to Know About Marsupials, Carnivores, Herbivores, and More!* Woodbridge, CT: Blackbirch Marketing, 1999.

**Other sources:**

Berry, Ruth, and Mark Chapman. ABC TV Documentaries: *Hypsi: The Forest Gardener* Aired: January 16, 2001. http://www.abc.net.au/tv/documentaries/stories/s231600.htm (Web site accessed on June 30, 2004).

WALLABIES AND KANGAROOS
**Macropodidae**

**Class:** Mammalia
**Order:** Diprotodontia
**Family:** Macropodidae
**Number of species:** 62 species

family

CHAPTER

phylum

class

subclass

order

monotypic order

suborder

▲ **famlly**

## PHYSICAL CHARACTERISTICS

Kangaroos and wallabies are marsupial mammals, meaning that they do not produce a well-developed placenta like many familiar mammals. A placenta is an organ that grows inside the mother's uterus (womb) during pregnancy and allows the developing baby to share the mother's food and oxygen. Marsupial mammals are born underdeveloped and they finish developing inside their mother's pouch.

Kangaroos and wallabies are some of the best known Australian marsupials. They have four legs, although their front legs are much smaller and weaker than their large back legs. They usually have long tails and large ears that are either pointed or rounded. They have a head and body length that varies in size from 11 to 91 inches (28 to 231 centimeters), and a tail that ranges in length from 6 to 43 inches (15 to 109 centimeters). They weigh between 3 and 187 pounds (1 to 85 kilograms). In some species the males are much larger than the females. Kangaroos and wallabies have fur that ranges in color from reddish orange to black.

Kangaroos and wallabies have very long, large, strong back feet that allow them to hop at speeds of up to 35 miles per hour (55 kilometers per hour). They have four toes on each of their front and back feet, and the second and third toes on their back feet are fused (attached) together. All of their toes have strong claws.

## GEOGRAPHIC RANGE

Kangaroos and wallabies live all over Australia, as well as in parts of New Guinea and some surrounding islands. They have been introduced into Hawaii, New Zealand, Great Britain, and Germany.

## HABITAT

Kangaroos and wallabies live in many different habitats. Some live in the tropical rainforest while others live in the grasslands or woodlands. There is almost no area of Australia where at least one species of kangaroo or wallaby does not live.

## DIET

Most kangaroos and wallabies are herbivores, which means that they eat only plants. They eat mostly leaves and grass, although some also eat fruit, seeds, and fungi. Some of the smaller species are omnivores, animals that eat both animals and plants. These species eat insects and other invertebrates.

## BEHAVIOR AND REPRODUCTION

Kangaroos and wallabies portray a very diverse set of behaviors. Larger species tend to be diurnal, or mostly active during the day. Smaller species tend to be nocturnal, or mostly active at night. Smaller species are often solitary, while larger species often live or feed in groups of up to fifty animals called mobs. A few species are thought to be territorial. They live alone and defend their home area.

When male kangaroos or wallabies fight, they often do so by supporting themselves on their back legs, or even sometimes just their tail for short periods, and attack each other with the strong claws on their front paws. Sometimes they use their strong hind legs to kick out when they are lying on their sides. Females sometimes do this if males try to mate with them and they are not interested.

Like all marsupials, kangaroos and wallabies give birth to young that are not fully developed. These tiny newborns are blind, hairless, and cannot survive on their own. When they are born, they crawl into their mother's pouch where they attach to one of her nipples. This nipple usually swells, keeping the young in place while the mother moves. In some species the mother will let the young out of the pouch for short periods when it gets older. After the young matures, the mother will no longer let it return to the pouch. In some species it becomes what is called a "young-at-foot." During the young-at-foot period, the young kangaroo or wallaby stays with the mother and often suckles, but no longer re-enters the pouch. In some species there is no young-at-foot period.

Kangaroos and wallabies usually give birth to one baby at a time. In some species the female gives birth the same day

## MEETING THE CHANGING NEEDS OF BABIES

When kangaroo newborns climb into their mother's pouches, they attach themselves to one of her nipples. From this nipple they get the milk that provides the nourishment they need to survive and grow. But the nutritional needs of a newborn are not the same as the nutritional needs of a young animal almost ready to leave the pouch. To make sure their young get the nutrients they need, female kangaroos have milk that changes in content as the young matures. When the young-at-foot and a young in the pouch are both suckling, the two different nipples actually produce two different types of milk, suited to the needs of the two different young.

another young leaves her pouch and becomes a young-at-foot. These species often mate the same day that they give birth, but the fertilized egg stops developing until the pouch-young is nearly old enough to leave the pouch. When the pouch-young is ready to leave, the next baby moves to the pouch.

## WALLABIES, KANGAROOS, AND PEOPLE

Many species of kangaroos and wallabies have been hunted for their meat and their skins both by aboriginal (native) Australians and by European settlers. These animals are also important in the Aboriginal culture, where they often play important roles in traditional dreamtime stories. Some sheep ranchers consider kangaroos and wallabies to be a nuisances, because they eat the grass and other plants that the farmers want for livestock grazing.

## CONSERVATION STATUS

Four species in this family have already gone extinct. Many others are Endangered, which means that they face a very high risk of extinction in the wild. Others are considered Vulnerable, which means that they face a high risk of extinction in the wild. Some actions are being taken to help particular species, including protecting their habitats and breeding them in captivity, so they may be later reintroduced into the wild.

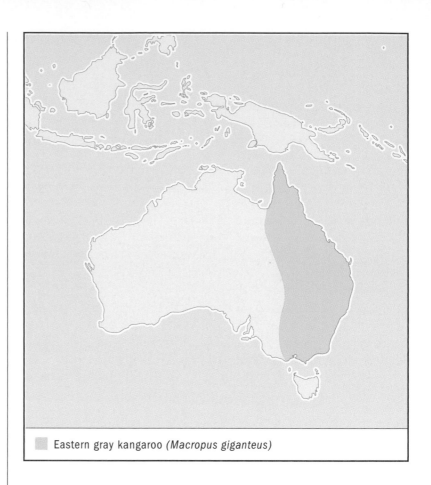

Eastern gray kangaroo (*Macropus giganteus*)

## EASTERN GRAY KANGAROO
### *Macropus giganteus*

**Physical characteristics:** Eastern gray kangaroos have a head and body length that ranges from 38 to 91 inches (97 to 231 centimeters). Their tails range in length from 18 to 43 inches (46 to 109 centimeters). They weigh from 8 to 146 pounds (4 to 66 kilograms). Eastern gray kangaroos have the characteristic body shape of all kangaroos with strong hind legs and large back feet. They have grayish brown fur that is paler on their bellies. Unlike other kangaroos, they have hairy snouts.

**Geographic range:** The eastern gray kangaroo lives in eastern Australia and in eastern Tasmania.

**Habitat:** The eastern gray kangaroo lives mainly in grassy woodlands, open grasslands, and forest.

**Diet:** The eastern gray kangaroo eats mainly grasses.

**Behavior and reproduction:** The eastern gray kangaroo is diurnal. It usually grazes during the early morning and late afternoon when temperatures are lower. Pregnancy usually lasts for thirty-six days, and the young stay in the pouch for 320 days.

**Eastern gray kangaroos and people:** It is thought that native Australians probably hunted the eastern gray kangaroo for food. Today, it is illegally hunted for skins and meat.

**Conservation status:** The eastern gray kangaroo is considered Near Threatened. This classification means that this kangaroo is not currently threatened, but could become threatened. This kangaroo has been affected by illegal hunting for its skins and meat, as well as the destruction of its habitat for agriculture. ■

*Eastern gray kangaroos may gather in large social groups, called "mobs." (© Bill Bachman/ Photo Researchers, Inc. Reproduced by permission.)*

Red kangaroo (*Macropus rufus*)

## RED KANGAROO
### *Macropus rufus*

**Physical characteristics:** Red kangaroos have fur that is reddish brown to blue-gray on most of their body, while their fur is white underneath. Red kangaroos have a head and body length that varies from 29 to 55 inches (74 to 140 centimeters). Their tail length is 25 to 39 inches (64 to 100 centimeters). Their weight varies between 37 and 187 pounds (17 to 85 kilograms). These are the largest kangaroos living today.

**Geographic range:** Most of Australia, except the coastal regions.

**Habitat:** Red kangaroos live in grasslands, open woodlands, and open forests.

**Diet:** Red kangaroos are herbivores. They eat grass and the leaves of shrubs and other plants.

**Behavior and reproduction:** Red kangaroos are pregnant for 33 days before giving birth. The young live in the pouch for 235 days.

**Red kangaroos and people:** Red kangaroos are hunted for their skins and meat in some places in Australia. The red kangaroo also has important cultural significance for native Australians, in whose traditional dreamtime stories they often play large parts.

**Conservation status:** Red kangaroos are not considered threatened. They have benefited from clearing of land for livestock grazing and are one of the few native Australian animals to have increased their population since the coming of European settlers. ■

*The male red kangaroo (on the right) has a rich red color, while the female red kangaroo (on the left) is smaller and less colorful. The males are called "boomers" and the females "blue flyers." (© Wayne Lawler/Photo Researchers, Inc. Reproduced by permission.)*

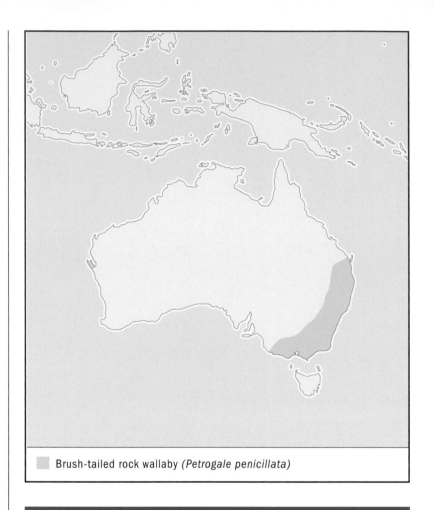

Brush-tailed rock wallaby *(Petrogale penicillata)*

## BRUSH-TAILED ROCK WALLABY
### *Petrogale penicillata*

**Physical characteristics:**   Brush-tailed rock wallabies have fur that is black-brown on their front section and red-brown on their rump. On their underside the fur is paler. They have a tail that is furry and dark colored, characteristics that have contributed to their name. These wallabies have distinctive markings on their heads consisting of a white stripe on their cheeks and a black stripe on their heads. Their head and body length ranges from 20 to 23 inches (51 to 58 centimeters). Their tails range in length from 20 to 28 inches (51 to 71 centimeters). Their weight ranges from 11 to 24 pounds (5 to 11 kilograms).

**Geographic range:** Brush-tailed rock wallabies live in eastern Australia. They have also been introduced successfully to Hawaii and New Zealand, where self-sustaining colonies now exist.

**Habitat:** Brush-tailed rock wallabies live in rocky areas in a variety of habitats such as rainforest and woodlands.

**Diet:** Brush-tailed rock wallabies mainly eat grass, but they also sometimes will eat herbs and fruits.

**Behavior and reproduction:** Brush-tailed rock wallabies are mostly nocturnal. They sleep in deep cracks in rocks and caves. Females are pregnant for thirty-one days before giving birth. Young live in the pouch for almost seven months before leaving.

**Brush-tailed rock wallabies and people:** Although brush-tailed rock wallabies have no current economic significance to humans, they were hunted in large numbers for their furs in the late nineteenth and early twentieth centuries.

**Conservation status:** The brush-tailed rock wallaby is considered Vulnerable, meaning that it faces a high risk of extinction. The main threats to these wallabies are destruction of their habitat from the grazing of livestock and predation from species of animals that are not native to Australian such as red foxes and dingoes (wild dogs). ■

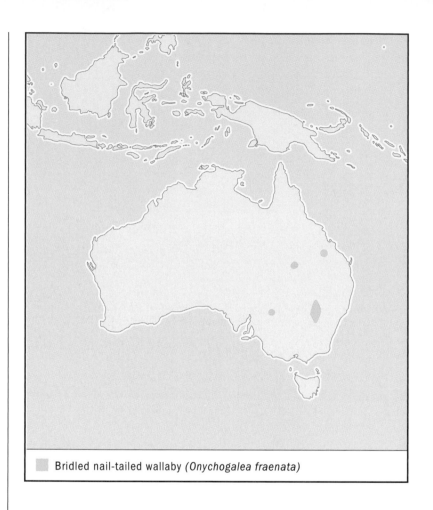

Bridled nail-tailed wallaby (*Onychogalea fraenata*)

## BRIDLED NAIL-TAILED WALLABY
### *Onychogalea fraenata*

**Physical characteristics:** Bridled nail-tailed wallabies have gray fur with paler gray fur on their bellies. They have a distinctive white stripe on both sides of their body extending from neck to forearms. On the end of the tail is a horny spur, probably inspiring their name. Bridled nail-tailed wallabies range in head and body length from 18 to 28 inches (46 to 71 centimeters), with a tail length that ranges from 15 to 21 inches (38 to 53 centimeters). They have a weight that ranges from 9 to 18 pounds (4 to 8 kilograms).

**Geographic range:** Currently bridled nail-tailed wallabies have significant populations only in a few places including one location in central Queensland, two places in eastern Australia where they have been reintroduced, two sanctuaries, and a zoo.

**Habitat:** Bridled nail-tailed wallabies live in areas of woodlands dominated by acacia trees and shrublands.

**Diet:** Bridled nail-tailed wallabies are herbivores. They eat soft-leaved grasses and other vegetation.

**Behavior and reproduction:** Bridled nail-tailed wallabies are nocturnal. They use dense vegetation as shelter during the day. Females are pregnant for twenty-three to sixty-two days before giving birth. The young live in the pouch for 119 to 126 days.

*Bridled nail-tailed wallabies are active at night and stay sheltered in thick vegetation during the day. (© Mitch Reardon/Photo Researchers, Inc. Reproduced by permission.)*

**Bridled nail-tailed wallabies and people:** There is no known significant relationship between the bridled nail-tailed wallabies and people, although scientists think that they have been hunted for their meat and skins.

**Conservation status:** Bridled nail-tailed wallabies are considered Endangered. This means that they are facing a very high risk of extinction in the wild. Scientists think that the main threats to these wallabies are probably clearing of their habitat for agriculture, and predation by species that are not native to Australia, such as the red fox. ■

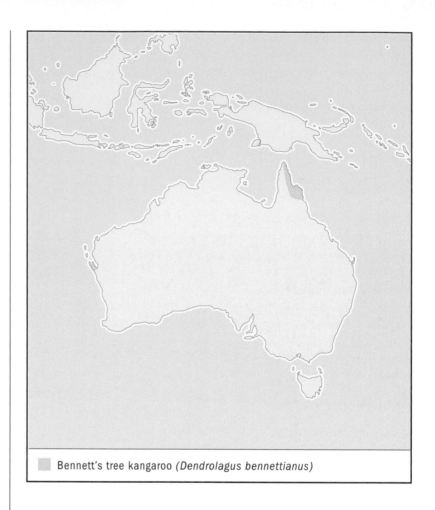

Bennett's tree kangaroo (*Dendrolagus bennettianus*)

## BENNETT'S TREE KANGAROO
### *Dendrolagus bennettianus*

**Physical characteristics:** Bennett's tree kangaroos have dark brown fur on most of their bodies although the fur on the top of their head and shoulders is reddish brown. Their foreheads and snouts are gray. Bennett's tree kangaroos have head and body lengths that range from 27 to 30 inches (69 to 76 centimeters). Their tails range in length from 29 to 33 inches (74 to 84 centimeters). They weigh between 18 and 30 pounds (8 to 14 kilograms).

**Geographic range:**  Bennett's tree kangaroos live on the eastern part of Cape York, which is a peninsula in the far northeast of Australia.

**Habitat:**  Bennett's tree kangaroos live in tropical rainforests.

**Diet:**  Bennett's tree kangaroos eat mainly leaves, although they sometimes also eat fruit.

**Behavior and reproduction:**  Male Bennett's tree kangaroos live alone. They are territorial, which means that they defend their living area against other males of their species, although their home range may overlap with that of several different females. The young remain in the pouch for about 270 days and are young-at-foot for up to two years.

**Bennett's tree kangaroo and people:**  Bennett's tree kangaroos were hunted by native Australians.

**Conservation status:**  Bennett's tree kangaroo is considered Near Threatened. This means that while these kangaroos are not in serious danger yet, they may soon become threatened.  ■

*Young Bennett's tree kangaroos are in their mother's pouch for seven months, and may stay with their mothers until they're two years old. (Illustration by Marguette Dongvillo. Reproduced by permission.)*

## FOR MORE INFORMATION

### Books:

Edwards, Bruce. *Kangaroos and Wallabies.* Hollywood, FL: Ralph Curtis Books, 1993.

Finney, Tim F. *Mammals of New Guinea,* 2nd ed. Ithaca, NY: Cornell University Press, 1995.

Menkhorst, Frank. *A Field Guide to the Mammals of Australia,* 2nd ed. Oxford, U.K.: Oxford University Press, 2001.

Triggs, Barbara. *Tracks, Scats and Other Traces: A Field Guide to Australian Mammals.* Oxford, U.K.: Oxford University Press, 1996.

Woods, Samuel G. *Sorting Out Mammals: Everything You Want to Know About Marsupials, Carnivores, Herbivores, and More!* Woodbridge, CT: Blackbirch Marketing, 1999.

**Web sites:**

Australian National Parks and Wildlife Service. "Kangaroos & Wallabies." http://www.nationalparks.nsw.gov.au/npws.nsf/Content/Kangaroos+and+wallabies (accessed on June 30, 2004).

**PYGMY POSSUMS**

**Burramyidae**

**Class:** Mammalia

**Order:** Diprotodontia

**Family:** Burramyidae

**Number of species:** 5 species

C H A P T E R

## PHYSICAL CHARACTERISTICS

Pygmy possums, like most animals native to Australia and New Guinea, are marsupial mammals. This type of mammal, unlike familiar eutherian (yoo-THEER-ee-an) mammals such as dogs, cats, or humans, does not have a well-developed placenta. A placenta is an organ that grows in the mother's uterus (womb) during pregnancy in order to share food and oxygen with the developing young. Since marsupial mammals like pygmy possums do not have a well-developed placenta, their young are born hairless, blind, and underdeveloped and must complete development inside their mother's pouch.

Pygmy possums look much like common mice. They are small, between 2 and 4 inches (5 to 10 centimeters) long, and they weigh between 0.2 and 1.4 ounces (7 to 40 grams). They are covered with soft fur that is brown on their backs and lighter underneath.

## GEOGRAPHIC RANGE

Pygmy possums live in central New Guinea, Tasmania, and southeastern and southwestern Australia.

## HABITAT

Most pygmy possums live in wet forest areas with evergreen or eucalyptus (yoo-kah-LIP-tus) trees. One species, the mountain pygmy possum, lives in the tropical mountain rainforest of New Guinea above 4,900 feet (1,500 meters).

## DIET

Different species of pygmy possums have different diets, ranging from plant pollen and nectar to insects to small lizards.

phylum

class

subclass

order

monotypic order

suborder

**family**

The long-tailed pygmy possum eats mainly insects, but will also feed on flowers. The eastern pygmy possum eats mainly pollen and nectar. The mountain pygmy possum eats seeds, fruit, insects, and other small animals. All species of pygmy possum are eaten by owls, feral (wild) cats, snakes, and carnivorous (meat-eating) marsupial mammals.

## BEHAVIOR AND REPRODUCTION

Pygmy possums are nocturnal, which means that they sleep during the day and are active at night, although a few species may come out on cloudy days. All but one species live in trees and are good climbers, using their prehensile (grasping) tail to help them climb. These tree-dwelling pygmy possums build nests inside tree hollows using leaves and other plant material. As many as five possums live in a shared nest.

The female pygmy possum has four teats, or nipples. This is the maximum number of young that she can raise, although the usual number is one to three young, once or twice a year. She raises the young without any help from the male. After birth, she carries the young in her pouch until they reach an appropriate size, around 0.2 ounces (7 grams). They then spend time in the nest until they reach about 0.35 ounces (10 grams), after which they become independent. Although not much is known about how long some species live, female mountain pygmy possums live about eleven years, while males live only four, an unusually large difference in lifespan.

The mountain pygmy possum lives in mountain meadows and rock fields. It is very different from other pygmy possums. It lives at high elevations between 4,265 and 7,300 feet (1,300 and 2,230 meters), where there is snow on the ground at least three months out of the year. It shares a nest with other possums of the same sex, and stores up fat to survive the winter. One individual was found in autumn that weighed almost three times its normal weight. In the winter, the mountain pygmy possum can reduce its heart rate, energy use, and body temperature and remain inactive for up to twenty days at a time.

## PYGMY POSSUMS AND PEOPLE

Pygmy possums are not known to have any significance to humans except to those interested in scientific study. Species that feed on plant nectar and pollen may be responsible for helping to extend the range of these plants.

## CONSERVATION STATUS

The mountain pygmy possum is considered Endangered because of the very limited area (only two places in Victoria, Australia) in which it lives. Disturbances to its habitat are considered the most important threat. A natural threat is the annual change in rainfall. The amount of rain affects the size of the Bogong moth population—this in turn affects the amount of food that is available for the mountain pygmy possum, which gorges on Bogong moths almost exclusively during the summer months.

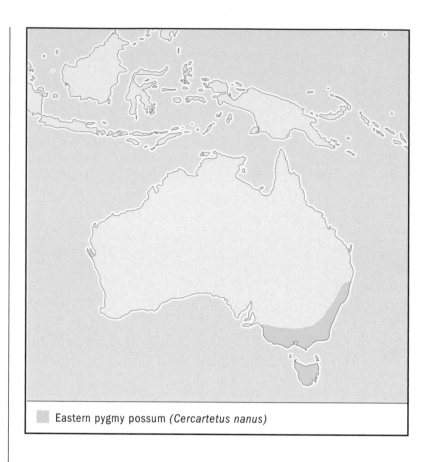

Eastern pygmy possum (*Cercartetus nanus*)

## EASTERN PYGMY POSSUM
### *Cercartetus nanus*

**Physical characteristics:**  Eastern pygmy possums grow to a length of between 7 and 8 inches (18 to 20 centimeters). They have brown fur, except on their belly, which has gray fur. The base of their tail is thick because of stored fat in that area. Eastern pygmy possums also have long tongues with bristles on the tip like a brush.

**Geographic range:**  This species lives in Tasmania and in eastern and southeastern regions of Australia.

**Habitat:**  Eastern pygmy possums live in open forests, shrubby woodlands, and rainforests.

**Diet:** These possums are omnivorous. They eat nectar and pollen as well as insects. More insects are eaten by individuals that live in wet areas where plants bloom less continuously.

**Behavior and reproduction:** Eastern pygmy possums are solitary animals. They build nests out of leaves and bark inside of tree-hollows. The female is mature at about five months of age. She gives birth to one to three young twice each year. The young are born after a month-long pregnancy. They remain in the pouch for about forty-two days, and stay in the nest another three weeks before becoming independent at the age of about two months.

**Eastern pygmy possums and people:** Eastern pygmy possums hold no known significance to humans beyond scientific interest.

**Conservation status:** This species is not considered to be threatened. ■

*Eastern pygmy possums have long tongues with bristles on the tip like a brush. This helps them feed on nectar from flowers. (© Pavel German. Reproduced by permission.)*

## FOR MORE INFORMATION

### Books:

Mansergh, I. M., Linda Broome, and Katrina Sandiford. *The Mountain-Pygmy Possum of the Australian Alps (Australian Natural History).* Kensington, Australia: New South Wales University Press, 1994.

Steiner, Barbara A. *A Field Guide to the Mammals of Australia.* Oxford, U.K.: Oxford University Press, 2001.

### Web sites:

Lamington National Park. "Eastern Pygmy Possum." http://lamington.nrsm.uq.edu.au/Documents/Anim/eastern_pygmy_possum.htm (accessed on June 30, 2004).

"Royal's Hidden Population of Pygmy Possums Astounds Researchers." Australian National Parks and Wildlife Service. http://www.nationalparks.nsw.gov.au/npws.nsf/Content/Royals+hidden+population+of+pygmy+possums+astounds+researchers (accessed on June 30, 2004).

**Class:** Mammalia

**Order:** Diprotodontia

**Family:** Pseudocheiridae

**Number of species:** 16 species

phylum

class

subclass

order

monotypic order

suborder

▲ **family**

family

CHAPTER

## PHYSICAL CHARACTERISTICS

Ringtail and greater gliding possums are marsupial mammals. They range in length from 13 to 37 inches (32 to 95 centimeters) and weigh between 4 ounces and 79 pounds (115 grams to 22.5 kilograms). In this family there are two distinct types of possums. The greater gliding possums have a membrane, or thin layer of skin, between their front legs and their back legs. They spread their arms and legs when they leap from tree to tree and the membrane acts like a parasail or parachute and allows them to glide. The other group, known as the ringtail possums, is much different. They do not have this membrane, and their legs are short and stocky. The greater gliding possums can be up to 37 inches (95 centimeters) long, including their long tail, and weigh up to 42 ounces (1,200 grams).

Ringtail possums are furry and can be light gray, cream, orange, or dark brown in color. One species, the green ringtail, even looks green because of a combination of yellow, black and white fur. Ringtail possums have short round ears and a tail that is bare near the end.

Because they are marsupial mammals, ringtail and greater gliding possums are different from most familiar mammals such as cats, horses and humans. These familiar mammals are all eutherian (yoo-THEER-ee-an) mammals, which means they have a well-developed placenta. A placenta is an organ that grows in the mother's uterus, womb, and lets the mother and developing baby share food and oxygen. Marsupial mammals do not have this type of placenta. Because of this, they give birth to young that are not physically developed enough to be able to survive on their own. Instead, the young are carried around either in a pouch or attached to the mother's teats, or nipples, on her underbelly until they have completed their development.

## GEOGRAPHIC RANGE

Ringtail and greater gliding possums live along the eastern coast of Australia from its northern-most tip near New Guinea to its southern-most tip near Tasmania. They can also be found in the more mountainous areas of New Guinea, as well as Tasmania, and the southwestern tip of Australia.

## HABITAT

Most of the species that live in New Guinea, live in mountain forests. In Australia there are a number of different species that occupy a variety of different habitats. One species known as the rock possum lives on the rocky ground. Most other ringtails are arboreal, meaning they live in trees. Some of these tree-dwelling possums live in Australia's rainforests while others live in more dry and less dense forests.

## DIET

Ringtail and greater gliding possums are herbivores, which means that they eat plants. Most of their diet is made up of leaves, especially eucalyptus (yoo-kah-LIP-tus) leaves. Some species also eat fruits and flowers. These animals have teeth that are specially suited to grinding up leaves. They also all have a large cecum (SEE-kum), which is a pouch in the digestive system. In order to get enough nutritional value from the leaves they eat—eucalyptus leaves, especially, have low nutritional value—the leaves must be broken down. In the cecum, these animals have special bacteria that break down the leaves, so that they can be used by the animal.

## BEHAVIOR AND REPRODUCTION

Ringtail and greater gliding possums are nocturnal, which means that they are active at night and sleep during the day. Almost all species live in trees. Social organization and interaction

## DIGESTIVE RECYCLING

Greater gliding and ringtail possums eat plants like eucalyptus leaves that are tough, difficult to digest, and do not contain a lot of nutrients or calories. To get enough energy out of these leaves, they pass them through their digestive system once. Chunks of undigested leaf are eliminated when they defecate, have a bowel movement, then they eat their waste and digest it again so that more nutrients can be removed.

are important to most species in this family. Some live in bonded pairs and raise their young together. Most of the rainforest species live alone, but some of the other species spend time in groups and share sleeping spots. These possums use vocal calls to communicate with each other and with their young. None of them are territorial or protect a particular area.

Ringtail and greater gliding possums give birth to one or two young once a year. The young are born underdeveloped and crawl into their mother's pouch to continue to grow and mature. After 90 to 120 days in the mother's pouch, they leave and are carried on her back for another three months. After ten months the young become independent.

## RINGTAIL AND GREATER GLIDING POSSUMS AND PEOPLE

Most ringtail and greater gliding possums do not have a significant impact on people, except for the scientists who study them. In New Guinea, some larger species are hunted for food. Some species living near people's homes have been known to eat flowers from gardens.

## CONSERVATION STATUS

Populations of ringtail and greater gliding possums vary in how threatened they are by extinction. Some species, like the lemuroid ringtail possum, are widespread and have large populations. They are not considered threatened. Other species are threatened by the shrinking size of their habitat. The d'Albertis's ringtail possum and the golden ringtail are among this group. No species in this family is currently considered endangered, and they are not protected under law on the island of New Guinea.

Greater glider (*Petauroides volans*)

## GREATER GLIDER
### *Petauroides volans*

**Physical characteristics:**   The greater glider is one of the largest of the gliding possums, with lengths that range between 35 and 41 inches (90 and 105 centimeters). They weigh between 2 and 3.8 pounds (0.9 and 1.7 kilograms). Their fur is dark brown on most of the body except the underside, which is white. They have a long bushy tail that allows them to turn in mid-air and a gliding membrane that runs from their elbows to their ankles and acts as a parasail.

**Geographic range:**   Greater gliders are found in eastern Australia.

**Habitat:**   Greater gliders live in the both dry and wet forests, but not rainforests.

*The greater glider is one of the largest gliding possums. This possum feeds in the trees at night. (© B. G. Thomson/Photo Researchers, Inc. Reproduced by permission..)*

**Diet:**   Greater gliders are herbivores. Their primary food is the leaves of trees and some parts of other plants.

**Behavior and reproduction:**   Greater gliders are able to glide for distances up to 330 feet (100 meters) and even make 90 degree turns while in the air by using their tail like a rudder. The female gives birth to one young each year between March and June. The young stay in their mother's pouch for 120 days, after which they ride on their mother's back for three more months.

**Greater gliders and people:**   Greater gliders have no known importance for people.

**Conservation status:**   Greater gliders are classified as Vulnerable, facing a high risk of extinction in the wild.   ■

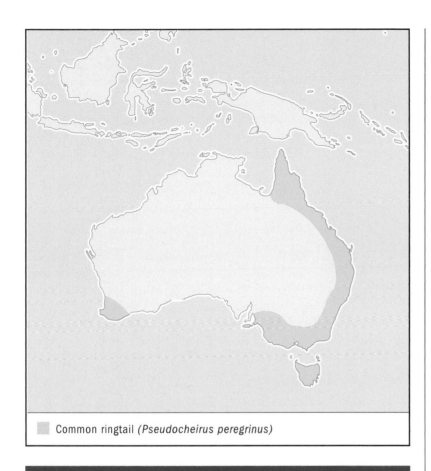

Common ringtail (*Pseudocheirus peregrinus*)

# COMMON RINGTAIL
## *Pseudocheirus peregrinus*

**Physical characteristics:** Common ringtails range in length from 24 to 28 inches (60 to 70 centimeters) and weigh between 1.5 and 2.4 pounds (0.7 and 1.1 kilograms). Ringtails have gray-brown fur with lighter fur on the belly. Their tail is long, thin, and pale on the end.

**Geographic range:** Common ringtails can be found along the eastern coast of Australia from the northern-most tip, down to the southern tip near Tasmania. They are also found throughout Tasmania and the Bass Straight islands.

**Habitat:** Common ringtails live among any type of vegetation with dense underbrush. This can mean a wide variety of locations, from rainforests to Australian coastal wasteland.

Common ringtails may build their large nests next to one or more other common ringtails.
(E. R. Degginger/Bruce Coleman Inc. Reproduced by permission.)

**Diet:** Common ringtails are herbivores meaning that they eat mainly leaves, fruits, and flowers.

**Behavior and reproduction:** Common ringtails are nocturnal. Common ringtails build large nests, often next to each other or in groups. Females give birth to two young at a time between April and November. After birth the young live in their mother's pouch for three months. Males take part in the care of the young after they leave the pouch. Once young are six months old, they leave their parents.

**Common ringtail and people:** Common ringtails in the areas around where people live have been known to eat flowers and other decorative plants in gardens.

**Conservation status:** Common ringtails are not threatened. ■

## FOR MORE INFORMATION

### Books:

Kerle, Anne. *Possums: The Brushtails, Ringtails and Greater Gliders.* Sydney, Australia: University of New South Wales Press, 2001.

Russell, Rupert. *Spotlight on Possums.* St. Lucia, Australia: University of Queensland Press, 1980.

Steiner, Barbara A. *A Field Guide to the Mammals of Australia.* Oxford, U.K.: Oxford University Press, 2001.

### Web sites:

"Common Ringtail Possum." Tasmanian Department of Primary Industries, Water and Environment: Parks & Wildlife. http://www.dpiwe.tas.gov.au/inter.nsf/WebPages/BHAN-53J3P5?open (accessed on June 30, 2004).

"Sugar Glider." Tasmanian Department of Primary Industries, Water and Environment: Parks & Wildlife. http://www.dpiwe.tas.gov.au/inter.nsf/WebPages/BHAN-53J8XS?open (accessed on June 30, 2004).

**Class:** Mammalia

**Order:** Diprotodontia

**Family:** Petauridae

**Number of species:** 12 species

family

C H A P T E R

## PHYSICAL CHARACTERISTICS

Gliding and striped possums are arboreal, which means that they live in trees. They are also nocturnal, meaning they are active at night and sleep during the day, often in hollow trees. Members of this family are medium-sized. They measure between 12 and 31 inches (32 to 78 centimeters) long and weigh between 3 and 25 ounces (95 to 720 grams).

As the name of this family suggests, there are two major types of Petauridae. These two types are organized into groups called subfamilies. One subfamily is called Petaurinae, and the other is called Dactylopsilinae. The Petaurinae subfamily is the group known as the gliding possums. The Dactylopsilinae are the striped possums. Although they are closely related, these two subfamilies look quite different from each other.

Gliding possums are gray, brown, or cream colored. They have a membrane (a thin layer of skin) between their front and rear legs that stretches from their wrist to their ankle. When they leap from branch to branch, they spread this membrane out like a bed sheet in order to glide. Gliding possums also have a bushy tail that is used for steering while in the air. The end of their tail is prehensile, which means that it can be used for grasping branches.

Striped possums are black with two white stripes that run along their back like a skunk. Also like a skunk, these animals have a strong and unpleasant odor that is produced by several glands or organs that secrete chemicals from the body. Striped possums have five toes on their front paws. The fourth toe is much longer than the rest. They use this to tap tree trunks to find hollow spaces where insects might be hiding. Once they find the insects, they use this toe to dig them out. They also have very strong front teeth that help them to puncture the bark of trees.

## GEOGRAPHIC RANGE

Striped possums live in New Guinea. One species is also found in the rainforest on the northern tip of Australia that is closest to New Guinea. Gliding possums also live in New Guinea and Australia, but are found in a much wider area. They live both on the northern and eastern coast of Australia and on the island of Tasmania.

## HABITAT

Gliding and striped possums live in many different types of forests, from dense rainforests to open forests where trees are spread far apart.

## DIET

Gliding possums are omnivorous meaning they eat both plants and animals. They feed mostly on sap from trees, as well as nectar and blossoms. Some species of gliding possums are able to bite into tree bark in order to get the sap. Others feed off sap that leaks from wounds in trees made by other species.

Striped possums are insectivorous, meaning that they mainly eat insects. They use their long fourth finger to tap trees and rotting logs to find the hollow spots where insect larvae (LAR-vee; young developing insects) are living. They then use their strong front teeth to dig into the tree and their fourth finger to pull out the larvae.

## BEHAVIOR AND REPRODUCTION

Striped possums live alone and do not form social groups. They are believed to be territorial. This means that they stay in a particular area and defend it against other members of their species. Gliding possums are more social and live in family groups and share their nests. These groups are made up of variable numbers of adult males and females. Within these groups, both males and females develop a system of ranking known as a hierarchy (HI-uh-raar-key). Females will aggressively bother other females that are below them in this hierarchy, sometimes causing the death of their babies. Males that are high in this system tend to care for the young when the females are away. Gliding possums are also territorial, because they protect their area from other gliding possums that are not in their group.

Gliding and striped possums are marsupial mammals, which means that they do not have a well-developed placenta. The placenta is an organ that allows the mother to share food and oxygen with developing offspring in her uterus (womb) during pregnancy. As a result, marsupials like these possums are born underdeveloped and need to continue to grow in their mother's pouch for some time after birth before they can survive in the outside world.

All female members of this family have a pouch with two teats (nipples). Two young are born at a time. After the young are born, they crawl to the pouch and attach themselves to one of their mother's teats. After many days, the young emerge from the pouch and live in a nest. During this time, they may be carried around on their mother's back. Information about reproduction is not known for all species, but it is known that for the sugar glider, pregnancy lasts only sixteen days. However, the young remain in the pouch for another sixty days after birth. The young then live in the nest until they are about four months old. In this species the males that live in the group help to care for the young.

**ODOR AND TERRITORY**

Animals produce odors for many different reasons. In some cases an animal uses odor as protection to ward off potential predators. They also use odor to attract potential mates. In other situations, animals use odors to let other animals know that a particular area is their territory. Gliding and striped possums use odors to mark territory for different reasons. While striped possums are most likely telling other striped possums to stay out of their area, gliding possums use odor to identify members of their group.

## GLIDING AND STRIPED POSSUMS AND PEOPLE

The sugar glider is becoming popular as an exotic pet. It is not clear whether these animals make appropriate pets and some countries have placed a ban on importing them from New Guinea. Beyond this species, there is no significant relationship between humans and the members of this family other than scientific study.

## CONSERVATION STATUS

Three species in this family are Endangered, facing a very high risk of extinction in the wild: Tate's triok, the mahogany glider, and Leadbeater's possum. Other species, such as the yellow-bellied glider and the squirrel glider are considered Vulnerable, facing a high risk of extinction in the wild. Conservation efforts are underway to identify and protect key habitats of a number of these animals.

Sugar glider *(Petaurus breviceps)*

## SUGAR GLIDER
### *Petaurus breviceps*

**Physical characteristics:**   Sugar gliders are part of the gliding group (Petaurinae) of this family. They have a membrane that extends from the fifth toe of their back legs to the first finger on their front legs. They spread their arms and legs to make a sail out of the membrane when leaping between branches. Sugar gliders are fairly small measuring between 12 and 15 inches (32 to 42 centimeters) long and weighing between 3.5 to 5.5 ounces (95 to 160 grams). They have two black stripes along the sides of the face, and one black stripe that runs along their back. The rest of their fur is blue-gray, except for on the belly, which has lighter fur.

**Geographic range:**   Sugar gliders live in New Guinea, Tasmania, and in the northern and eastern parts of Australia.

**Habitat:**   Sugar gliders are frequently found living in acacia and eucalyptus trees.

**Diet:**   The sugar glider is an omnivore. It eats tree sap, pollen, insect larvae, and insect-like animals such as spiders

**Behavior and reproduction:**   Sugar gliders are nocturnal. Using strong legs to launch themselves, they are able to glide up to 230 feet (70 meters). Sugar gliders, like many gliding possums, are social and they live in family groups that are territorial.

Sugar gliders give birth to one or two offspring twice a year. Their pregnancy lasts sixteen days. Pouch stay for the young is about two months, with another two months are spent in the nest. Their lifespan is about fourteen years.

**Sugar gliders and people:**   Despite controversy, sugar gliders are becoming popular as household pets, both in Asia and the United States.

**Conservation status:** This species is not threatened. There is no serious danger that they will become extinct in the foreseeable future. ■

## FOR MORE INFORMATION

### Books:

Steiner, Barbara A. *A Field Guide to the Mammals of Australia.* Oxford, U.K.: Oxford University Press, 2001.

Triggs, Barbara. *Tracks, Scats and Other Traces: A Field Guide to Australian Mammals.* Oxford, U.K.: Oxford University Press, 1996.

Robinson, Hannah. *Australia: An Ecotraveler's Guide.* New York: Interlink Books, 2003.

### Web sites:

Australian National Parks and Wildlife Service. "Gliding Possums." http://www.nationalparks.nsw.gov.au/npws.nsf/Content/Gliding+possums (accessed on June 30, 2004).

**HONEY POSSUM**

**Tarsipedidae**

**Class:** Mammalia

**Order:** Diprotodontia

**Family:** Tarsipedidae

**One species:** Honey possum
(*Tarsipes rostratus*)

family

C H A P T E R

## PHYSICAL CHARACTERISTICS

Honey possums are very small and highly specialized marsupial mammals. Despite their name, honey possums do not actually make or eat honey—instead, they have unique physical features that help them to feed primarily on the pollen and nectar from flowers. They are very small and have long tongues to pull the nectar or pollen out from inside a flower. Their heads are long and tapered, and they are covered in coarse, short hair. Except for three black stripes down the middle of their back, their coloring is a grayish brown.

Male honey possums weigh only 0.24 to 0.38 ounces (7 to 8 grams). Female possums weigh slightly more, between 0.28 and 0.56 ounces (8 to 16 grams). From the tip of their nose to the end of their body (excluding the tail) they are only between 2.6 and 3.5 inches (6.5 to 9 centimeters) long.

Honey possums have long tails, as long or longer than their bodies. They use this tail to help them climb along branches between flowers. The tip of the tail is prehensile, meaning that the honey possum can use it to grasp objects. It is almost hairless, which also helps to improve its grip. Honey possums are often seen hanging upside down by their tails. They also have very long tongues, which they can extend beyond their mouth even further than the length of their head. This helps them to retrieve their food from flowers. Their paws have four toes. The bones of the middle two toes on the back paws are fused (attached) but have separate claws that are used for grooming. Other toes are clawless.

phylum

class

subclass

order

monotypic order

suborder

▲ **family**

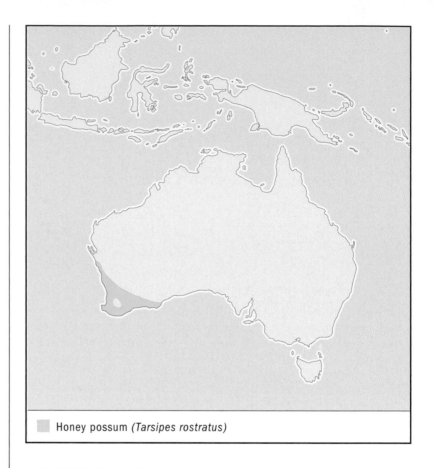

Honey possum (*Tarsipes rostratus*)

## GEOGRAPHIC RANGE

Honey possums live in a very small region in the south-western tip of Australia.

## HABITAT

The honey possum lives on uninhabited sandy beaches where the kinds of flowers that they feed on bloom almost all year round.

## DIET

Even though they are called honey possums, these animals do not eat honey. They feed upon the nectar and pollen from the flowers of plants such as myrtles (MER-tuhlz), proteas (PRO-tee-ahz), and banksias (BANK-see-ahz) that grow on the coast of southwestern Australia. Their teeth, which are stubby and short, are not used to chew or bite. In order to get the pollen and nectar, honey possums use their long tongue and tapered head to poke into the flowers. The end of their tongue is like a brush, and they use it to pull the food into their mouth. In order to maintain themselves, honey possums must consume large amounts of their sugary food and spend most of their time searching for flowers.

## BEHAVIOR AND REPRODUCTION

Because they require a large amount of energy to keep warm, honey possums spend most of their time in search of food. They are nocturnal, which means they are most active at night, and sleep during the day. Honey possums live alone and sleep in holes of trees or nests that birds have abandoned. While the flowers from which they eat pollen or nectar bloom most of the year, sometimes there is a scarcity of food. During this time, honey possums often gather in large groups and curl up together. They become inactive, as if they are hibernating. Their heart rate slows and their body temperature drops in order to conserve energy. When more food is available, the honey possums become active again.

Honey possums feed on the nectar from flowers, like this Banksia *flower*. (© *Jiri Lochman/Lochman Transparencies. Reproduced by permission.*)

To get from flower to flower, honey possums run quickly along the sandy ground and climb very skillfully up branches in order to reach the blossoms. They use their long tails to grasp branches in case they lose their balance. Often they hang upside down in order to reach a flower. Once they have reached the flower, they use their front toes to pull it apart and then push their snout inside. Their long tongues can extend far into the flower and scrape out the pollen inside.

Honey possums are marsupial mammals, which means that they do not have a well-developed placenta. The placenta is an organ that allows the mother to share food and oxygen with developing offspring in her uterus (womb) during pregnancy. As a result, their young are born underdeveloped and need to continue to grow in their mother's pouch for some time after birth before they can survive in the outside world.

Honey possums live only for a year or two, but they reproduce almost continuously. After only six months, both male and female honey possums are able to produce offspring. After about a two-month pregnancy, the mother gives birth. The

## EVOLVING ALIKE

Even though monkeys and honey possums are not related, and they are so different in size, they share many characteristics. For example, honey possums have long tails, which they use for grabbing and balancing on branches like monkeys. Both monkeys and honey possums have toes that are good for grasping and climbing. When two animals are not related by evolution but develop similar characteristics, scientists call this "convergent evolution." Since both monkeys and honey possums needed to be able to climb efficiently, they have evolved similar features to help them.

newborns then spend another two months inside her pouch attached to one of her four nipples. At birth, the young weigh only 0.00002 ounces (0.0005 grams), and they are the smallest of all known mammals. Inside the pouch they grow to 0.09 ounces (2.5 grams). Their eyes open, and they grow hair.

The mother usually mates shortly after the litter (a group of young born at the same time) is born and enters her pouch. Because of this, she is able to give birth to another litter as the first litter is leaving her pouch. After a litter leaves the pouch, they spend a week or two following their mother around and even riding on her back. They are then ready to leave and begin looking for food on their own. A female will usually give birth to two litters, or eight young, but she will not often live long enough to give birth to a third litter.

## HONEY POSSUMS AND PEOPLE

Honey possums have little direct relation to humans, although they do help to spread flowers along the coast because of their pollen diet. Despite their nocturnal lifestyle, which makes them hard to find, honey possums are also popular with ecotourists. Ecotourists are people who want to observe nature without disturbing it.

## CONSERVATION STATUS

In 1992, much of the habitat and food supply of the honey possum was disappearing because humans were developing their habitat with little regard to this small animal. Today, with increased awareness, the number of honey possums has rebounded and they are not considered threatened.

## FOR MORE INFORMATION

**Books:**

Robinson, Hannah. *Australia: An Ecotraveler's Guide.* New York: Interlink Books, 2003.

Steiner, Barbara A. *A Field Guide to the Mammals of Australia.* Oxford, U.K.: Oxford University Press, 2001.

Triggs, Barbara. *Tracks, Scats and Other Traces: A Field Guide to Australian Mammals.* Oxford, U.K.: Oxford University Press, 1996.

**Web sites:**

Australian Association for Environmental Education. "Case Study 3—Honey Possums and Wildflowers." https://olt.qut.edu.au/udf/aaee/gen/index.cfm?fa=displayPage&rNum=475152 (accessed on June 30, 2004).

The University of Michigan Museum of Zoology. "*Tarsipes rostratus.*" http://animaldiversity.ummz.umich.edu/site/accounts/information/Tarsipes_rostratus.html (accessed on June 30, 2004).

Watson, Ian, and Craig Owen. "Honey Possum." Quantum, ABC Television. http://www.abc.net.au/quantum/s244451.htm (accessed on June 30, 2004).

family

C H A P T E R

phylum

class

subclass

order

monotypic order

suborder

▲ **family**

## PHYSICAL CHARACTERISTICS

The family Acrobatidae is made up of two species: the pygmy glider and the feather-tailed possum. Although they are very different in many ways, these two species have similarities that make them part of the same family.

The pygmy glider is the smaller of the two species. Their heads and bodies are usually between 2.5 and 3 inches (6.5 to 8 centimeters). They have tails that are also between 2.5 and 3 inches (6.5 to 8 centimeters) in length. The pygmy glider weighs less than 0.5 ounces (14 grams). Feather-tailed possums are larger, with a head and body length that ranges from 4 to 5 inches (10 to 13 centimeters). Their tail is longer than their body, with a length of between 5 and 6 inches (12 to 15 centimeters). They weigh between 1 and 2 ounces (30 to 60 grams).

Pygmy gliders and feather-tailed possums both have tails that are long and have long straight hairs sticking off both sides of their tail. These hairs make the tail look like a feather, which is how they got their name. Both species have large eyes and round ears. They both also have gray fur. The feather-tailed possum has black and white stripes on its face. The pygmy glider does not have these stripes and has a white belly.

Both species of this family have sharp claws that help them grip trees. They also have six pads on their feet to help them grip. The pygmy glider has a thin membrane, or piece of skin, that goes from its front legs to its back legs. This membrane allows it to glide. The feather-tailed possum does not glide and does not have this membrane.

Both species are marsupial mammals. This makes them different from most familiar mammals such as cats, dogs, and horses. These familiar mammals are all eutherian (yoo-THEER-ee-an) mammals, which means they have a well-developed placenta. A placenta is an organ that grows in the mother's uterus, womb, and lets the mother and developing baby share food and oxygen. Marsupial mammals do not have this type of placenta. Because of this, they give birth to young that are not physically developed enough to be able to survive on their own. Instead, the young are carried around either in a pouch or attached to the mother's teats, or nipples, on her underside until they have developed more fully and can survive on their own.

## GEOGRAPHIC RANGE

The pygmy glider lives in eastern Australia. The feather-tailed possum lives in New Guinea.

## HABITAT

Both species in this family live in trees. Feather-tailed possums live in tropical rainforests and woodland areas. They are also sometimes found in suburban gardens. Pygmy gliders prefer forests that contain many eucalyptus (yoo-kah-LIP-tus) trees. They also live in other woodland areas.

## DIET

Pygmy gliders and feather-tailed possums eat insects, fruit, flowers, and nectar.

## BEHAVIOR AND REPRODUCTION

Both the pygmy glider and the feather-tailed possum are nocturnal, which means they are active mainly at night. They have flexible prehensile tails that allow them to grab hold of branches. Feather-tailed possums usually live alone or in pairs, but pygmy gliders often live in groups and make nests out of dry leaves in branches or hollows in trees.

## WHAT MAKES A FAMILY?

Pygmy gliders and feather-tailed possums are in the same family, but they are different in many ways. Pygmy gliders have a special membrane that allows them to glide, while feather-tailed possums do not. Scientists look at many different clues to decide what species are similar enough to belong in the same family. These possums have ears that are very complex and unique to these two species. This is the kind of information scientists used to decide that these two species belonged in the same family, even though they may not look very similar.

Feather-tailed possums have one or two offspring at a time, while pygmy gliders usually have three or four offspring. They both give birth to young that are underdeveloped and spend time in the pouch while they grow and mature. After they leave the pouch, the young spend time in the nest before being weaned, no longer dependent on their mother's milk, and are ready to fend for themselves.

**FEATHER-TAILED POSSUMS AND PEOPLE**

Feather-tailed possums do not have any known significance to humans except to the scientists who study them.

**CONSERVATION STATUS**

Neither species of feather-tailed possum is considered threatened. They do not face a high risk of extinction in the wild in the near future.

Pygmy glider (*Acrobates pygmaeus*)

## PYGMY GLIDER
### *Acrobates pygmaeus*

**Physical characteristics:** The pygmy glider is the smallest marsupial that is able to glide. They weigh less than 0.5 ounces (14 grams). Their head and body measure between 2.5 and 3 inches (6.5 to 8 centimeters) in length. Their tail is also usually about 2.5 to 3 inches (6.5 to 8 centimeters) long. Females have pouches that contain four nipples.

Pygmy gliders have fur that is soft and gray. Around their large eyes are circles of black fur. Their belly is white. The pygmy glider's tail is about as long as its body and has long stiff hairs on each side of it. A membrane with fur on it is attached to either side of the pygmy glider's body from its front feet to its back feet.

**Geographic range:** Pygmy gliders are found in eastern Australia.

**Habitat:**  Pygmy gliders live in forest areas where there are many eucalyptus trees. They also live in woodland areas.

**Diet:**  Pygmy gliders eat mainly insects. They also eat nectar from flowers.

**Behavior and reproduction:**  Pygmy gliders are nocturnal. They live in trees and rarely spend any time on the forest floor, where they would be vulnerable to predators. Pygmy gliders are very social animals. They build nests out of leaves in branches and holes in trees. Many pygmy gliders live together in one nest. When it gets cold, they often huddle together to share warmth. When it gets especially cold or there is not enough food, pygmy gliders can go into torpor. Torpor is when the animal purposely lowers its body temperature and heart rate temporarily to conserve energy, similar to hibernation.

Pygmy gliders glide by jumping and then spreading their hands and feet so that their special membrane becomes stretched out. This membrane acts like a parachute so that the pygmy glider glides instead of falling. The feather-like tail is used to help control the glide. This way they are able to glide distances of up to 65 feet (20 meters) or more at a time. Because they live in trees and almost never go down to ground level, gliding is an important way for this species to move from tree to tree.

Pygmy gliders usually have three or four offspring at a time. The mother gives birth to young that are not able to fend for themselves.

The young crawl into her pouch where they continue to grow. Once the young have fur and are a little older, they sometimes ride around on their mother's back. After about sixty days, they leave the pouch and stay in the nest alone. They stay in the nest for another thirty-five or forty days. At this time the young are weaned, although they might not leave the nest. The day that the babies are born, the mother mates and gets pregnant again. The new fetuses stop developing until just before the young have been weaned. This means that the mother gives birth again just a day or two after the last set of young has stopped nursing.

**Pygmy gliders and people:**   Pygmy gliders are not known to have special significance to people except to the scientists who study them.

**Conservation status:**   Pygmy gliders are not considered threatened. They are not at risk of extinction in the wild in the foreseeable future.   ■

## FOR MORE INFORMATION

### Books:

Smith, Andrew, and John Winter. *A Key and Field Guide to the Australian Possums, Gliders and Koala.* Chipping Norton, Australia: Surrey Beatty and Sons, 1997.

Fenton, Julie A. *Kangaroos and Other Marsupials.* Chicago: World Book Inc., 2000.

### Web sites:

Australian National Parks and Wildlife. "Gliding possums." http://www.nationalparks.nsw.gov.au/npws.nsf/Content/Gliding+possums (accessed on June 30, 2004).

## SLOTHS, ANTEATERS, AND ARMADILLOS
### Xenarthra

**Class:** Mammalia
**Order:** Xenarthra
**Number of families:** 4 families

# order
## CHAPTER

## PHYSICAL CHARACTERISTICS

The order Xenarthra consists of sloths, anteaters, armadillos, and the extinct glyptodonts. The glyptodont, which became extinct 10,000 years ago, belonged to the armadillo family. It was 10 feet (3 meters) long. Modern-day xenarthrans (ZEN-arthranz) range from the pink fairy armadillo, which is 6 inches (15 centimeters) long, to the giant anteater, which is up to 7 feet (2.1 meters) long.

Sloths move slowly and spend most of their lives upside down in trees. They hold onto branches and trunks with their long limbs. Sloths have small heads, slim bodies, and tiny tails. Their hair is long and rough. Fur is mainly gray or brown, with green coloring in the outer hair. The green color is caused by algae (AL-jee), which are tiny water plants. Sloths aren't bothered by algae growing in their fur. They lick the algae when hungry, and the color helps sloths blend in with trees. This camouflage (KAM-uh-flaj) protects sloths from predators, animals that hunt them for food.

Two-toed tree sloths are up to 3 feet (0.9 meters) long and weigh 18 pounds (8 kilograms). There is a claw, approximately 3 inches (7.5 centimeters) long, on each of two digits (toes) of the sloth's front feet. Three-toed tree sloths are about 2 feet (0.6 meters) long and weigh 11 pounds (5 kilograms). They have three digits with claws on the front feet.

In the anteater family, two species have tiny heads and long snouts. The giant anteater and tamandua (tuh-MAN-duh-wah) use their tube-shaped snouts to dig into ant nests, and lick up ants with their tongues. The giant anteater weighs up to 88 pounds (39 kilograms) and its tongue is 2 feet (0.6 meters) long. The anteater's long, coarse fur is black, white, gray, and brown. Because its claws are long, the anteater walks on the side of its feet.

Tamandua is the scientific and common name of the lesser anteater. Length ranges from 3 to 5 feet (0.9 to 1.5 meters), and weight ranges from 8 to 13 pounds (3.5 to 6 kilograms). The northern tamandua is brown with black fur on its back. Southern tamandua fur color ranges from blonde to brown.

Tamandua and the silky anteater have prehensile tails that they use to hold objects or hang onto trees. The silky anteater is up to 20 inches (50 centimeters) long and weighs 17 ounces (480 grams) and up. Its fur is soft, and colors range from gray to yellow. In comparison to its size, the silky anteater's mouth is larger than that of other anteaters.

Armadillos' size ranges from the tiny fairy armadillo to the giant armadillo, which is 4.9 feet (1.5 meters) long and weighs 66 pounds (30 kilograms). Armadillos have long tails, and their bodies are covered by shells, "armor" formed out of bony plates. Hair grows between the plates, and the number of these bands varies by species. Shell color includes brown, white, and yellow. Body color is usually gray or brown. However, the pink fairy armadillo has a pink shell and white body. The armadillo shell covers most of its body.

## GEOGRAPHIC RANGE

Xenarthrans originated in the New World and live primarily in Central and South America. Sloths, anteaters, and armadillos live in Bolivia, Brazil, Colombia, Costa Rica, French Guiana, Guyana, Nicaragua, Panama, Peru, Suriname, and Venezuela. Sloths are also found in Ecuador and Honduras. Anteaters range in Belize, Guatemala, El Salvador, Honduras, Suriname, Paraguay, and Uruguay. Sloths and armadillos live in Mexico, and the nine-banded armadillo is the only xenarthran living in the United States.

## HABITAT

Sloths live in trees in the rainforest, an area where there is much rain throughout the year. This rain leads to the growth of many trees and plants. Anteaters live in rainforests or in the savanna, an area of grassland with few trees. Giant anteaters live on the ground, and pygmy anteaters live in trees. Tamanduas live in trees or on the ground.

Armadillos live in the rainforest, grasslands, desert, and in deciduous forests where leaves fall off trees during a certain season. Most armadillos burrow, using their claws to dig holes or tunnels that serve as their homes.

## DIET

Sloths are primarily herbivores, eating mostly leaves and twigs. Anteaters are insectivores, feeding mainly on insects. Armadillos are omnivores; their diet includes plants, insects, and other animals.

Sloths sleep most of the day and spend about seven hours eating. They develop a taste for the leaves that their mothers eat. This is because the mother sloth carries the cub with her. The young sloth feeds itself by reaching for leaves in the trees where its mother eats. The sloth diet includes leaves, flowers, buds, and twigs. Two-toed sloths may also eat bird eggs and insects.

The anteater's name describes its diet. A giant anteater must consume about 30,000 ants each day. The tamandua eats about 9,000 a day, and the silky anteater can eat 5,000 ants in a day. Giant anteaters and tamandua also consume termites. If tamandua can't locate ants and termites, they feed on bees, honey, and small fruit. The pygmy anteater eats beetles and fruit.

Armadillos eat plants and dig into the ground to find insects and worms to eat. They also eat small animals like snakes and frogs. Diet is based on habitat.

## BEHAVIOR AND REPRODUCTION

Xenarthrans are usually solitary. However, armadillos sometimes travel in pairs or small groups. Sloths, anteaters, and armadillos are thought to be polygynous (puh-LIH-juh-nus), meaning males mate with more than one female. After mating, the males leave, and the females raise the young.

A female sloth bears one young that she carries with her for up to a year. A female anteater usually gives birth to one cub. Very rarely, twins are born. The cub stays on the mother's back for six to nine months. Females of most armadillo species bear a litter of one to three young. However, some species bear up to twelve cubs.

When the armadillo is faced by predators, it bends its head down to protect its flesh from attack. The three-banded armadillo rolls itself into a hard-shelled ball. Sloths and anteaters use claws as protection. Predators of xenarthrans include jaguars, lions, and humans.

## SLOTHS, ANTEATERS, ARMADILLOS, AND PEOPLE

Humans have various relationships with sloths, anteaters, and armadillos. People hunt xenarthrans for food, and they make pets of some species. Sometimes people keep anteaters at home to help get rid of ants. People kill some sloths for their fur pelts. Tamandua is hunted for the tendon, a cord-like tissue that attaches muscle to bone, in its tail. The tendon is used to make rope.

In addition, medical researchers are studying armadillos. They are the only mammals besides humans that contract leprosy, a skin disease. Research on armadillos helps to develop treatment of this condition in people.

### AN UNUSUAL ORDER

Sloths, anteaters, and armadillos were once thought to belong to the order Edentata, a word that means "toothless." Some xenarthrans have teeth, and they all have skeletons that are different from other mammals. "Xenarthra" is a combination of Greek words meaning "strange joints." In xenarthrans, three pairs of joints connect some vertebrae (backbone segments) in the backbone. In addition, xenarthrans don't have separate pelvic bones. Pelvic bones are unconnected in the hips of most mammals.

## CONSERVATION STATUS

The three-toed sloth, giant armadillo, and pink fairy armadillo are considered Endangered, according to the World Conservation Union (IUCN). These mammals face a very high risk of extinction. Considered Vulnerable, facing a high risk of extinction, by the IUCN are the giant anteater and several species of armadillos in South America. Risk to these xenarthrans is caused mainly by loss of habitat as the rainforest is cleared of trees. Farming and hunting also threaten these populations.

## FOR MORE INFORMATION

### Books:

Attenborough, David. *The Life of Mammals*. Princeton, NJ: Princeton University Press, 2002.

Dollar, Sam. *Anteaters*. Austin, TX: Raintree Steck-Vaughn Publishers, 2001.

Squire, Ann O. *Anteaters, Sloths, and Armadillos*. New York: Franklin Watts, 1999.

**Web sites:**

Animal Diversity Web. The University of Michigan Museum of Zoology. http://animaldiversity.ummz.umich.edu/index.html (accessed on June 30, 2004).

BBC Science & Nature: Animals. "Wildfacts." http://www.bbc.co.uk/nature/wildfacts/ (accessed on June 30, 2004).

**Class:** Mammalia

**Order:** Xenarthra

**Family:** Megalonychidae

**Number of species:** 2 species

family
CHAPTER

## PHYSICAL CHARACTERISTICS

The family Megalonychidae consists of one living genus (JEE-nus), *Choloepus*, the two-toed tree sloths. A genus is a group of animals within a family that have some similar characteristics. Megalonychidae also includes eleven or more extinct genera (JEN-uh-rah; the plural of genus). Since the last of the West Indian sloths is dead, scientists have learned about them by studying fossils. From skeletons found in Haiti, researchers determined that the lesser Haitian ground sloth weighed about 50 pounds (23 kilograms) and was as large as a medium-sized dog. It lived on the ground, and probably also spent time in trees.

The lesser Haitian sloth, like the living *Choloepus* species, had long limbs, long claws, and a broad body. While tree sloths have tiny tails or none at all, this extinct sloth had a long tail that touched the ground. The ground sloth could balance with its tail and then stand on two feet to reach into trees.

Within *Choloepus* are two living species, Hoffmann's two-toed sloth and Linné's two-toed sloth (also called the southern two-toed sloth). Both use their limbs to hang upside down in trees. Front limbs are slightly longer than back limbs.

Two-toed sloths have small heads and shaggy fur ranging in color from brown to gray. There is a green tint to sloth fur. The color comes from algae (AL-jee), tiny water plants growing in the sloth's hair. The algae, along with the sloth's natural fur color, camouflage (KAM-uh-flaj) the tree-dweller and keep it hidden from predators, animals that hunt it for food. When hungry, sloths may lick the algae on their fur.

phylum

class

subclass

order

monotypic order

suborder

▲ **family**

The head and body length of two-toed tree sloths ranges from 2 to 3 feet (60 to 90 centimeters). They weigh from 9 to 18 pounds (4 to 8 kilograms). Sloths have eighteen teeth and 3-inch (7.5-centimeter) claws on each digit of their feet. There are two digits, or toes, on the front feet and three on the back feet. Sloths use their hook-shaped claws to hang from trees and to move.

Sloths may have as many as eight neck vertebrae, or bone segments. Other mammals, including humans, have seven. Two-toed sloths can turn their heads 180 degrees (a half-circle), which gives the sloths a very broad view of their surroundings.

## GEOGRAPHIC RANGE

The extinct West Indian sloths lived in the West Indies, in island countries including Haiti. Living two-toed sloth species reside in Bolivia, Brazil, Colombia, Costa Rica, Ecuador, French Guiana, Guyana, Honduras, Nicaragua, Panama, Peru, Suriname, and Venezuela.

## HABITAT

The earliest West Indian sloths were arboreal, living in trees. Later species lived both on the ground and in trees. Most two-toed sloths live in trees in the rainforest, an area where there is much rain throughout the year. Sloths also range in cloud forests, forests in high altitude areas that are kept moist by the clouds at that height.

## DIET

West Indian sloths probably ate leaves. Two-toed sloths are herbivores, eating mostly leaves and twigs. They also eat fruit. Since sloths move from tree to tree, their diet is as varied as the trees they live in.

## BEHAVIOR AND REPRODUCTION

Two-toed sloths are also known as *unau*. Their English name, sloth, means laziness. Sloths' diet of leaves produces little energy, so the animals move slowly to preserve that energy. The lack of energy also results in a low body temperature that ranges from 75° to 95°F (24° to 33°C). This wide range is the most varied of any mammal.

The two-toed tree sloths are solitary and remain alone unless breeding or raising their young. After mating, the male leaves. The female gives birth to one young after about eleven months. Gestation, the time a mother carries the baby inside her, may vary by species. A female Linné's two-toed sloth in captivity gave birth five months after mating. Mothers of both species keep the offspring with them for almost a year.

Two-toed sloths spend most of their lives upside down. They eat, mate, and sleep in that position. The low-energy animals may sleep fifteen hours or more a day. These sloths are nocturnal, and are most active at night. During that time, they eat and move from one tree to another. Sloths usually change locations by climbing on tree branches and vines. If this is not possible, the sloth will climb down and move to another tree.

### SLOW BUT NOT LAZY

Sloth is often understood to mean laziness, an undesirable trait. The word "sloth" is a version of the word "slow," which better describes sloths. Their limbs can't support their bodies, so sloths drag themselves on the ground at the rate of 45 feet (13.7 meters) per minute. In trees, sloths move no more than 125 feet (38 meters) per day.

## TWO-TOED TREE SLOTHS AND PEOPLE

From the earliest times, people probably hunted ground sloths for food and used their fur pelts to make clothing. Scientists study West Indian sloth fossils to learn how these animals evolved and changed over thousands of years. Two-toed sloths were occasionally hunted for their meat.

## CONSERVATION STATUS

West Indian sloths became extinct two thousand years ago, after people came to the area where they lived. Two-toed sloths lose habitat as forest land is used for lumbering and farms. There is not sufficient information available to determine whether sloths are at risk of extinction, according to the World Conservation Union (IUCN).

Hoffmann's two-toed sloth (*Choloepus hoffmanni*)

## HOFFMAN'S TWO-TOED SLOTH
### *Choloepus hoffmanni*

**Physical characteristics:** Hoffmann's two-toed sloths are about 2 feet (60 centimeters) long and weigh up to 18 pounds (8 kilograms). They have coarse fur that is tan colored or grayish brown. Hair color is lighter on the face. Algae adds a green color to the shaggy fur.

**Geographic range:** Hoffman's two-toed sloths live in Bolivia, Brazil, Columbia, Costa Rica, Ecuador, Honduras, Nicaragua, Panama, Peru, and Venezuela.

**Habitat:** Hoffmann's sloths live in the tree canopies, near the top of trees in rainforests and cloud forests. They often stay in liana (lee-AN-uh) tangles, twisted vines that provide shelter. The tangle also serves as an alarm. If a predator is approaching, the leaves move and the sloth is alerted about a possible attack.

**Diet:** Hoffmann's sloths eat leaves, shoots, flowers, and fruit.

**Behavior and reproduction:** Two-toed sloths are nocturnal, and do not become active until about an hour after the sun sets. Like other sloths, Hoffmann's sloth is solitary. However, a group of sloths may live in one tree. These groups are formed of only female sloths. Males stay on their own unless they are breeding.

After mating, the female sloth gives birth to one offspring in about eleven and a half months. Newborn sloths weigh from 12 to 16 ounces (340 to 454 grams). The mother carries the young sloth on her stomach. Since the offspring eats the same leaves as its mother, the young sloth develops a taste for those leaves. At the age of five months, the young sloth may feed on its own. However, it remains close to its mother for about a year.

Young and adult sloths use their claws and teeth as defenses against predators like harpy eagles, jaguars, and ocelots.

**Hoffman's two-toed sloths and people:** Sloths are known to heal quickly, so studying them could help scientists understand how to help people heal more quickly.

**Conservation status:** There is not enough information to determine whether Hoffmann's sloth faces a threat of extinction, according to IUCN. ∎

*Hoffmann's two-toed sloth spends its time in the tree canopy, near the top of the trees in rainforests and cloud forests. (Tom Brakefield/Bruce Coleman Inc. Reproduced by permission.)*

## FOR MORE INFORMATION

### Books:

Attenborough, David. *The Life of Mammals.* Princeton, NJ: Princeton University Press, 2002.

Squire, Ann O. *Anteaters, Sloths, and Armadillos.* New York: Franklin Watts, 1999.

**Web sites:**

Animal Diversity Web. http://animaldiversity.ummz.umich.edu/index.html (accessed on June 30, 2004).

Giacalone, Jacalyn. "Sloths." *Mammal Directory.* http://www.csam.montclair.edu/ceterms/mammals/sloths.html (accessed on June 30, 2004).

Walker's Mammals of the World Online. http://www.press.jhu.edu/books/walkers_mammals_of_the_world (accessed on June 30, 2004).

## THREE-TOED TREE SLOTHS
### Bradypodidae

**Class:** Mammalia
**Order:** Xenarthra
**Family:** Bradypodidae
**Number of species:** 4 species

## PHYSICAL CHARACTERISTICS

The three-toed tree sloth family consists of four species, groups within the family that share similar characteristics. All species have eighteen peg-like teeth, slim bodies, long limbs, and tiny tails. Front limbs are longer than their back limbs.

Sloths' fur ranges in color from gray to brown. The brown-throated three-toed sloth has brown fur in its throat area and may also have white or red fur. The pale-throated sloth has dark fur on its back and lighter colored fur on its front. The maned sloth has long, black hair on its back and neck. The monk sloth has a tan face.

All species of sloths may have green in their fur. This is caused by algae (AL-jee), tiny water plants growing in sloths' hair. Algae are a food source, and sloths lick their fur when hungry. Sloths live in trees, and the green and brown in their fur helps them blend in with the trees and hide from predators, animals that hunt them for food.

The head and body length of three-toed tree sloths ranges from 15.8 to 30.3 inches (40 to 77 centimeters). Tail length ranges from 1.9 to 3.5 inches (4.7 to 9 centimeters). They weigh from 5.1 to 12.1 pounds (2.3 to 5.5 kilograms). The monk sloth is about 20 percent smaller than other sloth species.

Three-toed tree sloths have three long, hooked claws on the digits (toes) of each foot. Sloths use the claws measuring from 3.2 to 3.9 inches (8 to 10 centimeters) to hang upside down from tree branches. Sloths can see a great distance because sloths can turn their heads 270°. They can turn so far because sloths

phylum

class

subclass

order

monotypic order

suborder

▲ **family**

have eight or nine neck vertebrae (bone segments)—most mammals, including humans, have seven vertebrae.

## GEOGRAPHIC RANGE

Three-toed tree sloths live in Central and South America. Species are found in Mexico, Argentina, Bolivia, Brazil, Colombia, Costa Rica, Ecuador, El Salvador, Honduras, Nicaragua, Panama, Paraguay, Suriname, Venezuela, French Guiana, and Guyana. Monk sloths live only on Escudo de Veraguas Island off the coast of Panama.

## HABITAT

Three-toed sloths live primarily in forests. They are located in rainforests, where heavy rain throughout the year produces abundant growth. Some species also live in dry forests and coniferous forests where leaves are green year-round. In addition, sloths have been found living in trees in parks and pastures.

## DIET

Three-toed sloths are herbivores and eat the leaves and shoots of trees. Sloths move slowly because their diet of leaves produces little energy. To make up for the lack of energy, sloths have a low body temperature of 86° to 90°F (30° to 34°C).

## BEHAVIOR AND REPRODUCTION

Three-toed sloths live upside down. They sleep, mate, and give birth in that position. Sloths are solitary. They are also polygynous (puh-LIH-juh-nus), meaning that males mate with more than one female. Sloths breed at any time during the year. The male leaves after mating, and the female bears usually one young within five to six months. She carries this offspring with her for up to a year. During this time, the young sloth develops a taste for the leaves on which its mother feeds.

Three-toed sloths are active during the day and night. During the day, they position themselves in trees so that the sun warms them. They sleep as much as eighteen hours each day.

Sloths use their claws as hooks to move through trees. They move slowly and travel at most 125 feet (38 meters) in a day. Their on-ground speed is 15 yards (13.7 meters) per minute. In the water, three-toed sloths swim well. Sloths also use their claws as a defense against predators like hawks, harpy eagles, boa constrictors, and anacondas, a type of snake.

## THREE-TOED TREE SLOTHS AND PEOPLE

Three-toed sloths can be important to medical research because they heal quickly and do not get infections easily. Scientists are interested to know why this is.

## CONSERVATION STATUS

The maned sloth is ranked as Endangered by the World Conservation Union (IUCN). This species faces threats of becoming extinct in the future because habitat is lost as trees are cut down in forests. Hunting also reduces the population.

Brown-throated three-toed sloth (*Bradypus variegatus*)

## BROWN-THROATED THREE-TOED SLOTH
### *Bradypus variegatus*

**Physical characteristics:** The brown-throated three-toed sloth is named for the brown fur around its throat. Chest fur is also brown, and adult males have a patch of yellow or orange fur on their backs between their shoulder blades. On this patch are thin stripes of black fur. These tree sloths have dark fur "masks" around their eyes and the area where fur covers their ears.

Other fur color varies, depending on where the sloths live and mate. Just as human parents pass along traits like eye color to their children, sloth offspring inherit the coloring of their parents. Brown-throated sloths may have grayish brown or reddish brown hair. While some have patches of white hair in their fur, other sloths are almost completely white.

These sloths range in length from 1.5 to 2 feet (45 to 60 centimeters) and weigh from 7 to 11 pounds (3 to 5 kilograms). They have tiny tails and three digits with claws on each of their four feet.

*The algae growing on the brown throated three-toed sloth's fur helps to keep it hidden in the trees. (Michael P. L. Fogden/ Bruce Coleman Inc. Reproduced by permission.)*

**Geographic range:** Brown-throated tree sloths live in Mexico, throughout Central America, and in parts of South America. They are found in Argentina, Bolivia, Brazil, Colombia, Costa Rica, Ecuador, El Salvador, Honduras, Nicaragua, Panama, and Paraguay.

**Habitat:** Brown-throated sloths adapt to a variety of habitats. They live in rainforests, evergreen forests, parks, and pastures. They may spend up to three days in a tree before moving to another tree.

**Diet:** Since people frequently saw brown-throated sloths in *Cecropia* (sih-KROPE-ee-uh) trees, it was thought that sloths only fed on these trees. However, the tree-toed sloths eat leaves and twigs from up to thirty different species of trees. Since the sloth learns feeding habits from its mother, it prefers to eat from the same type of tree that its mother does.

**Behavior and reproduction:** Three-toed sloths are also known as *ai* by the Guarani people of South America. The name comes from the noise made when sloths are in trouble—they make a whistling sound and hiss.

Brown-throated sloths are solitary except while they're breeding. Once they mate, the male leaves. The female gives birth in five to six months. The female typically has one young. However, there have been a few cases of twin births. At birth, a sloth weighs from 0.4 to 0.6 pounds (0.2 to 0.25 kilograms).

The mother sloth carries her baby on her stomach. The offspring nurses for about six weeks. After that, it feeds itself by reaching up for food in the trees where its mother lives. The young sloth also learns its range, the area where it will travel to live and feed. By the age of six months, the sloth keeps one foot on its mother while reaching for food. After about nine months, the mother leaves her offspring to live on its own.

**Brown-throated three-toed sloths and people:** Sloths are of interest to medical researchers because they heal quickly. The brown-throated sloths have also been hunted as food.

**Conservation status:** Brown-throated sloths are not threatened. ■

## FOR MORE INFORMATION

### Books:

Attenborough, David. *The Life of Mammals.* Princeton, NJ: Princeton University Press, 2002.

Squire, Ann O. *Anteaters, Sloths, and Armadillos.* New York: Franklin Watts, 1999.

### Web sites:

Animal Diversity Web, University of Michigan Zoology Department. http://animaldiversity.ummz. umich.edu/index.html (accessed on June 30, 2004).

Giacalone, Jacalyn. "Sloths." http://www.csam.montclair.edu/ceterms/ mammals/sloths.html (accessed on June 30, 2004).

Walker's Mammals of the World Online. http://www.press.jhu.edu/ books/walkers_mammals_of_the_world (accessed on June 30, 2004).

**Class:** Mammalia
**Order:** Xenarthra
**Family:** Myrmecophagidae
**Number of species:** 4 species

family
CHAPTER

## PHYSICAL CHARACTERISTICS

The anteater has a long snout, the part of the face that includes the nose, mouth, and jaw. While the anteater is toothless, it has a long tongue that it uses to catch the ants that make up the major part of its diet. The anteater uses its snout and claws to reach into ant nests. Long hair on the anteater's body is a protection against bites from the ants that they hunt and eat.

The anteater family includes three genera (JEN-uh-rah) and four species. A genus (JEE-nus), the singular of genera, is a group of animals with similar characteristics. Size is the primary difference in each anteater genus, and that difference is represented in the animals' common names.

From head to tail, the giant anteater measures a total of 110 inches (280 centimeters), and weighs from 48 to 88 pounds (22 to 39 kilograms).

Next in size are the tamanduas (tuh-MAN-duh-wahz), which are also known as the "lesser anteaters." Tamandua translates to "ant catcher" in Portuguese. The northern tamandua is brown with black fur on its back, and the southern tamandua's fur color ranges from blond to brown.

The silky anteater is also called the pygmy anteater. The maximum head-to-tail length is 21 inches (52 centimeters). Weight ranges from 6 to 13 ounces (175 to 357 grams).

The silky anteater and tamandua have prehensile tails that they use to grab and hold onto objects like trees. Both species have soft, silky hair in contrast to the coarse (rough) fur of the giant anteater.

phylum
class
subclass
order
monotypic order
suborder
▲ **family**

## DECIDING WHERE TO EAT

Giant anteaters use their sense of smell to find underground ant nests or termite mounds that can be up to 12 feet (4 meters) above ground. After using their claws to break into the mounds, anteaters use their long tongues to scoop up the insects. They can flick their tongues 150 times a minute into nests.

## GEOGRAPHIC RANGE

Anteaters live in Central and South America, in Belize, Bolivia, Brazil, Colombia, Costa Rica, Ecuador, El Salvador, French Guiana, Guatemala, Guyana, Honduras, Nicaragua, Panama, Peru, Suriname, and Venezuela.

## HABITAT

Silky anteaters live in trees in rainforests, areas where abundant rainfall produces heavy growth. They also inhabit grassland, areas where there are few trees. Giant anteaters live on the ground and are found mainly on grassland. They also live in wetlands, where the land is flat and wet. They live in moist forests and may live near rainforests. Tamandua live in trees or on the ground. They are found in rainforests, grassland, and dry forests.

## DIET

A giant anteater eats about 30,000 ants each day. The tamandua eat about 9,000 in a day, and the silky anteater can eat 5,000 in one day. The giant anteater and tamandua also consume termites.

## BEHAVIOR AND REPRODUCTION

All anteaters are believed to be solitary, only meeting up to breed. They are thought to be polygynous (puh-LIH-juh-nus), meaning males mate with more than one female. After giant anteaters mate, the male leaves, but the male silky anteater helps to feed its young while it's in the nest. The gestation period, the amount of time before the female gives birth, is 120 to 150 days for silky anteaters and tamandua. The giant anteater gives birth after about 190 days.

Female anteaters usually give birth to one young. The female's claws are so sharp that she cannot touch her cub. It climbs onto her back and lives there for six to nine months.

Silky anteaters are nocturnal, meaning that they are active at night. The other anteaters are active at night and during the day.

Anteaters use their claws to protect themselves against predators including hawks, mountain lions, and people.

## ANTEATERS AND PEOPLE

People sometimes keep anteaters to eliminate ants and termites from their homes, as well as keeping them as pets. In addition, people kill giant anteaters and eat their meat. People kill tamandua to make rope out of the tendon, a cord-like tissue that attaches muscle to bone, in the tail.

## CONSERVATION STATUS

Giant anteaters are Vulnerable, facing a high risk of extinction in the wild, according to the World Conservation Union (IUCN). Threats to giant anteaters' survival include the loss of habitat, and lack of food as trees are cut down and insect nests are destroyed. Habitat loss could threaten other anteaters in the future.

Silky anteater *(Cyclopes didactylus)*

## SILKY ANTEATER
### *Cyclopes didactylus*

**Physical characteristics:** The hair of silky anteaters is soft like silk. Their fur is gray or gold with a brown stripe on the back. Silky anteaters are 12 to 21 inches (32 to 52 centimeters) long. They have pink noses, tube-shaped muzzles, and long tongues.

These animals are also called two-toed anteaters because the anteaters have two toes on each of their front feet. Each toe has a long, curved claw. There is a smaller claw on each of the four toes on the back feet.

Tail length ranges from 6 to 12 inches (16 to 30 centimeters). Anteaters use their prehensile tails to hold on as they move through trees.

**Geographic range:** Silky anteaters live in Mexico, Belize, Costa Rica, El Salvador, Guatemala, Honduras, Nicaragua, Panama, Colombia, Venezuela, Guyana, Suriname, French Guiana, Brazil, Peru, Ecuador, Bolivia, and Trinidad and Tobago.

**Habitat:** Silky anteaters spend most of their lives in trees, in rainforests where deciduous trees undergo seasonal changes. The anteaters live mainly in kapok (KAY-pock) trees, where pods (dry seed vessels) are fluffy and gold and silver. The anteaters resemble the pods in appearance, helping the animals to hide from predators.

**Diet:** Silky anteaters eat ants off of leaves and from the insides of tree nests.

**Behavior and reproduction:** Silky anteaters are nocturnal. After they mate, the female gives birth to one young in 120 to 150 days. She keeps the cub in a nest made of leaves in a hole in a tree trunk. Both parents raise the cub, feeding it and carrying it on their backs.

Silky anteaters are hunted by birds like the harpy eagle and hawk eagle. While anteaters strike out with their claws at predators, their best defense is their appearance, since they blend in with kapok pods.

**Silky anteaters and people:** Silky anteaters are sometimes hunted by people as a source of meat.

**Conservation status:** The silky anteater is not a threatened animal. ■

Giant anteater *(Myrmecophaga tridactyla)*

## GIANT ANTEATER
### *Myrmecophaga tridactyla*

**Physical characteristics:** Giant anteaters range in length from 5 feet, 7 inches to 9.1 feet (174 to 280 centimeters). That length includes tails, which are from 25 to 35 inches (64 to 90 centimeters) long. Tail fur is about 16 inches (40.6 centimeters) long.

The anteater's long fur is gray with bands of black and white. The animals have tiny heads, and small eyes and ears. Although their vision is poor, their sense of smell is forty times stronger than that of humans. Giant anteaters have long tube-shaped snouts that they use

to reach into underground ant nests. Their tongues look like worms and can extend 2 feet (0.6 meters) into nests.

Antcaters' claws are 4 to 6 inches (10 to 15 centimeters) long. Although useful for digging for food, the claws are so long that anteaters have to walk on the side of their feet.

**Geographic range:** Giant anteaters live in Belize, Guatemala, El Salvador, Nicaragua, Honduras, Costa Rica, Panama, Paraguay, Uruguay, Colombia, Venezuela, Guyana, Suriname, French Guiana, Argentina, Brazil, Ecuador, Peru, and Bolivia.

**Habitat:** The giant anteater lives on the ground in nearly treeless grasslands and in forests. They also range in wetland swamps.

**Diet:** Giant anteaters eat ants and termites. They lick wet plants to get water.

**Behavior and reproduction:** Giant anteaters are usually active during the day. However, they become nocturnal when people are around. They do not climb trees, but are talented swimmers.

Anteaters are solitary unless breeding or raising young. After mating, the male leaves and the female gives birth after 190 days to one cub. Very rarely, twins are born. The cub rides on the mother's back for up to nine months.

Anteaters use their claws to fight predators like jaguars.

*Giant anteaters' worm-like tongues are up to 2 feet (0.6 meters) long. They use them to reach into underground ant nests. (Illustration by Joseph E. Trumpey. Reproduced by permission.)*

**Giant anteaters and people:** People hunt giant anteaters and kill them for their meat and skin. Giant anteaters may be trapped to keep as pets.

**Conservation status:** Giant anteaters are Vulnerable, facing a high risk of extinction in the wild. Threats to their survival include loss of habitat as land is developed, in addition, to being hunted and killed by people. ■

## FOR MORE INFORMATION

### Books:

Attenborough, David. *The Life of Mammals.* Princeton, NJ: Princeton University Press, 2002.

Dollar, Sam. *Anteaters.* New York: Raintree Steck-Vaughn Publishers, 2001.

### Web sites:

Animal Diversity Web. http://animaldiversity.ummz.umich.edu/index.html (accessed on June 21, 2004).

**Class:** Mammalia
**Order:** Xenarthra
**Family:** Dasypodidae
**Number of species:** 20 species

CHAPTER

## PHYSICAL CHARACTERISTICS

The smallest armadillo is the pink fairy armadillo, which is 5 to 6 inches (12.7 to 15.2 centimeters) long and weighs 4.2 ounces (120 grams). The largest family member is the giant armadillo, which is 4.9 feet (1.5 meters) long and weighs 66 pounds (30 kilograms).

"Armadillo" is Spanish for "little armored one." The armadillo's protective armor is the turtle-like shell, or carapace, made up of round, bony plates. Between the hard plates on the armadillo are bands of softer skin. Hair grows between the plates. Shell colors include brown, gray, and yellow. Body color is usually gray or brown. Hair is usually white and pale yellow. The pink fairy armadillo has a pink shell and white hair.

Armadillos have bony plates on their backs. Some have plates on their heads, and plates cover some armadillos' tails. The shell protects the armadillo from predators, animals that hunt and kill armadillos for food.

The arrangement of plates and bands in the Dasypodidae family varies within subgroups called genera (JEN-uh-rah) and species. The family is divided into eight genera. A genus (JEE-nus), the singular of genera, is a group that shares similar characteristics. For example, members of the genus *Tolypeutes* are three-banded armadillos.

Armadillos have tiny eyes and poor eyesight. Some species have short snouts, or noses, while others have long, tube-shaped snouts. Armadillos have long tails and short limbs. They

phylum

class

subclass

order

monotypic order

suborder

▲ **family**

## ARMADILLOS ENJOY WATER

People in Texas have seen nine-banded armadillos playing in shallow water. However, armadillos can do more than splash and take mud baths. Armadillos can swim across a body of water or walk underneath water. Armadillos swim by taking in air to inflate their stomachs. Then they float while paddling with their paws. In addition, armadillos can sink and remain on the ground below water for six to ten minutes.

use claws on their limbs to dig for food and to burrow, digging a hole or tunnel for sleeping or hiding from predators.

## GEOGRAPHIC RANGE

The nine-banded armadillo is the only armadillo living in the United States. Armadillos live in the South American countries of Argentina, Bolivia, Brazil, Colombia, Ecuador, French Guiana, Guyana, Paraguay, Peru, Suriname, Uruguay, and Venezuela. Some armadillo species range in Mexico and the Central American countries of Belize, Costa Rica, El Salvador, Guatemala, Honduras, Nicaragua, and Panama.

## HABITAT

Armadillos live in the desert, grassland areas with few trees, and various types of forests, including rainforests, coniferous forests, and deciduous forests. In all habitats, armadillos sleep in burrows, holes, or tunnels they make by burrowing.

## DIET

Armadillos eat beetles, ants, termites, and worms. They sometimes eat snakes, frogs, and plants. Their diet is based on what is available in their habitat.

## BEHAVIOR AND REPRODUCTION

Armadillos are usually crepuscular (kri-PUS-kyuh-lur), active at dawn and dusk, and nocturnal, active at night. Some species are active during the day, and many species look for food during the day when the weather is colder.

Armadillos are solitary, staying alone until they mate. Armadillos are thought to be polygamous (puh-LIH-gah-mus), having more than one mating partner. After mating, the male leaves, and the female raises the young. Females bear from two to twelve pups, depending on the species.

Predators that hunt armadillos include jaguars, wolves, wild dogs, and alligators. As a defense, the armadillo burrows and curls up so that little of its soft flesh is exposed. The three-banded armadillo can roll itself into a ball.

## ARMADILLOS AND PEOPLE

People have found various uses for armadillos. They have eaten their meat and made purses and baskets out of their shells. Some people keep armadillos as pets.

While sometimes resented for the burrows they dig, armadillos eat insects that cause damage. In addition, doctors study nine-banded armadillos because they are the only mammals besides humans that contract leprosy (LEH-pruh-see), a skin disease. Research of armadillos could help treat people diagnosed with leprosy.

## CONSERVATION STATUS

The giant armadillo and pink fairy armadillo are Endangered, facing a very high risk of extinction, or dying out, according to the World Conservation Union (IUCN). The main threat is habitat loss as trees are cut down. The use of land for farming reduces fairy armadillo habitat and development has cut into the amount of giant armadillo habitat. Furthermore, domestic dogs kill small armadillos, and people hunt giant armadillos for their meat.

Four other armadillo species are Vulnerable, facing a high risk of extinction in the wild.

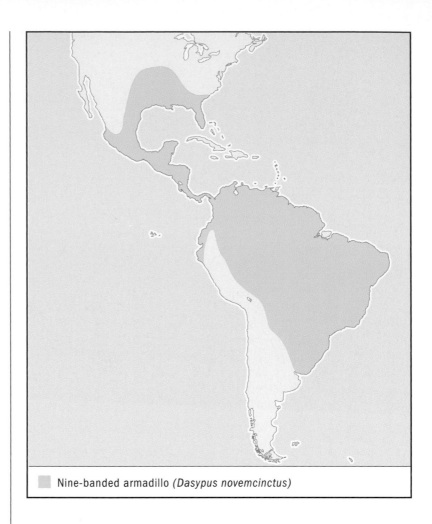

Nine-banded armadillo (Dasypus novemcinctus)

## NINE-BANDED ARMADILLO
### *Dasypus novemcinctus*

**Physical characteristics:** Although named nine-banded armadillos, these brown and gray mammals have from seven to eleven bands on their backs. Nine-banded armadillos are about 25.4 inches (64.6 centimeters) long and weigh up to 15 pounds (6.8 kilograms). Tails measure 9.5 to 14.6 inches (24 to 37 centimeters) in length. They have protective armor on their tails and heads, and have visible ears and small eyes. Nine-banded armadillos have strong claws, a powerful sense of hearing, and poor vision.

Also known as common long-nosed armadillos, nine-banded armadillos use their long noses to smell ants and other prey hunted for food.

**Geographic range:** Nine-banded armadillos live in the United States, Mexico, Belize, Bolivia, Brazil, Colombia, Costa Rica, Ecuador, El Salvador, French Guiana, Grenada, Guatemala, Guyana, Honduras, Nicaragua, Panama, Paraguay, and Peru.

**Habitat:** Nine-banded armadillos live in coniferous forests, and also range in grassland areas like prairies, where there are fewer trees.

**Diet:** These armadillos eat ants, beetles, other insects, snails, and worms. They also eat larvae (LAR-vee), the early, often worm-like forms of insects, such as a caterpillar that later changes into a butterfly. They sometimes eat fruit.

**Behavior and reproduction:** Nine-banded armadillos are crepuscular and nocturnal, but may also be active in the daytime during the winter. They are solitary unless breeding.

The female can give birth only once a year. She usually mates with one male, but males may mate with other females. After the male fertilizes the female's egg, it takes four months or longer before the egg is implanted (attached) in the uterus. After implantation, the female gives birth in about two months to four young.

When frightened, armadillos can jump 3 to 4 feet (0.9 to 1.2 meters) in the air. This action can scare predators like dogs, coyotes, wildcats, and bears. Cars are a threat to armadillos; a vehicle may pass over an armadillo without hurting it, but if the motion startles the armadillo, it may jump, hit the underside of the car, and die.

**Nine-banded armadillos and people:**   The nine-banded armadillo became the Texas state mascot in 1981. In the 1930s, people ate armadillos during the Great Depression, a time of high unemployment. People called armadillos "Hoover hogs" and "Texas turkeys." The first name referred to President Herbert Hoover, who people blamed for the Depression. Some people still eat armadillo—barbecuing the meat or cooking armadillo chili. Texans began holding armadillo races during the 1970s. Researchers also study the armadillo to develop treatments for leprosy.

**Conservation status:**   Nine-banded armadillos are not threatened.   ■

Pink fairy armadillo (*Chlamyphorus truncatus*)

## PINK FAIRY ARMADILLO
### *Chlamyphorus truncatus*

**Physical characteristics:** Pink fairy armadillos are approximately 5.9 inches (15 centimeters) long and weigh 4.2 ounces (120 grams). The armadillo has a pink shell and thick, white fur on its sides. The shell is attached to the backbone and covers the top of the armadillo's head. The shell extends on the back but doesn't cover the armadillo's rear.

Pink fairy armadillos have small eyes and ears, and pointed noses. They cannot move their tail up and down, so the tail drags on the ground.

*Pink fairy armadillos live in the central grasslands of Argentina. They dig their burrows near ant nests. (© N. Smythe/Photo Researchers, Inc. Reproduced by permission.)*

**Geographic range:** Pink fairy armadillos are found in Argentina.

**Habitat:** Pink fairy armadillos live in central Argentina in grassland and sandy plains where thorn bushes and cacti (KACK-tie, or KACK-tee; plural of cactus) grow. The armadillos often dig burrows in dry soil near ant nests. When rain wets the ground where they live, armadillos move to another place.

**Diet:** Pink fairy armadillos eat ants most of the time. Their diet also includes snails, worms, roots, and other plant material. The armadillos sometimes eat carrion, the flesh of dead animals.

**Behavior and reproduction:** Pink fairy armadillos are nocturnal and are strong diggers. They eat at night and spend the day in their burrows. The armadillos are solitary until they mate. They are thought to be polygamous. The female gives birth to one young. The pup's shell does not become completely hard until it is fully grown.

**Pink fairy armadillos and people:** There is no known relationship between pink fairy armadillos and people.

**Conservation status:** Pink fairy armadillos are Endangered, facing a very high risk of extinction in the wild, and the major threat to their survival is agriculture. Habitat is lost as land is plowed for farming. Another threat comes from domestic dogs that kill the tiny armadillos. ■

## FOR MORE INFORMATION

**Books:**

Squire, Ann O. *Anteaters, Sloths, and Armadillos.* New York: Franklin Watts, 1999.

**Periodicals:**

Myers, Kathy. "The Armor-Plated Armadillos." *ZooNooz* (September 2003): 12–17.

Smith, Dwight G. "The Armored Pig." *World and I* (August 1999): 174.

**Web sites:**

"Armadillo." The Handbook of Texas Online. http://www.tsha. utexas.edu/handbook/online/articles/view/AA/tca2.html (accessed on June 30, 2004).

"Everyday Mysteries." The Library of Congress. http://www.loc.gov/rr/ scitech/mysteries/armadillo.html (accessed on June 30, 2004).

# Species List by Biome

## CONIFEROUS FOREST

American black bear
American pika
American water shrew
Asian elephant
Bobcat
Brown-throated three-toed
  sloth
Chimpanzee
Common bentwing bat
Coypu
Desert cottontail
Eastern mole
Edible dormouse
Ermine
Gambian rat
Geoffroy's spider monkey
Giant panda
Gray squirrel
Gray wolf
Greater sac-winged bat
Hairy-footed jerboa
Human
Indian crested porcupine
Kirk's dikdik
Lar gibbon
Little brown bat
Malayan moonrat
Mandrill
Moose

Mountain beaver
Mountain hare
Nine-banded armadillo
North American beaver
North American porcupine
Northern pika
Pacarana
Pallas's long-tongued bat
Pallid bat
Pileated gibbon
Puma
Red deer
Red panda
Red-shanked douc langur
Reindeer
Rhesus macaque
Serow
Siamang
Siberian musk deer
Snow leopard
Snowshoe hare
South African porcupine
Southern tree hyrax
Star-nosed mole
Striped skunk
Tasmanian devil
Three-striped night monkey
Tiger
Valley pocket gopher
Venezuelan red howler monkey

Virginia opossum
Weeper capuchin
Western barbastelle
White-tailed deer
White-throated capuchin

## DECIDUOUS FOREST

Aardvark
African civet
American bison
American black bear
American least shrew
American pika
American water shrew
Ashy chinchilla rat
Asian elephant
Aye-aye
Bobcat
Bornean orangutan
Bridled nail-tailed wallaby
Brush-tailed phascogale
Brush-tailed rock wallaby
Capybara
Central American agouti
Chimpanzee
Collared peccary
Common bentwing bat
Common brush-tailed possum
Common genet

Common ringtail
Common tenrec
Common wombat
Cotton-top tamarin
Coypu
Crowned lemur
Degu
Desert cottontail
Eastern chipmunk
Eastern gray kangaroo
Eastern mole
Eastern pygmy possum
Edible dormouse
Ermine
Eurasian wild pig
European badger
Forest elephant
Forest hog
Funnel-eared bat
Gambian rat
Geoffroy's spider monkey
Giant panda
Goeldi's monkey
Gray squirrel
Gray wolf
Greater dog-faced bat
Greater glider
Greater horseshoe bat
Greater sac-winged bat
Ground pangolin
Human
Indian crested porcupine
Indian muntjac
Indian rhinoceros
Koala
Lar gibbon
Lesser Malay mouse deer
Lesser New Zealand short-
  tailed bat
Lion
Little brown bat
Lord Derby's anomalure
Lowland tapir
Malayan moonrat
Mara
Mountain beaver
Mountain hare

North American beaver
North American porcupine
Northern raccoon
Numbat
Paca
Pacarana
Pallas's long-tongued bat
Parnell's moustached bat
Pileated gibbon
Puma
Pygmy glider
Red deer
Red fox
Red kangaroo
Red panda
Red-tailed sportive lemur
Rhesus macaque
Ringtailed lemur
Rock cavy
Senegal bushbaby
Serow
Siamang
Silky anteater
South African porcupine
Southern flying squirrel
Spotted hyena
Star-nosed mole
Striped skunk
Sugar glider
Three-striped night monkey
Tiger
Valley pocket gopher
Venezuelan red howler
  monkey
Virginia opossum
Water buffalo
Weeper capuchin
Western barbastelle
Western European hedgehog
White rhinoceros
White-tailed deer
White-throated capuchin

## DESERT
Australian jumping mouse
Bighorn sheep

Bobcat
Brazilian free-tailed bat
California leaf-nosed bat
Collared peccary
Damaraland mole-rat
Dassie rat
Desert cottontail
Dromedary camel
Egyptian slit-faced bat
Egyptian spiny mouse
Grant's desert golden mole
Gray wolf
Hairy-footed jerboa
Hardwicke's lesser mouse-
  tailed bat
Human
Kirk's dikdik
Lion
Mzab gundi
Naked mole-rat
North American porcupine
Pallid bat
Parnell's moustached bat
Pink fairy armadillo
Pronghorn
Puma
Red fox
Rhesus macaque
San Joaquin pocket mouse
Savanna elephant
Short-beaked echidna
Southern marsupial mole
Spotted hyena
Striped skunk
Trident leaf-nosed bat
Valley pocket gopher
Virginia opossum
White-footed sportive lemur

## GRASSLAND
Aardvark
Aardwolf
African civet
Alpaca
Alpine marmot
American bison

American black bear
American least shrew
American pika
Ashy chinchilla rat
Asian elephant
Australian false vampire bat
Australian jumping mouse
Black wildebeest
Black-bellied hamster
Black-tailed prairie dog
Brazilian free-tailed bat
Bridled nail-tailed wallaby
California leaf-nosed bat
Capybara
Central American agouti
Chimpanzee
Common bentwing bat
Common genet
Common tenrec
Coypu
Degu
Dwarf epauletted fruit bat
Eastern barred bandicoot
Eastern chipmunk
Eastern gray kangaroo
Eastern mole
Egyptian rousette
Egyptian slit-faced bat
Egyptian spiny mouse
Ermine
Eurasian wild pig
Forest elephant
Gambian rat
Giant anteater
Giant kangaroo rat
Giraffe
Grant's desert golden mole
Gray wolf
Greater bilby
Greater dog-faced bat
Greater horseshoe bat
Grevy's zebra
Ground pangolin
Hardwicke's lesser mouse-
    tailed bat
Hispaniolan solenodon
Hispid cotton rat

Human
Indian crested porcupine
Indian muntjac
Indian rhinoceros
Kiang
Lesser New Zealand short-
    tailed bat
Lion
Llama
Long-tailed chinchilla
Lowland tapir
Maned wolf
Mara
Naked bat
Nine-banded armadillo
Northern pika
Numbat
Paca
Pallas's long-tongued bat
Pallid bat
Parnell's moustached bat
Pearson's tuco-tuco
Pink fairy armadillo
Pronghorn
Przewalski's horse
Puma
Red deer
Red fox
Red kangaroo
Rock cavy
Rock hyrax
San Joaquin pocket mouse
Savanna elephant
Senegal bushbaby
Short-beaked echidna
Smoky bat
Snow leopard
South African porcupine
Spix's disk-winged bat
Spotted hyena
Springhare
Star-nosed mole
Striped skunk
Tasmanian wolf
Thomson's gazelle
Tiger
Valley pocket gopher

Vampire bat
Virginia opossum
Water buffalo
Western European hedgehog
Western red colobus
White rhinoceros
Yellow-streaked tenrec

## LAKE AND POND
American water shrew
Babirusa
Capybara
Central American agouti
Common hippopotamus
Coypu
Duck-billed platypus
European otter
Greater bulldog bat
Malayan tapir
Muskrat
North American beaver
North American porcupine
Prehensile-tailed porcupine
Tiger

## OCEAN
Antarctic fur seal
Beluga
Blue whale
Burmeister's porpoise
California sea lion
Common bottlenosed dolphin
Dugong
Franciscana dolphin
Galápagos sea lion
Gray whale
Harbor porpoise
Harp seal
Hawaiian monk seal
Humpback whale
Killer whale
Narwhal
North Atlantic right whale
Northern bottlenosed whale
Northern elephant seal
Northern minke whale

Pygmy right whale
Pygmy sperm whale
Shepherd's beaked whale
Sperm whale
Spinner dolphin
Steller's sea cow
Walrus
West Indian manatee

## RAINFOREST
Australian false vampire bat
Aye-aye
Babirusa
Bald uakari
Bennett's tree kangaroo
Bornean orangutan
Brazilian free-tailed bat
Brown-throated three-toed
  sloth
Brush-tailed rock wallaby
Central American agouti
Checkered sengi
Chevrotains
Chimpanzee
Collared peccary
Colombian woolly monkey
Common brush-tailed possum
Common ringtail
Common squirrel monkey
Common tenrec
Common tree shrew
Cotton-top tamarin
Coypu
Crowned lemur
Cuban hutia
Eastern pygmy possum
Eurasian wild pig
Forest elephant
Fossa
Funnel-eared bat
Geoffroy's spider monkey
Giant anteater
Goeldi's monkey
Greater sac-winged bat
Ground cuscus
Hispaniolan solenodon

Hoffman's two-toed sloth
Human
Indian crested porcupine
Indian flying fox
Indian muntjac
Indri
Kitti's hog-nosed bat
Lar gibbon
Lesser New Zealand short-
  tailed bat
Lord Derby's anomalure
Lowland tapir
Malayan colugo
Malayan tapir
Mandrill
Masked titi
Milne-Edwards's sifaka
Monito del monte
Mountain beaver
Musky rat-kangaroo
Naked bat
North American beaver
Northern bettong
Northern greater bushbaby
Okapi
Old World sucker-footed bat
Paca
Pacarana
Philippine tarsier
Pileated gibbon
Potto
Prehensile-tailed porcupine
Proboscis monkey
Pygmy hippopotamus
Pygmy marmoset
Pygmy slow loris
Queensland tube-nosed bat
Red mouse lemur
Red-shanked douc langur
Rhesus macaque
Ring-tailed mongoose
Rock hyrax
Rufous spiny bandicoot
Short-beaked echidna
Siamang
Siberian musk deer
Silky anteater

Silky shrew opossum
Smoky bat
Southern pudu
Spiny rat
Spix's disk-winged bat
Sugar glider
Sumatran rhinoceros
Three-striped night monkey
Valley pocket gopher
Vampire bat
Venezuelan red howler
  monkey
Virginia opossum
Water opossum
Weeper capuchin
Western gorilla
Western red colobus
Western tarsier
White bat
White-faced saki
White-tailed deer
White-throated capuchin
Yellow-streaked tenrec

## RIVER AND STREAM
American water shrew
Aye-aye
Babirusa
Baiji
Black-bellied hamster
Boto
Capybara
Central American agouti
Common hippopotamus
Common squirrel monkey
Coypu
Duck-billed platypus
European otter
Ganges and Indus dolphin
Greater bulldog bat
Greater cane rat
Lowland tapir
Malayan tapir
Mountain beaver
Muskrat
North American beaver

North American porcupine
Northern raccoon
Old World sucker-footed bat
Paca
Prehensile-tailed porcupine
Pygmy hippopotamus
Smoky bat
Tiger
Virginia opossum
Water opossum
West Indian manatee
White-footed sportive lemur

## SEASHORE
Antarctic fur seal
California sea lion
Cape horseshoe bat
European otter
Galápagos sea lion
Grant's desert golden mole
Greater bulldog bat
Harp seal
Hawaiian monk seal
Honey possum
Lesser New Zealand short-
  tailed bat

Marianas fruit bat
Northern elephant seal
Pearson's tuco-tuco
Walrus

## TUNDRA
American black bear
Ermine
Gray wolf
Hairy-footed jerboa
Human
Long-tailed chinchilla
Moose
Mountain hare
North American porcupine
Northern pika
Norway lemming
Polar bear
Red fox
Reindeer
Snowshoe hare
Striped skunk

## WETLAND
American black bear

Bobcat
Bornean orangutan
Brazilian free-tailed bat
Capybara
Common squirrel monkey
Coypu
European otter
Giant anteater
Greater bulldog bat
Greater cane rat
Greater dog-faced bat
Indian flying fox
Malayan moonrat
Marianas fruit bat
North American beaver
Northern raccoon
Old World sucker-footed bat
Pacarana
Parnell's moustached bat
Proboscis monkey
Puma
Rhesus macaque
Spix's disk-winged bat
Star-nosed mole
Tiger
Valley pocket gopher

# Species List by Geographic Range

### AFGHANISTAN
Common bentwing bat
Dromedary camel
Eurasian wild pig
Gray wolf
Greater horseshoe bat
Hardwicke's lesser mouse-
 tailed bat
Red deer
Red fox
Rhesus macaque
Snow leopard
Trident leaf-nosed bat

### ALBANIA
Blue whale
Common bentwing bat
Common bottlenosed dolphin
Edible dormouse
Eurasian wild pig
European badger
European otter
Gray wolf
Greater horseshoe bat
Humpback whale
Northern minke whale
Pygmy sperm whale
Red deer
Red fox
Sperm whale

### ALGERIA
Blue whale
Common bentwing bat
Common bottlenosed dolphin
Common genet
Dromedary camel
Eurasian wild pig
European otter
Greater horseshoe bat
Humpback whale
Killer whale
Mzab gundi
Northern bottlenosed whale
Northern minke whale
Pygmy sperm whale
Red deer
Red fox
Sperm whale
Trident leaf-nosed bat

### ANDORRA
European badger
Red fox

### ANGOLA
Aardvark
African civet
Blue whale
Common bentwing bat

Common bottlenosed dolphin
Common genet
Dassie rat
Egyptian slit-faced bat
Gambian rat
Giraffe
Ground pangolin
Humpback whale
Kirk's dikdik
Lion
Northern minke whale
Pygmy sperm whale
South African porcupine
Sperm whale
Spinner dolphin
Spotted hyena
Springhare
Western gorilla
White rhinoceros

### ANTARCTICA
Antarctic fur seal
Blue whale
Northern minke whale

### ARGENTINA
Blue whale
Brazilian free-tailed bat
Brown-throated three-toed sloth

Burmeister's porpoise
Capybara
Central American agouti
Collared peccary
Common bottlenosed dolphin
Coypu
Franciscana dolphin
Giant anteater
Greater bulldog bat
Humpback whale
Killer whale
Llama
Lowland tapir
Maned wolf
Mara
Monito del monte
Northern minke whale
Pallas's long-tongued bat
Pearson's tuco-tuco
Pink fairy armadillo
Prehensile-tailed porcupine
Puma
Pygmy right whale
Red deer
Shepherd's beaked whale
Southern pudu
Sperm whale
Three-toed tree sloths
Vampire bat
Water opossum

## ARMENIA
Common bentwing bat
Edible dormouse
Eurasian wild pig
European badger
Gray wolf
Red deer
Red fox

## AUSTRALIA
Australian false vampire bat
Australian jumping mouse
Bennett's tree kangaroo
Blue whale
Bridled nail-tailed wallaby

Brush-tailed phascogale
Brush-tailed rock wallaby
Common bentwing bat
Common bottlenosed dolphin
Common brush-tailed possum
Common ringtail
Common wombat
Duck-billed platypus
Dugong
Eastern barred bandicoot
Eastern gray kangaroo
Eastern pygmy possum
Greater bilby
Greater glider
Honey possum
Humpback whale
Killer whale
Koala
Musky rat-kangaroo
Northern bettong
Northern minke whale
Numbat
Pygmy glider
Pygmy right whale
Pygmy sperm whale
Queensland tube-nosed bat
Red fox
Red kangaroo
Rufous spiny bandicoot
Short-beaked echidna
Southern marsupial mole
Sperm whale
Spinner dolphin
Sugar glider
Tasmanian devil
Tasmanian wolf

## AUSTRIA
Alpine marmot
Common bentwing bat
Edible dormouse
Ermine
Eurasian wild pig
European badger
Greater horseshoe bat
Mountain hare

Red deer
Red fox
Western European hedgehog

## AZERBAIJAN
Common bentwing bat
Edible dormouse
Eurasian wild pig
European badger
Gray wolf
Red deer
Red fox

## BANGLADESH
Asian elephant
Blue whale
Common bentwing bat
Common bottlenosed dolphin
Eurasian wild pig
Ganges and Indus dolphin
Gray wolf
Greater horseshoe bat
Humpback whale
Indian crested porcupine
Indian flying fox
Indian muntjac
Indian rhinoceros
Northern minke whale
Pygmy sperm whale
Red fox
Rhesus macaque
Serow
Sperm whale
Spinner dolphin
Tiger

## BELARUS
Black-bellied hamster
Edible dormouse
Ermine
Eurasian wild pig
European badger
Gray wolf
Moose
Mountain hare

Red deer
Red fox

## BELGIUM
Black-bellied hamster
Blue whale
Common bottlenosed dolphin
Edible dormouse
Ermine
Eurasian wild pig
European badger
Greater horseshoe bat
Harbor porpoise
Humpback whale
Killer whale
North Atlantic right whale
Northern minke whale
Pygmy sperm whale
Sperm whale
Western European hedgehog

## BELIZE
Blue whale
Brazilian free-tailed bat
Central American agouti
Collared peccary
Common bottlenosed dolphin
Funnel-eared bat
Geoffroy's spider monkey
Giant anteater
Greater bulldog bat
Greater dog-faced bat
Greater sac-winged bat
Hispid cotton rat
Humpback whale
Nine-banded armadillo
Northern minke whale
Paca
Pallas's long-tongued bat
Parnell's moustached bat
Pygmy sperm whale
Silky anteater
Sperm whale
Spinner dolphin
Spix's disk-winged bat
Vampire bat

Virginia opossum
Water opossum
White-tailed deer

## BENIN
Aardvark
African civet
Blue whale
Common bottlenosed dolphin
Common genet
Gambian rat
Humpback whale
Lord Derby's anomalure
Northern minke whale
Pygmy sperm whale
Rock hyrax
Senegal bushbaby
South African porcupine
Sperm whale
Spinner dolphin

## BHUTAN
Asian elephant
Common bentwing bat
Gray wolf
Greater horseshoe bat
Indian crested porcupine
Red fox
Red panda
Rhesus macaque
Serow
Snow leopard
Water buffalo

## BOLIVIA
Alpaca
Ashy chinchilla rat
Boto
Brazilian free-tailed bat
Brown-throated three-toed
  sloth
Capybara
Central American agouti
Collared peccary
Coypu
Giant anteater
Goeldi's monkey

Greater bulldog bat
Greater dog-faced bat
Greater sac-winged bat
Hoffman's two-toed sloth
Llama
Lowland tapir
Maned wolf
Nine-banded armadillo
Pacarana
Pallas's long-tongued bat
Puma
Pygmy marmoset
Silky anteater
Spix's disk-winged bat
Three-toed tree sloths
Vampire bat
White-faced saki
White-tailed deer

## BOSNIA AND HERZEGOVINA
Common bentwing bat
Edible dormouse
Eurasian wild pig
European badger
Greater horseshoe bat
Red deer
Red fox

## BOTSWANA
Aardvark
Aardwolf
African civet
Common genet
Common hippopotamus
Damaraland mole-rat
Egyptian slit-faced bat
Giraffe
Ground pangolin
Lion
Savanna elephant
Springhare

## BRAZIL
Bald uakari
Blue whale

Boto
Brazilian free-tailed bat
Brown-throated three-toed
  sloth
Burmeister's porpoise
Capybara
Central American agouti
Collared peccary
Common bottlenosed dolphin
Common squirrel monkey
Coypu
Franciscana dolphin
Funnel-eared bat
Giant anteater
Goeldi's monkey
Greater bulldog bat
Greater dog-faced bat
Greater sac-winged bat
Hoffman's two-toed sloth
Humpback whale
Killer whale
Lowland tapir
Maned wolf
Masked titi
Nine-banded armadillo
Northern minke whale
Paca
Pacarana
Pallas's long-tongued bat
Parnell's moustached bat
Prehensile-tailed porcupine
Pygmy marmoset
Pygmy right whale
Pygmy sperm whale
Red deer
Rock cavy
Silky anteater
Smoky bat
Sperm whale
Spinner dolphin
Spix's disk-winged bat
Three-striped night monkey
Three-toed tree sloths
Vampire bat
Venezuelan red howler
  monkey
Water opossum

Weeper capuchin
White-faced saki
White-tailed deer

## BULGARIA
Common bentwing bat
Edible dormouse
Eurasian wild pig
European badger
Gray wolf
Greater horseshoe bat
Harbor porpoise
Red deer
Red fox

## BURKINA FASO
Aardvark
African civet
Common genet
Egyptian slit-faced bat
Rock hyrax
Senegal bushbaby

## BURUNDI
Aardvark
African civet
Common bentwing bat
Common genet
Egyptian slit-faced bat
Gambian rat
Lord Derby's anomalure
Senegal bushbaby
South African porcupine

## CAMBODIA
Asian elephant
Blue whale
Common bentwing bat
Common bottlenosed dolphin
Dugong
Eurasian wild pig
Greater horseshoe bat
Humpback whale
Indian muntjac
Lesser Malay mouse deer

Malayan tapir
Northern minke whale
Pileated gibbon
Pygmy sperm whale
Serow
Sperm whale
Spinner dolphin

## CAMEROON
Aardvark
African civet
Blue whale
Chimpanzee
Common bottlenosed dolphin
Common genet
Dwarf epauletted fruit bat
Egyptian rousette
Forest elephant
Forest hog
Gambian rat
Greater cane rat
Humpback whale
Lord Derby's anomalure
Mandrill
Northern minke whale
Potto
Pygmy sperm whale
Rock hyrax
Senegal bushbaby
South African porcupine
Sperm whale
Spinner dolphin
Western gorilla
Western red colobus

## CANADA
American bison
American black bear
American least shrew
American pika
American water shrew
Beluga
Bighorn sheep
Black-tailed prairie dog
Bobcat
California sea lion

Eastern chipmunk
Eastern mole
Ermine
Gray squirrel
Gray wolf
Harbor porpoise
Harp seal
Killer whale
Little brown bat
Moose
Mountain beaver
Muskrat
Narwhal
North American beaver
North American porcupine
North Atlantic right whale
Northern bottlenosed whale
Northern raccoon
Pallid bat
Polar bear
Pronghorn
Puma
Red deer
Red fox
Reindeer
Snowshoe hare
Southern flying squirrel
Star-nosed mole
Striped skunk
Virginia opossum
Walrus
White-tailed deer

## CENTRAL AFRICAN REPUBLIC
Aardvark
African civet
Chimpanzee
Common genet
Dwarf epauletted fruit bat
Egyptian rousette
Forest elephant
Gambian rat
Giraffe
Greater cane rat
Lord Derby's anomalure

Rock hyrax
Senegal bushbaby
South African porcupine
Western gorilla
White rhinoceros

## CHAD
Aardvark
African civet
Common genet
Dromedary camel
Egyptian slit-faced bat
Gambian rat
Ground pangolin
Mzab gundi
Rock hyrax
Senegal bushbaby
Spotted hyena
Trident leaf-nosed bat
White rhinoceros

## CHILE
Alpaca
Ashy chinchilla rat
Blue whale
Brazilian free-tailed bat
Burmeister's porpoise
Common bottlenosed dolphin
Coypu
Degu
Humpback whale
Killer whale
Llama
Long-tailed chinchilla
Monito del monte
Northern minke whale
Pallas's long-tongued bat
Pearson's tuco-tuco
Pygmy right whale
Pygmy sperm whale
Red deer
Shepherd's beaked whale
Southern pudu
Sperm whale
Vampire bat

## CHINA
Asian elephant
Baiji
Blue whale
Common bentwing bat
Common bottlenosed dolphin
Dugong
Edible dormouse
Ermine
European badger
Giant panda
Gray wolf
Greater horseshoe bat
Hairy-footed jerboa
Humpback whale
Indian muntjac
Kiang
Killer whale
Lar gibbon
Lesser Malay mouse deer
Moose
Mountain hare
Northern minke whale
Northern pika
Pygmy slow loris
Pygmy sperm whale
Red deer
Red fox
Red panda
Reindeer
Rhesus macaque
Serow
Siberian musk deer
Snow leopard
Sperm whale
Spinner dolphin
Tiger

## COLOMBIA
Bald uakari
Blue whale
Boto
Brazilian free-tailed bat
Brown-throated three-toed sloth
Capybara

Central American agouti
Collared peccary
Colombian woolly monkey
Common bottlenosed dolphin
Common squirrel monkey
Cotton-top tamarin
Funnel-eared bat
Giant anteater
Goeldi's monkey
Greater bulldog bat
Greater sac-winged bat
Hispid cotton rat
Hoffman's two-toed sloth
Humpback whale
Killer whale
Llama
Lowland tapir
Nine-banded armadillo
Northern minke whale
Paca
Pacarana
Pallas's long-tongued bat
Parnell's moustached bat
Prehensile-tailed porcupine
Pygmy marmoset
Pygmy sperm whale
Silky anteater
Silky shrew opossum
Smoky bat
Sperm whale
Spinner dolphin
Spiny rat
Spix's disk-winged bat
Three-striped night monkey
Three-toed tree sloths
Vampire bat
Water opossum
White-faced saki
White-tailed deer
White-throated capuchin

## CONGO
African civet
Blue whale
Common bottlenosed dolphin
Common genet

Dwarf epauletted fruit bat
Egyptian rousette
Egyptian slit-faced bat
Forest elephant
Forest hog
Humpback whale
Lord Derby's anomalure
Northern minke whale
Potto
Pygmy sperm whale
South African porcupine
Sperm whale
Spinner dolphin
Springhare
Western gorilla

## COSTA RICA
American least shrew
Blue whale
Brazilian free-tailed bat
Brown-throated three-toed
  sloth
Central American agouti
Collared peccary
Common bottlenosed dolphin
Funnel-eared bat
Geoffroy's spider monkey
Giant anteater
Greater bulldog bat
Greater dog-faced bat
Greater sac-winged bat
Hispid cotton rat
Hoffman's two-toed sloth
Humpback whale
Killer whale
Nine-banded armadillo
Northern minke whale
Paca
Pallas's long-tongued bat
Parnell's moustached bat
Puma
Pygmy sperm whale
Silky anteater
Smoky bat
Sperm whale
Spinner dolphin

Spiny rat
Spix's disk-winged bat
Three-toed tree sloths
Vampire bat
Virginia opossum
Water opossum
White bat
White-tailed deer
White-throated capuchin

## CROATIA
Blue whale
Common bentwing bat
Common bottlenosed dolphin
Edible dormouse
Eurasian wild pig
European badger
Greater horseshoe bat
Humpback whale
Northern minke whale
Pygmy sperm whale
Red deer
Red fox
Sperm whale

## CUBA
Blue whale
Brazilian free-tailed bat
Central American agouti
Collared peccary
Common bottlenosed dolphin
Cuban hutia
Funnel-eared bat
Greater bulldog bat
Humpback whale
Killer whale
Northern minke whale
Pallid bat
Parnell's moustached bat
Pygmy sperm whale
Sperm whale
Spinner dolphin

## CYPRUS
Blue whale

Common bottlenosed dolphin
Humpback whale
Northern minke whale
Pygmy sperm whale
Sperm whale

## CZECH REPUBLIC
Black-bellied hamster
Common bentwing bat
Edible dormouse
Ermine
European badger
Greater horseshoe bat
Red deer
Red fox

## DEMOCRATIC REPUBLIC OF THE CONGO
Aardvark
African civet
Blue whale
Checkered sengi
Chimpanzee
Common bentwing bat
Common bottlenosed dolphin
Common genet
Common hippopotamus
Dwarf epauletted fruit bat
Egyptian rousette
Egyptian slit-faced bat
Forest elephant
Forest hog
Gambian rat
Giraffe
Humpback whale
Lord Derby's anomalure
Mandrill
Northern minke whale
Okapi
Potto
Pygmy sperm whale
Rock hyrax
South African porcupine
Sperm whale

Spinner dolphin
Western gorilla
Western red colobus
White rhinoceros

## DENMARK
Blue whale
Common bottlenosed dolphin
Ermine
Eurasian wild pig
European badger
Harbor porpoise
Humpback whale
Killer whale
North Atlantic right whale
Northern minke whale
Norway lemming
Pygmy sperm whale
Red deer
Red fox
Sperm whale
Western European hedgehog

## DJIBOUTI
Aardvark
Blue whale
Common bottlenosed dolphin
Common genet
Dromedary camel
Dugong
Humpback whale
Northern minke whale
Rock hyrax
Senegal bushbaby
Sperm whale
Spinner dolphin

## DOMINICAN REPUBLIC
Blue whale
Brazilian free-tailed bat
Common bottlenosed dolphin
Funnel-eared bat
Greater bulldog bat
Hispaniolan solenodon

Humpback whale
Killer whale
Northern minke whale
Parnell's moustached bat
Pygmy sperm whale
Sperm whale
Spinner dolphin

## ECUADOR
Blue whale
Boto
Brazilian free-tailed bat
Brown-throated three-toed sloth
Capybara
Central American agouti
Collared peccary
Common bottlenosed dolphin
Galápagos sea lion
Giant anteater
Goeldi's monkey
Greater bulldog bat
Greater dog-faced bat
Greater sac-winged bat
Hoffman's two-toed sloth
Humpback whale
Killer whale
Llama
Lowland tapir
Nine-banded armadillo
Northern minke whale
Pacarana
Pallas's long-tongued bat
Pygmy marmoset
Pygmy sperm whale
Silky anteater
Silky shrew opossum
Sperm whale
Spinner dolphin
Spiny rat
Spix's disk-winged bat
Three-toed tree sloths
Vampire bat
Water opossum
White-faced saki
White-tailed deer

## EGYPT
Blue whale
Common bottlenosed dolphin
Common genet
Dromedary camel
Egyptian rousette
Egyptian slit-faced bat
Egyptian spiny mouse
Eurasian wild pig
Greater horseshoe bat
Hardwicke's lesser mouse-
  tailed bat
Humpback whale
Northern minke whale
Pygmy sperm whale
Red fox
Rock hyrax
Sperm whale
Trident leaf-nosed bat

## EL SALVADOR
Blue whale
Brazilian free-tailed bat
Brown-throated three-toed
  sloth
Collared peccary
Common bottlenosed dolphin
Funnel-eared bat
Geoffroy's spider monkey
Giant anteater
Greater bulldog bat
Greater sac-winged bat
Hispid cotton rat
Humpback whale
Killer whale
Nine-banded armadillo
Northern minke whale
Paca
Pallas's long-tongued bat
Parnell's moustached bat
Pygmy sperm whale
Silky anteater
Sperm whale
Spinner dolphin
Spix's disk-winged bat
Three-toed tree sloths

Vampire bat
Virginia opossum
Water opossum
White-tailed deer

## EQUATORIAL GUINEA
African civet
Blue whale
Common bottlenosed dolphin
Common genet
Forest elephant
Humpback whale
Lord Derby's anomalure
Mandrill
Northern minke whale
Potto
Pygmy sperm whale
South African porcupine
Sperm whale
Spinner dolphin
Western gorilla

## ERITREA
Aardvark
Blue whale
Common bottlenosed dolphin
Common genet
Dromedary camel
Dugong
Egyptian slit-faced bat
Humpback whale
Northern minke whale
Rock hyrax
Sperm whale
Spinner dolphin

## ESTONIA
Blue whale
Common bottlenosed dolphin
Ermine
Eurasian wild pig
European badger
Gray wolf
Harbor porpoise
Humpback whale

Moose
Mountain hare
Northern minke whale
Red deer
Red fox
Sperm whale

## ETHIOPIA
Aardvark
Common genet
Dromedary camel
Egyptian slit-faced bat
Forest hog
Grevy's zebra
Lion
Naked mole-rat
Rock hyrax
Senegal bushbaby
Thomson's gazelle

## FINLAND
Blue whale
Common bottlenosed dolphin
Ermine
Eurasian wild pig
European badger
European otter
Gray wolf
Humpback whale
Moose
Mountain hare
Northern minke whale
Norway lemming
Red fox
Reindeer
Sperm whale
Western European hedgehog

## FRANCE
Alpine marmot
Blue whale
Common bentwing bat
Common bottlenosed dolphin
Common genet
Edible dormouse

Ermine
Eurasian wild pig
European badger
European otter
Greater horseshoe bat
Harbor porpoise
Humpback whale
Killer whale
North Atlantic right whale
Northern bottlenosed whale
Northern minke whale
Pygmy sperm whale
Red deer
Red fox
Sperm whale
Western European hedgehog

## FRENCH GUIANA
Blue whale
Capybara
Collared peccary
Common bottlenosed dolphin
Common squirrel monkey
Funnel-eared bat
Giant anteater
Greater bulldog bat
Greater dog-faced bat
Greater sac-winged bat
Humpback whale
Lowland tapir
Nine-banded armadillo
Northern minke whale
Paca
Pallas's long-tongued bat
Parnell's moustached bat
Prehensile-tailed porcupine
Pygmy sperm whale
Silky anteater
Smoky bat
Sperm whale
Spinner dolphin
Spix's disk-winged bat
Three-toed tree sloths
Vampire bat
Water opossum
Weeper capuchin

White-faced saki
White-tailed deer

## GABON
African civet
Blue whale
Common bottlenosed dolphin
Common genet
Common hippopotamus
Dwarf epauletted fruit bat
Egyptian rousette
Forest elephant
Forest hog
Humpback whale
Lord Derby's anomalure
Mandrill
Northern minke whale
Potto
Pygmy sperm whale
South African porcupine
Sperm whale
Spinner dolphin
Western gorilla

## GAMBIA
Aardvark
African civet
Blue whale
Common bottlenosed dolphin
Common genet
Gambian rat
Greater cane rat
Humpback whale
Killer whale
Northern minke whale
Pygmy sperm whale
Senegal bushbaby
South African porcupine
Sperm whale
Spinner dolphin
Western red colobus

## GEORGIA
Common bentwing bat
Edible dormouse

Eurasian wild pig
European badger
Gray wolf
Harbor porpoise
Red deer
Red fox

## GERMANY
Alpine marmot
Black-bellied hamster
Blue whale
Common bentwing bat
Common bottlenosed dolphin
Edible dormouse
Ermine
Eurasian wild pig
European badger
Greater horseshoe bat
Harbor porpoise
Humpback whale
Killer whale
North Atlantic right whale
Northern minke whale
Northern raccoon
Pygmy sperm whale
Red deer
Red fox
Sperm whale
Western European hedgehog

## GHANA
Aardvark
African civet
Blue whale
Chimpanzee
Common bottlenosed dolphin
Common genet
Dwarf epauletted fruit bat
Egyptian rousette
Forest elephant
Forest hog
Gambian rat
Humpback whale
Lord Derby's anomalure
Northern minke whale
Potto

Pygmy sperm whale
Rock hyrax
Senegal bushbaby
South African porcupine
Sperm whale
Spinner dolphin
Western red colobus

## GREECE
Blue whale
Common bentwing bat
Common bottlenosed dolphin
Edible dormouse
European badger
European otter
Gray wolf
Greater horseshoe bat
Harbor porpoise
Humpback whale
Northern minke whale
Pygmy sperm whale
Red deer
Red fox
Sperm whale

## GREENLAND
Blue whale
Ermine
Harbor porpoise
Harp seal
Humpback whale
Killer whale
North Atlantic right whale
Northern bottlenosed whale
Northern minke whale
Polar bear
Reindeer
Walrus

## GRENADA
Nine-banded armadillo
Pallas's long-tongued bat

## GUAM
Marianas fruit bat

## GUATEMALA
American least shrew
Blue whale
Brazilian free-tailed bat
Central American agouti
Collared peccary
Common bottlenosed dolphin
Funnel-eared bat
Geoffroy's spider monkey
Giant anteater
Greater bulldog bat
Greater dog-faced bat
Greater sac-winged bat
Hispid cotton rat
Humpback whale
Killer whale
Nine-banded armadillo
Northern minke whale
Paca
Pallas's long-tongued bat
Parnell's moustached bat
Puma
Pygmy sperm whale
Silky anteater
Sperm whale
Spinner dolphin
Spix's disk-winged bat
Vampire bat
Virginia opossum
Water opossum
White-tailed deer

## GUINEA
Aardvark
African civet
Blue whale
Chimpanzee
Common bottlenosed dolphin
Common genet
Egyptian slit-faced bat
Forest hog
Gambian rat
Humpback whale
Killer whale
Northern minke whale
Pygmy hippopotamus

Pygmy sperm whale
Rock hyrax
Senegal bushbaby
South African porcupine
Sperm whale
Spinner dolphin

## GUINEA-BISSAU
Aardvark
African civet
Blue whale
Common bottlenosed dolphin
Common genet
Forest hog
Gambian rat
Humpback whale
Killer whale
Northern minke whale
Pygmy sperm whale
Rock hyrax
Senegal bushbaby
South African porcupine
Sperm whale
Spinner dolphin
Western red colobus

## GUYANA
Blue whale
Boto
Capybara
Collared peccary
Common bottlenosed dolphin
Common squirrel monkey
Funnel-eared bat
Giant anteater
Greater bulldog bat
Greater dog-faced bat
Greater sac-winged bat
Humpback whale
Lowland tapir
Nine-banded armadillo
Northern minke whale
Paca
Pallas's long-tongued bat
Parnell's moustached bat
Prehensile-tailed porcupine

Pygmy sperm whale
Silky anteater
Smoky bat
Sperm whale
Spinner dolphin
Spix's disk-winged bat
Three-toed tree sloths
Vampire bat
Water opossum
Weeper capuchin
White-faced saki
White-tailed deer

## HAITI
Blue whale
Brazilian free-tailed bat
Common bottlenosed dolphin
Funnel-eared bat
Greater bulldog bat
Hispaniolan solenodon
Humpback whale
Killer whale
Northern minke whale
Parnell's moustached bat
Pygmy sperm whale
Sperm whale
Spinner dolphin

## HONDURAS
American least shrew
Blue whale
Brazilian free-tailed bat
Brown-throated three-toed
 sloth
Central American agouti
Collared peccary
Common bottlenosed dolphin
Funnel-eared bat
Geoffroy's spider monkey
Giant anteater
Greater bulldog bat
Greater dog-faced bat
Greater sac-winged bat
Hispid cotton rat
Hoffman's two-toed sloth
Humpback whale

Killer whale
Nine-banded armadillo
Northern minke whale
Paca
Pallas's long-tongued bat
Parnell's moustached bat
Pygmy sperm whale
Silky anteater
Sperm whale
Spinner dolphin
Spiny rat
Spix's disk-winged bat
Three-toed tree sloths
Vampire bat
Virginia opossum
Water opossum
White bat
White-tailed deer
White-throated capuchin

## HUNGARY
Black-bellied hamster
Common bentwing bat
Edible dormouse
Ermine
Eurasian wild pig
European badger
Greater horseshoe bat
Red deer
Red fox

## ICELAND
Blue whale
Harbor porpoise
Humpback whale
Killer whale
North Atlantic right whale
Northern bottlenosed whale
Northern minke whale
Norway lemming

## INDIA
Asian elephant
Blue whale
Common bentwing bat

Common bottlenosed dolphin
Dromedary camel
Dugong
Ermine
Eurasian wild pig
Ganges and Indus dolphin
Gray wolf
Greater horseshoe bat
Hardwicke's lesser mouse-
 tailed bat
Humpback whale
Indian crested porcupine
Indian flying fox
Indian muntjac
Indian rhinoceros
Kiang
Killer whale
Lion
Northern minke whale
Pygmy sperm whale
Red fox
Red panda
Rhesus macaque
Serow
Snow leopard
Sperm whale
Spinner dolphin
Tiger
Water buffalo

## INDONESIA
Asian elephant
Babirusa
Blue whale
Bornean orangutan
Common bentwing bat
Common bottlenosed dolphin
Common tree shrew
Dugong
Eurasian wild pig
European otter
Humpback whale
Indian muntjac
Killer whale
Lar gibbon
Lesser Malay mouse deer

Malayan colugo
Malayan moonrat
Malayan tapir
Naked bat
Northern minke whale
Proboscis monkey
Pygmy sperm whale
Serow
Siamang
Sperm whale
Spinner dolphin
Sumatran rhinoceros
Tiger
Western tarsier

## IRAN
Blue whale
Common bentwing bat
Common bottlenosed dolphin
Dromedary camel
Dugong
Edible dormouse
Egyptian rousette
Egyptian spiny mouse
Eurasian wild pig
European badger
Gray wolf
Greater horseshoe bat
Hairy-footed jerboa
Humpback whale
Indian crested porcupine
Killer whale
Northern minke whale
Pygmy sperm whale
Red deer
Red fox
Sperm whale
Spinner dolphin
Trident leaf-nosed bat

## IRAQ
Dromedary camel
Egyptian spiny mouse
Eurasian wild pig
Gray wolf
Greater horseshoe bat

Red fox
Trident leaf-nosed bat

## IRELAND
Blue whale
Common bottlenosed dolphin
Ermine
Eurasian wild pig
European badger
European otter
Harbor porpoise
Humpback whale
Killer whale
Mountain hare
North Atlantic right whale
Northern bottlenosed whale
Northern minke whale
Red deer
Red fox
Sperm whale
Western European hedgehog

## ISRAEL
Blue whale
Common bottlenosed dolphin
Dromedary camel
Egyptian rousette
Egyptian slit-faced bat
Egyptian spiny mouse
Eurasian wild pig
Gray wolf
Hardwicke's lesser mouse-
  tailed bat
Humpback whale
Indian crested porcupine
Northern minke whale
Pygmy sperm whale
Red fox
Rock hyrax
Sperm whale
Trident leaf-nosed bat

## ITALY
Alpine marmot
Blue whale

Common bentwing bat
Common bottlenosed dolphin
Edible dormouse
Ermine
Eurasian wild pig
European badger
Gray wolf
Greater horseshoe bat
Humpback whale
Killer whale
Mountain hare
Northern minke whale
Pygmy sperm whale
Red deer
Red fox
Sperm whale
Western European hedgehog

## IVORY COAST
Aardvark
African civet
Blue whale
Chimpanzee
Common bottlenosed dolphin
Common genet
Dwarf epauletted fruit bat
Egyptian rousette
Forest elephant
Forest hog
Gambian rat
Humpback whale
Lord Derby's anomalure
Northern minke whale
Pygmy hippopotamus
Pygmy sperm whale
Rock hyrax
Senegal bushbaby
South African porcupine
Sperm whale
Spinner dolphin
Western red colobus

## JAMAICA
Blue whale
Brazilian free-tailed bat
Common bottlenosed dolphin

Funnel-eared bat
Greater bulldog bat
Humpback whale
Killer whale
Northern minke whale
Pallas's long-tongued bat
Parnell's moustached bat
Pygmy sperm whale
Sperm whale
Spinner dolphin

## JAPAN
Blue whale
Common bentwing bat
Common bottlenosed dolphin
Dugong
Ermine
Eurasian wild pig
European badger
European otter
Gray whale
Greater horseshoe bat
Harbor porpoise
Humpback whale
Killer whale
Marianas fruit bat
Mountain hare
Northern minke whale
Northern pika
Pygmy sperm whale
Reindeer
Siberian musk deer
Sperm whale
Spinner dolphin

## JORDAN
Dromedary camel
Egyptian slit-faced bat
Egyptian spiny mouse
Eurasian wild pig
Gray wolf
Hardwicke's lesser mouse-
   tailed bat
Red fox
Rock hyrax
Trident leaf-nosed bat

## KAZAKHSTAN
Black-bellied hamster
Common bentwing bat
Edible dormouse
Ermine
Eurasian wild pig
European badger
Gray wolf
Hairy-footed jerboa
Moose
Mountain hare
Red deer
Red fox
Snow leopard

## KENYA
Aardvark
Aardwolf
African civet
Blue whale
Common bentwing bat
Common bottlenosed dolphin
Common genet
Dugong
Egyptian rousette
Egyptian slit-faced bat
Forest hog
Gambian rat
Giraffe
Greater cane rat
Grevy's zebra
Ground pangolin
Humpback whale
Kirk's dikdik
Lion
Lord Derby's anomalure
Naked mole-rat
Northern greater bushbaby
Northern minke whale
Potto
Pygmy sperm whale
Rock hyrax
Senegal bushbaby
South African porcupine
Sperm whale
Spinner dolphin

Springhare
Thomson's gazelle

## KUWAIT
Egyptian spiny mouse
Gray wolf
Trident leaf-nosed bat

## KYRGYZSTAN
Common bentwing bat
Edible dormouse
Ermine
Eurasian wild pig
European badger
Gray wolf
Red deer
Red fox
Snow leopard

## LAOS
Asian elephant
Common bentwing bat
Eurasian wild pig
Greater horseshoe bat
Indian muntjac
Lesser Malay mouse deer
Malayan tapir
Pileated gibbon
Pygmy slow loris
Red fox
Red-shanked douc langur
Rhesus macaque
Serow

## LATVIA
Blue whale
Common bottlenosed dolphin
Ermine
Eurasian wild pig
European badger
Gray wolf
Harbor porpoise
Humpback whale
Moose
Mountain hare

Northern minke whale
Red deer
Red fox
Sperm whale

## LEBANON
Blue whale
Common bottlenosed dolphin
Dromedary camel
Egyptian spiny mouse
Hardwicke's lesser mouse-
 tailed bat
Humpback whale
Northern minke whale
Pygmy sperm whale
Sperm whale
Trident leaf-nosed bat

## LESOTHO
Aardvark
African civet
Common bentwing bat
Common genet
Egyptian slit-faced bat
South African porcupine

## LESSER ANTILLES
Blue whale
Brazilian free-tailed bat
Common bottlenosed dolphin
Funnel-eared bat
Greater bulldog bat
Humpback whale
Killer whale
Northern minke whale
Pygmy sperm whale
Sperm whale
Spinner dolphin

## LIBERIA
Aardvark
African civet
Blue whale
Common bottlenosed dolphin

Common genet
Forest elephant
Forest hog
Humpback whale
Killer whale
Lord Derby's anomalure
Northern minke whale
Pygmy hippopotamus
Pygmy sperm whale
Rock hyrax
South African porcupine
Sperm whale
Spinner dolphin
Western red colobus

## LIBYA
Blue whale
Common bottlenosed dolphin
Dromedary camel
Egyptian spiny mouse
Eurasian wild pig
Greater horseshoe bat
Humpback whale
Mzab gundi
Northern minke whale
Pygmy sperm whale
Red fox
Sperm whale
Trident leaf-nosed bat

## LIECHTENSTEIN
Ermine
Eurasian wild pig
Greater horseshoe bat
Red deer
Red fox

## LITHUANIA
Blue whale
Common bottlenosed dolphin
Edible dormouse
Ermine
Eurasian wild pig
European badger
Harbor porpoise

Humpback whale
Moose
Mountain hare
Northern minke whale
Red deer
Red fox
Sperm whale

## LUXEMBOURG
Edible dormouse
Ermine
Eurasian wild pig
European badger
Greater horseshoe bat
Red deer
Red fox

## MACEDONIA
Common bentwing bat
Edible dormouse
Eurasian wild pig
European badger
Gray wolf
Greater horseshoe bat
Red deer
Red fox

## MADAGASCAR
Aye-aye
Blue whale
Common bentwing bat
Common bottlenosed dolphin
Common tenrec
Crowned lemur
Dugong
Fossa
Humpback whale
Indri
Killer whale
Milne-Edwards's sifaka
Northern minke whale
Old World sucker-footed bat
Pygmy sperm whale
Red mouse lemur

Red-tailed sportive lemur
Ringtailed lemur
Ring-tailed mongoose
Sperm whale
Spinner dolphin
White-footed sportive lemur
Yellow-streaked tenrec

## MALAWI
Aardvark
African civet
Checkered sengi
Common bentwing bat
Common genet
Egyptian slit-faced bat
Gambian rat
Ground pangolin
South African porcupine

## MALAYSIA
Asian elephant
Blue whale
Bornean orangutan
Common bentwing bat
Common bottlenosed dolphin
Common tree shrew
Dugong
Eurasian wild pig
Humpback whale
Indian muntjac
Killer whale
Lar gibbon
Lesser Malay mouse deer
Malayan colugo
Malayan moonrat
Malayan tapir
Naked bat
Northern minke whale
Proboscis monkey
Pygmy sperm whale
Serow
Siamang
Sperm whale
Spinner dolphin
Sumatran rhinoceros

## MALI
Aardvark
African civet
Common genet
Dromedary camel
Egyptian rousette
Egyptian slit-faced bat
Gambian rat
Mzab gundi
Rock hyrax
Savanna elephant
Senegal bushbaby

## MARIANA ISLANDS
Marianas fruit bat

## MAURITANIA
Aardvark
Blue whale
Common bottlenosed dolphin
Dromedary camel
Humpback whale
Killer whale
Northern minke whale
Pygmy sperm whale
Sperm whale
Spinner dolphin

## MEXICO
American black bear
American least shrew
Bighorn sheep
Black-tailed prairie dog
Blue whale
Bobcat
Brazilian free-tailed bat
Brown-throated three-toed
  sloth
California leaf-nosed bat
California sea lion
Central American agouti
Collared peccary
Common bottlenosed dolphin
Desert cottontail
Eastern mole

Funnel-eared bat
Geoffroy's spider monkey
Gray whale
Greater bulldog bat
Greater dog-faced bat
Greater sac-winged bat
Hispid cotton rat
Humpback whale
Killer whale
Little brown bat
Muskrat
Nine-banded armadillo
North American beaver
North American porcupine
Northern elephant seal
Northern minke whale
Northern raccoon
Paca
Pallas's long-tongued bat
Pallid bat
Parnell's moustached bat
Pronghorn
Puma
Pygmy sperm whale
Silky anteater
Sperm whale
Spinner dolphin
Spix's disk-winged bat
Striped skunk
Three-toed tree sloths
Valley pocket gopher
Vampire bat
Virginia opossum
Water opossum
White-tailed deer

## MOLDOVA
Black-bellied hamster
Common bentwing bat
Edible dormouse
Eurasian wild pig
European badger
Gray wolf
Greater horseshoe bat
Red deer
Red fox

## MONACO
European badger
Red fox

## MONGOLIA
Ermine
Eurasian wild pig
Gray wolf
Hairy-footed jerboa
Moose
Mountain hare
Northern pika
Przewalski's horse
Red deer
Red fox
Reindeer
Siberian musk deer
Snow leopard

## MOROCCO
Blue whale
Common bentwing bat
Common bottlenosed dolphin
Dromedary camel
Eurasian wild pig
European otter
Greater horseshoe bat
Harbor porpoise
Hardwicke's lesser mouse-
 tailed bat
Humpback whale
Killer whale
North Atlantic right whale
Northern bottlenosed whale
Northern minke whale
Pygmy sperm whale
Red deer
Red fox
Sperm whale
Spinner dolphin
Trident leaf-nosed bat

## MOZAMBIQUE
Aardvark
African civet
Blue whale
Checkered sengi
Common bentwing bat
Common bottlenosed dolphin
Common genet
Common hippopotamus
Dugong
Egyptian rousette
Egyptian slit-faced bat
Gambian rat
Ground pangolin
Humpback whale
Killer whale
Lord Derby's anomalure
Northern minke whale
Pygmy sperm whale
Rock hyrax
South African porcupine
Sperm whale
Spinner dolphin
Springhare
White rhinoceros

## MYANMAR
Asian elephant
Blue whale
Common bentwing bat
Common bottlenosed dolphin
Eurasian wild pig
Gray wolf
Greater horseshoe bat
Humpback whale
Indian flying fox
Indian muntjac
Kitti's hog-nosed bat
Lar gibbon
Lesser Malay mouse deer
Malayan moonrat
Malayan tapir
Northern minke whale
Pygmy sperm whale
Red fox
Red panda
Rhesus macaque
Serow

Sperm whale
Spinner dolphin
Tiger

## NAMIBIA
Aardvark
African civet
Blue whale
Common bentwing bat
Common bottlenosed dolphin
Common genet
Common hippopotamus
Damaraland mole-rat
Dassie rat
Egyptian slit-faced bat
Giraffe
Grant's desert golden mole
Ground pangolin
Humpback whale
Killer whale
Kirk's dikdik
Northern minke whale
Pygmy sperm whale
Rock hyrax
Savanna elephant
Sperm whale
Springhare

## NEPAL
Asian elephant
Common bentwing bat
Eurasian wild pig
Ganges and Indus dolphin
Gray wolf
Greater horseshoe bat
Indian crested porcupine
Indian muntjac
Indian rhinoceros
Kiang
Red fox
Red panda
Rhesus macaque
Serow
Snow leopard
Water buffalo

## NETHERLANDS

Black-bellied hamster
Blue whale
Common bottlenosed dolphin
Ermine
Eurasian wild pig
European badger
Harbor porpoise
Humpback whale
Killer whale
Northern minke whale
Northern raccoon
Pygmy sperm whale
Red deer
Red fox
Sperm whale
Western European hedgehog

## NEW ZEALAND

Blue whale
Brush-tailed rock wallaby
Common bottlenosed dolphin
Common brush-tailed possum
Dugong
Humpback whale
Killer whale
Lesser New Zealand short-
  tailed bat
Northern minke whale
Pygmy right whale
Pygmy sperm whale
Shepherd's beaked whale
Sperm whale

## NICARAGUA

American least shrew
Blue whale
Brazilian free-tailed bat
Brown-throated three-toed
  sloth
Central American agouti
Collared peccary
Common bottlenosed dolphin
Funnel-eared bat
Geoffroy's spider monkey

Giant anteater
Greater bulldog bat
Greater dog-faced bat
Greater sac-winged bat
Hispid cotton rat
Hoffman's two-toed sloth
Humpback whale
Killer whale
Nine-banded armadillo
Northern minke whale
Paca
Pallas's long-tongued bat
Parnell's moustached bat
Pygmy sperm whale
Silky anteater
Sperm whale
Spinner dolphin
Spiny rat
Spix's disk-winged bat
Three-toed tree sloths
Vampire bat
Virginia opossum
Water opossum
White bat
White-tailed deer
White-throated capuchin

## NIGER

Aardvark
Dromedary camel
Egyptian slit-faced bat
Gambian rat
Mzab gundi
Rock hyrax
Senegal bushbaby
Trident leaf-nosed bat

## NIGERIA

Aardvark
African civet
Blue whale
Chimpanzee
Common bottlenosed dolphin
Common genet
Dwarf epauletted fruit bat

Egyptian rousette
Egyptian slit-faced bat
Gambian rat
Humpback whale
Lord Derby's anomalure
Northern minke whale
Potto
Pygmy sperm whale
Rock hyrax
Senegal bushbaby
South African porcupine
Sperm whale
Spinner dolphin
Western gorilla
Western red colobus

## NORTH KOREA

Blue whale
Common bentwing bat
Common bottlenosed dolphin
Eurasian wild pig
Humpback whale
Killer whale
Northern minke whale
Northern pika
Pygmy sperm whale
Red deer
Siberian musk deer
Sperm whale
Spinner dolphin

## NORWAY

Blue whale
Common bottlenosed dolphin
Ermine
Eurasian wild pig
European badger
European otter
Harbor porpoise
Humpback whale
Killer whale
Moose
Mountain hare
North Atlantic right whale
Northern bottlenosed whale

Northern minke whale
Norway lemming
Polar bear
Red deer
Red fox
Reindeer
Sperm whale
Western European hedgehog

## OMAN
Blue whale
Common bottlenosed dolphin
Dromedary camel
Dugong
Egyptian rousette
Egyptian spiny mouse
Gray wolf
Humpback whale
Killer whale
Northern minke whale
Pygmy sperm whale
Rock hyrax
Sperm whale
Spinner dolphin
Trident leaf-nosed bat

## PAKISTAN
Blue whale
Common bentwing bat
Common bottlenosed dolphin
Dromedary camel
Dugong
Eurasian wild pig
Ganges and Indus dolphin
Gray wolf
Greater horseshoe bat
Hardwicke's lesser mouse-
  tailed bat
Humpback whale
Indian flying fox
Indian muntjac
Indian rhinoceros
Kiang
Killer whale
Northern minke whale

Pygmy sperm whale
Red fox
Rhesus macaque
Snow leopard
Sperm whale
Spinner dolphin
Trident leaf-nosed bat

## PANAMA
American least shrew
Blue whale
Brazilian free-tailed bat
Brown-throated three-toed
  sloth
Capybara
Central American agouti
Collared peccary
Common bottlenosed dolphin
Funnel-eared bat
Geoffroy's spider monkey
Giant anteater
Greater bulldog bat
Greater dog-faced bat
Greater sac-winged bat
Hispid cotton rat
Hoffman's two-toed sloth
Humpback whale
Killer whale
Nine-banded armadillo
Northern minke whale
Northern raccoon
Paca
Pallas's long-tongued bat
Parnell's moustached bat
Puma
Pygmy sperm whale
Silky anteater
Smoky bat
Sperm whale
Spinner dolphin
Spiny rat
Spix's disk-winged bat
Three-toed tree sloths
Vampire bat
Water opossum
White bat

White-tailed deer
White-throated capuchin

## PAPUA NEW GUINEA
Blue whale
Common bentwing bat
Common bottlenosed dolphin
Dugong
Ground cuscus
Humpback whale
Killer whale
Northern minke whale
Pygmy sperm whale
Rufous spiny bandicoot
Short-beaked echidna
Sperm whale
Spinner dolphin
Sugar glider

## PARAGUAY
Brazilian free-tailed bat
Brown-throated three-toed
  sloth
Capybara
Collared peccary
Coypu
Giant anteater
Greater bulldog bat
Maned wolf
Nine-banded armadillo
Paca
Pallas's long-tongued bat
Prehensile-tailed porcupine
Three-toed tree sloths
Vampire bat
Water opossum

## PERU
Alpaca
Ashy chinchilla rat
Bald uakari
Blue whale
Boto
Brazilian free-tailed bat
Burmeister's porpoise

Capybara
Central American agouti
Collared peccary
Common bottlenosed
  dolphin
Giant anteater
Goeldi's monkey
Greater bulldog bat
Greater dog-faced bat
Greater sac-winged bat
Hoffman's two-toed sloth
Humpback whale
Killer whale
Llama
Lowland tapir
Maned wolf
Nine-banded armadillo
Northern minke whale
Pacarana
Pallas's long-tongued bat
Parnell's moustached bat
Pearson's tuco-tuco
Pygmy marmoset
Pygmy sperm whale
Silky anteater
Sperm whale
Spinner dolphin
Spix's disk-winged bat
Vampire bat
Water opossum
White-faced saki
White-tailed deer

## PHILIPPINES
Blue whale
Common bentwing bat
Common bottlenosed
  dolphin
Dugong
Humpback whale
Naked bat
Northern minke whale
Philippine tarsier
Pygmy sperm whale
Sperm whale
Spinner dolphin

## POLAND
Black-bellied hamster
Blue whale
Common bentwing bat
Common bottlenosed
  dolphin
Edible dormouse
Ermine
Eurasian wild pig
European badger
Greater horseshoe bat
Harbor porpoise
Humpback whale
Moose
Northern minke whale
Red deer
Red fox
Sperm whale

## PORTUGAL
Blue whale
Common bentwing bat
Common bottlenosed
  dolphin
Common genet
Eurasian wild pig
European badger
European otter
Greater horseshoe bat
Harbor porpoise
Humpback whale
Killer whale
North Atlantic right whale
Northern bottlenosed whale
Northern minke whale
Pygmy sperm whale
Red deer
Red fox
Sperm whale
Western barbastelle
Western European hedgehog

## PUERTO RICO
Blue whale
Brazilian free-tailed bat

Common bottlenosed
  dolphin
Funnel-eared bat
Greater bulldog bat
Humpback whale
Killer whale
Northern minke whale
Pygmy sperm whale
Sperm whale
Spinner dolphin

## QATAR
Egyptian spiny mouse

## ROMANIA
Black-bellied hamster
Common bentwing bat
Edible dormouse
Eurasian wild pig
European badger
Gray wolf
Greater horseshoe bat
Harbor porpoise
Red deer
Red fox

## RUSSIA
Beluga
Black-bellied hamster
Blue whale
Common bentwing bat
Common bottlenosed
  dolphin
Edible dormouse
Ermine
Eurasian wild pig
European otter
Gray whale
Gray wolf
Harbor porpoise
Harp seal
Humpback whale
Killer whale
Moose
Mountain hare
Narwhal

Northern minke whale
Northern pika
Northern raccoon
Polar bear
Red deer
Red fox
Reindeer
Siberian musk deer
Snow leopard
Sperm whale
Tiger
Walrus
Western European hedgehog

## RWANDA
Aardvark
African civet
Chimpanzee
Common bentwing bat
Common genet
Egyptian slit-faced bat
Gambian rat
Lord Derby's anomalure
Rock hyrax
Senegal bushbaby
South African porcupine

## SAUDI ARABIA
Blue whale
Common bottlenosed dolphin
Dromedary camel
Dugong
Egyptian slit-faced bat
Egyptian spiny mouse
Gray wolf
Hardwicke's lesser mouse-
    tailed bat
Humpback whale
Indian crested porcupine
Northern minke whale
Pygmy sperm whale
Rock hyrax
Sperm whale
Spinner dolphin
Trident leaf-nosed bat

## SENEGAL
Aardvark
African civet
Blue whale
Chimpanzee
Common bottlenosed dolphin
Common genet
Egyptian slit-faced bat
Gambian rat
Hardwicke's lesser mouse-
    tailed bat
Humpback whale
Killer whale
Northern minke whale
Pygmy sperm whale
Rock hyrax
Senegal bushbaby
South African porcupine
Sperm whale
Spinner dolphin
Western red colobus

## SIERRA LEONE
Aardvark
African civet
Blue whale
Chimpanzee
Common bottlenosed dolphin
Common genet
Egyptian slit-faced bat
Forest hog
Gambian rat
Humpback whale
Killer whale
Lord Derby's anomalure
Northern minke whale
Potto
Pygmy hippopotamus
Pygmy sperm whale
Rock hyrax
Senegal bushbaby
South African porcupine
Sperm whale
Spinner dolphin
Western red colobus

## SINGAPORE
Lesser Malay mouse deer

## SLOVAKIA
Black-bellied hamster
Edible dormouse
Ermine
European badger
Greater horseshoe bat
Red deer
Red fox

## SLOVENIA
Blue whale
Common bentwing bat
Common bottlenosed dolphin
Edible dormouse
Ermine
Eurasian wild pig
European badger
Greater horseshoe bat
Humpback whale
Northern minke whale
Pygmy sperm whale
Red deer
Red fox
Sperm whale

## SOMALIA
Aardwolf
African civet
Blue whale
Common bentwing bat
Common bottlenosed dolphin
Common genet
Dromedary camel
Dugong
Egyptian slit-faced bat
Humpback whale
Kirk's dikdik
Naked mole-rat
Northern greater bushbaby
Northern minke whale
Pygmy sperm whale

Rock hyrax
Senegal bushbaby
South African porcupine
Sperm whale
Spinner dolphin

## SOUTH AFRICA
Aardvark
Aardwolf
African civet
Black wildebeest
Blue whale
Cape horseshoe bat
Common bentwing bat
Common bottlenosed dolphin
Common genet
Damaraland mole-rat
Dassie rat
Egyptian rousette
Egyptian slit-faced bat
Gambian rat
Giraffe
Grant's desert golden mole
Ground pangolin
Humpback whale
Killer whale
Northern minke whale
Pygmy right whale
Pygmy sperm whale
Rock hyrax
Savanna elephant
Shepherd's beaked whale
South African porcupine
Southern tree hyrax
Sperm whale
Spinner dolphin
Springhare

## SOUTH KOREA
Blue whale
Common bentwing bat
Common bottlenosed dolphin
Eurasian wild pig
Humpback whale
Killer whale

Northern minke whale
Pygmy sperm whale
Sperm whale
Spinner dolphin

## SPAIN
Alpine marmot
Blue whale
Common bentwing bat
Common bottlenosed dolphin
Common genet
Edible dormouse
Eurasian wild pig
European badger
European otter
Gray wolf
Greater horseshoe bat
Harbor porpoise
Humpback whale
Killer whale
North Atlantic right whale
Northern bottlenosed whale
Northern minke whale
Pygmy sperm whale
Red deer
Red fox
Sperm whale
Western barbastelle
Western European hedgehog

## SRI LANKA
Asian elephant
European otter
Indian crested porcupine
Indian flying fox
Indian muntjac

## SUDAN
Aardvark
African civet
Blue whale
Chimpanzee
Common bottlenosed dolphin
Common genet

Common hippopotamus
Dromedary camel
Dugong
Dwarf epauletted fruit bat
Egyptian slit-faced bat
Gambian rat
Giraffe
Greater cane rat
Ground pangolin
Humpback whale
Northern minke whale
Pygmy sperm whale
Rock hyrax
Senegal bushbaby
South African porcupine
Sperm whale
Spinner dolphin
Spotted hyena
Thomson's gazelle
Trident leaf-nosed bat
White rhinoceros

## SURINAME
Blue whale
Collared peccary
Common bottlenosed dolphin
Common squirrel monkey
Funnel-eared bat
Giant anteater
Greater bulldog bat
Greater dog-faced bat
Greater sac-winged bat
Humpback whale
Lowland tapir
Northern minke whale
Paca
Pallas's long-tongued bat
Parnell's moustached bat
Prehensile-tailed porcupine
Pygmy sperm whale
Silky anteater
Smoky bat
Sperm whale
Spinner dolphin
Spix's disk-winged bat
Three-toed tree sloths

Vampire bat
Water opossum
Weeper capuchin
White-faced saki
White-tailed deer

## SWAZILAND
Aardvark
African civet
Common bentwing bat
Common genet
Egyptian slit-faced bat
Gambian rat
Giraffe
Ground pangolin
South African porcupine

## SWEDEN
Blue whale
Common bottlenosed dolphin
Ermine
Eurasian wild pig
European badger
Gray wolf
Harbor porpoise
Humpback whale
Moose
Mountain hare
Northern minke whale
Norway lemming
Red deer
Red fox
Sperm whale
Western European hedgehog

## SWITZERLAND
Alpine marmot
Common bentwing bat
Edible dormouse
Ermine
Eurasian wild pig
European badger
Greater horseshoe bat
Mountain hare
Red deer

Red fox
Western European hedgehog

## SYRIA
Blue whale
Common bottlenosed dolphin
Dromedary camel
Egyptian spiny mouse
Eurasian wild pig
Gray wolf
Greater horseshoe bat
Hardwicke's lesser mouse-
   tailed bat
Humpback whale
Northern minke whale
Pygmy sperm whale
Red deer
Red fox
Sperm whale
Trident leaf-nosed bat

## TAJIKISTAN
Common bentwing bat
Edible dormouse
Ermine
Eurasian wild pig
European badger
Gray wolf
Greater horseshoe bat
Red deer
Red fox
Snow leopard

## TANZANIA
Aardvark
African civet
Blue whale
Checkered sengi
Chimpanzee
Common bentwing bat
Common bottlenosed dolphin
Common genet
Common hippopotamus
Dugong
Egyptian rousette

Egyptian slit-faced bat
Gambian rat
Giraffe
Greater cane rat
Ground pangolin
Humpback whale
Killer whale
Kirk's dikdik
Lion
Lord Derby's anomalure
Northern greater bushbaby
Northern minke whale
Pygmy sperm whale
Rock hyrax
Senegal bushbaby
South African porcupine
Sperm whale
Spinner dolphin
Springhare
Thomson's gazelle

## THAILAND
Asian elephant
Blue whale
Common bentwing bat
Common bottlenosed dolphin
Common tree shrew
Dugong
Eurasian wild pig
Greater horseshoe bat
Humpback whale
Indian muntjac
Kitti's hog-nosed bat
Lar gibbon
Lesser Malay mouse deer
Malayan colugo
Malayan moonrat
Malayan tapir
Northern minke whale
Pileated gibbon
Pygmy sperm whale
Red fox
Rhesus macaque
Serow
Sperm whale

Spinner dolphin
Water buffalo

## TOGO
Aardvark
African civet
Blue whale
Common bottlenosed dolphin
Common genet
Forest hog
Gambian rat
Humpback whale
Lord Derby's anomalure
Northern minke whale
Pygmy sperm whale
Rock hyrax
Senegal bushbaby
South African porcupine
Sperm whale
Spinner dolphin

## TRINIDAD AND TOBAGO
Pallas's long-tongued bat
Prehensile-tailed porcupine
Silky anteater
Smoky bat
Vampire bat

## TUNISIA
Blue whale
Common bentwing bat
Common bottlenosed dolphin
Common genet
Dromedary camel
Eurasian wild pig
European otter
Greater horseshoe bat
Humpback whale
Killer whale
Northern minke whale
Pygmy sperm whale
Red deer
Red fox
Sperm whale
Trident leaf-nosed bat

## TURKEY
Blue whale
Common bentwing bat
Common bottlenosed dolphin
Edible dormouse
Egyptian rousette
Eurasian wild pig
European badger
Gray wolf
Greater horseshoe bat
Harbor porpoise
Humpback whale
Northern minke whale
Pygmy sperm whale
Red deer
Sperm whale

## TURKMENISTAN
Common bentwing bat
Edible dormouse
Eurasian wild pig
European badger
Gray wolf
Greater horseshoe bat
Hairy-footed jerboa
Red deer
Red fox

## UGANDA
Aardvark
African civet
Checkered sengi
Chimpanzee
Common bentwing bat
Common genet
Dwarf epauletted fruit bat
Egyptian rousette
Egyptian slit-faced bat
Forest hog
Gambian rat
Giraffe
Greater cane rat
Ground pangolin
Lord Derby's anomalure
Potto

Senegal bushbaby
South African porcupine
White rhinoceros

## UKRAINE
Alpine marmot
Black-bellied hamster
Common bentwing bat
Edible dormouse
Ermine
Eurasian wild pig
European badger
Gray wolf
Greater horseshoe bat
Harbor porpoise
Moose
Red deer
Red fox

## UNITED ARAB EMIRATES
Dromedary camel
Egyptian spiny mouse
Gray wolf
Trident leaf-nosed bat

## UNITED KINGDOM
Blue whale
Common bottlenosed dolphin
Ermine
Eurasian wild pig
European badger
European otter
Greater horseshoe bat
Harbor porpoise
Humpback whale
Killer whale
Mountain hare
North Atlantic right whale
Northern bottlenosed whale
Northern minke whale
Pygmy sperm whale
Red deer
Red fox
Sperm whale

Western barbastelle
Western European hedgehog

## UNITED STATES
American bison
American black bear
American least shrew
American pika
American water shrew
Beluga
Bighorn sheep
Black-tailed prairie dog
Blue whale
Bobcat
Brazilian free-tailed bat
California leaf-nosed bat
California sea lion
Collared peccary
Common bottlenosed dolphin
Desert cottontail
Eastern chipmunk
Eastern mole
Ermine
Giant kangaroo rat
Gray squirrel
Gray whale
Gray wolf
Harbor porpoise
Hawaiian monk seal
Hispid cotton rat
Humpback whale
Killer whale
Little brown bat
Moose
Mountain beaver
Muskrat
Narwhal
Nine-banded armadillo
North American beaver
North American porcupine
North Atlantic right whale
Northern bottlenosed whale
Northern elephant seal
Northern minke whale
Northern raccoon
Pallid bat

Polar bear
Pronghorn
Puma
Pygmy sperm whale
Red deer
Red fox
Reindeer
San Joaquin pocket mouse
Snowshoe hare
Southern flying squirrel
Sperm whale
Spinner dolphin
Star-nosed mole
Steller's sea cow
Striped skunk
Valley pocket gopher
Virginia opossum
Walrus
West Indian manatee
White-tailed deer

## URUGUAY
Blue whale
Brazilian free-tailed bat
Burmeister's porpoise
Capybara
Collared peccary
Common bottlenosed dolphin
Coypu
Franciscana dolphin
Giant anteater
Humpback whale
Killer whale
Maned wolf
Northern minke whale
Pearson's tuco-tuco
Prehensile-tailed porcupine
Pygmy right whale
Red deer
Sperm whale
Vampire bat

## UZBEKISTAN
Common bentwing bat
Edible dormouse

Eurasian wild pig
European badger
Gray wolf
Hairy-footed jerboa
Red deer
Red fox
Snow leopard

## VENEZUELA
Blue whale
Boto
Brazilian free-tailed bat
Capybara
Collared peccary
Colombian woolly monkey
Common bottlenosed dolphin
Common squirrel monkey
Funnel-eared bat
Giant anteater
Greater bulldog bat
Greater dog-faced bat
Greater sac-winged bat
Hispid cotton rat
Hoffman's two-toed sloth
Humpback whale
Lowland tapir
Northern minke whale
Paca
Pacarana
Pallas's long-tongued bat
Parnell's moustached bat
Prehensile-tailed porcupine
Puma
Pygmy sperm whale
Silky anteater
Silky shrew opossum
Smoky bat
Sperm whale
Spinner dolphin
Spix's disk-winged bat
Three-striped night monkey
Three-toed tree sloths
Vampire bat
Venezuelan red howler
  monkey
Water opossum

Weeper capuchin
White-tailed deer

## VIETNAM

Asian elephant
Blue whale
Common bentwing bat
Common bottlenosed dolphin
Dugong
Eurasian wild pig
Greater horseshoe bat
Humpback whale
Indian muntjac
Malayan tapir
Northern minke whale
Pygmy slow loris
Pygmy sperm whale
Red fox
Red-shanked douc langur
Rhesus macaque
Serow
Sperm whale
Spinner dolphin

## YEMEN

Blue whale
Common bottlenosed dolphin
Dromedary camel
Dugong
Egyptian rousette

Egyptian slit-faced bat
Egyptian spiny mouse
Gray wolf
Hardwicke's lesser mouse-
   tailed bat
Humpback whale
Northern minke whale
Pygmy sperm whale
Rock hyrax
Sperm whale
Spinner dolphin
Trident leaf-nosed bat

## YUGOSLAVIA

Alpine marmot
Blue whale
Common bentwing bat
Common bottlenosed dolphin
Edible dormouse
Ermine
Gray wolf
Greater horseshoe bat
Humpback whale
Northern minke whale
Pygmy sperm whale
Red deer
Sperm whale

## ZAMBIA

Aardvark

Aardwolf
African civet
Checkered sengi
Common bentwing bat
Common genet
Common hippopotamus
Egyptian rousette
Egyptian slit-faced bat
Gambian rat
Giraffe
Ground pangolin
Lord Derby's anomalure
South African porcupine
Spotted hyena
Springhare

## ZIMBABWE

Aardvark
African civet
Common bentwing bat
Common genet
Damaraland mole-rat
Egyptian rousette
Egyptian slit-faced bat
Gambian rat
Ground pangolin
Savanna elephant
South African porcupine
Spotted hyena
Springhare

# Index

*Italic* type indicates volume number; **boldface** type indicates entries and their pages; (ill.) indicates illustrations.

Ant catchers. *See* Tamanduas

Antarctic fur seals, *3:* 675–76, 675 (ill.), 676 (ill.)

Antarctic minke whales, *4:* 786

**Anteaters,** *1:* 9, 178–82, **195–202**
> *See also* Echidnas; Numbats; Pangolins

Antechinus, *1:* 53

**Antelopes,** *4:* **969–87**

*Antilocapra americana. See* Pronghorn

Antilocapridae. *See* Pronghorn

*Antrozous pallidus. See* Pallid bats

Ants
> eating, *1:* 9
> formacid, *5:* 991

Aotidae. *See* Night monkeys

*Aotus trivirgatus. See* Three-striped night monkeys

**Apes, great,** *3:* 423, **563–77**

*Aplodontia rufa. See* Mountain beavers

Aplodontidae. *See* Mountain beavers

Aquatic tenrecs, *2:* 232, 234

Arctic foxes, *3:* 583

*Arctocephalus gazella. See* Antarctic fur seals

**Armadillos,** *1:* 178–82, **203–11**

Armored rats, *5:* 1182

Arnoux's beaked whales, *4:* 751

Arra-jarra-ja. *See* Southern marsupial moles

Artiodactyla. *See* Even-toed ungulates

*Asellia tridens. See* Trident leaf-nosed bats

Ashy chinchilla rats, *5:* 1178, 1179–80, 1179 (ill.), 1180 (ill.)

Asian chevrotains, *4:* 927

Asian elephants, *4:* 813–14, 813 (ill.), 814 (ill.), 817

Asian false vampire bats, *2:* 324

Asian rhinoceroses, *4:* 849

Asiatic black bears, *3:* 593, 594, 595

Asiatic water shrews, *2:* 213–14

**Asses,** *4:* 848, 850, **854–64**

*Astonishing Elephant* (Alexander), *4:* 811

*Ateles geoffroyi. See* Geoffroy's spider monkeys

Atelidae. *See* Howler monkeys; Spider monkeys

*Atherura* species, *5:* 1111, 1112

Atlantic bottlenosed dolphins. *See* Common bottlenosed dolphins

Atlantic bottlenosed whales. *See* Northern bottlenosed whales

**Australasian carnivorous marsupials,** *1:* **51–55,** 75

Australian Bilby Appreciation Society, *1:* 77

Australian false vampire bats, *2:* 323, 324–25, 326–28, 326 (ill.), 327 (ill.)

Australian ghost bats. *See* Australian false vampire bats

Australian jumping mice, *5:* 1062–63, 1062 (ill.), 1063 (ill.)

Australian Koala Foundation, *1:* 109

Australian Platypus Conservancy, *1:* 22

Australian sea lions, *3:* 674

Australian water rats, *5:* 998

**Avahis,** *3:* **458–65**

**Aye-ayes,** *3:* 424, **475–79,** 477 (ill.), 478 (ill.)

Azara's agoutis, *5:* 1155


**B**

Babirusas, *4:* 894, 897–98, 897 (ill.), 899 (ill.)

Baboon lemurs, *3:* 459

Baboons, *3:* 424, 425, 426

*Babyrousa babyrussa. See* Babirusas

Bactrian camels, *4:* 917, 918

**Badgers,** *3:* 579, **614–27,** 629, 637

Bahaman funnel-eared bats, *2:* 379

Bahamian hutias, *5:* 1189

**Baijis,** *4:* 707, **714–18,** 716 (ill.), 717 (ill.)

Baird's beaked whales, *4:* 751

*Balaena mysticetus. See* Bowhead whales

Balaenidae. *See* Bowhead whales; Right whales

*Balaenoptera acutorostrata. See* Northern minke whales

*Balaenoptera musculus. See* Blue whales

Balaenopteridae. *See* Rorquals

Bald uakaris, *3:* 516, 520–22, 520 (ill.), 521 (ill.)

Baleen whales, *4:* 704–6, 777, 783–84, 787, 789, 795

Bamboo lemurs, *3:* 451

Banded anteaters. *See* Numbats

**Bandicoots,** *1:* 74–78, **79–87**
> *See also* Spiny bandicoots

Barbados raccoons, *3:* 581

Barbara's titis, *3:* 517

*Barbastella barbastellus. See* Western barbastelles

Barbastelles, western, *2:* 415–16, 415 (ill.), 416 (ill.)

Barred bandicoots. *See* Eastern barred bandicoots

Bathyergidae. *See* African mole-rats

**Bats,** *2:* **275–81**
> **American leaf-nosed,** *2:* **345–57**
> **bulldog,** *2:* **364–70**
> **disk-winged,** *2:* 384, **388–94,** 396
> **false vampire,** *2:* **323–29**
> **free-tailed,** *2:* 278, 279, **399–408**
> fruit, *2:* 277, 280, 282–97, 315, 345

Cougars. *See* Pumas

Cows, mountain. *See* Tapirs

**Cows, sea,** *4:* 828–32, **833–40**

**Coyotes,** *1:* 72, *3:* **583–92**

**Coypus,** *5:* **1194–99,** 1195 (ill.), 1196 (ill.)

Crab-eater seals, *3:* 580

Craseonycteridae. *See* Kitti's hog-nosed bats

*Craseonycteris thonglongyai.* *See* Kitti's hog-nosed bats

Crested capuchins, *3:* 488

Crested genets, *3:* 629

Crested porcupines
Indian, *5:* 1115–16, 1115 (ill.), 1116 (ill.)
North African, *5:* 1114

*Cricetomys gambianus. See* Gambian rats

*Cricetus cricetus. See* Black-bellied hamsters

*Crocuta crocuta. See* Spotted hyenas

Crowned lemurs, *3:* 455–57, 455 (ill.), 456 (ill.)

*Cryptomys damarensis. See* Damaraland mole-rats

*Cryptoprocta ferox. See* Fossa

*Cryptoprocta spelea, 3:* 646

*Cryptotis parva. See* American least shrews

Ctenodactylidae. *See* Gundis

Ctenomyidae. *See* Tuco-tucos

*Ctenomys pearsoni. See* Pearson's tuco-tucos

Cuban hutias, *5:* 1188, 1189, 1191–93, 1191 (ill.), 1192 (ill.)

Cuban solenodons, *2:* 240, 242

*Cuniculus brisson. See* Pacas

*Cuscomys ashaninki, 5:* 1178

*Cuscomys oblativa, 5:* 1178

**Cuscuses,** *1:* 99, **116–23**

Cuvier's whales, *4:* 751

*Cyclopes didactylus. See* Silky anteaters

Cynocephalidae. *See* Colugos

*Cynocephalus variegatus. See* Malayan colugos

*Cynomys ludovicianus. See* Black-tailed prairie dogs


**D**

Dactylopsilinae. *See* Striped possums

d'Albertis's ringtail possums, *1:* 156

Dall's porpoises, *4:* 729–30

Damaraland mole-rats, *5:* 1106–7, 1106 (ill.), 1107 (ill.)

Dance of death, *3:* 615

**Dassie rats,** *5:* **1093–96,** 1094 (ill.), 1095 (ill.)

Dasypodidae. *See* Armadillos

*Dasyprocta punctata. See* Central American agoutis

*Dasyprocta* species, *5:* 1153

Dasyproctidae. *See* Agoutis

*Dasypus novemcinctus. See* Nine-banded armadillos

Dasyuridae. *See* Marsupial cats; Marsupial mice; Tasmanian devils

Dasyuromorphia. *See* Australasian carnivorous marsupials

*Daubentonia madagascariensis. See* Aye-ayes

Daubentoniidae. *See* Aye-ayes

Davis Mountains cottontails, *5:* 1215

De-stressing behavior, *3:* 517

De Winton's golden moles, *2:* 227

Death, dance of, *3:* 615

Decompression sickness, *3:* 691

**Deer,** *4:* 889–90, **933–53**
*See also* Mouse deer

Degus, *5:* 1172, 1173, 1174–75, 1174 (ill.), 1175 (ill.)

Delacour langurs, *3:* 537

*Delphinapterus leucas. See* Belugas

Delphinidae. *See* Dolphins

Demidoff's bushbabies, *3:* 436

*Dendrohyrax arboreus. See* Southern tree hyraxes

*Dendrolagus bennettianus. See* Bennett's tree kangaroos

Dermoptera. *See* Colugos

Desert bandicoots, *1:* 77, 82

Desert cottontails, *5:* 1220–21, 1220 (ill.), 1221 (ill.)

Desert golden moles, Grant's, *2:* 226, 229–31, 229 (ill.), 230 (ill.)

Desert rat-kangaroos, *1:* 131–32

**Desmans,** *2:* **255–62**

Desmarest's hutias. *See* Cuban hutias

*Desmodus rotundus. See* Vampire bats

Devil fish. *See* Gray whales

Dian's tarsiers, *3:* 481

Dibblers, southern, *1:* 54

*Dicerorhinus sumatrensis. See* Sumatran rhinoceroses

*Diclidurus* species, *2:* 304

Didelphidae. *See* New World opossums

Didelphimorphia. *See* New World opossums

*Didelphis virginiana. See* Virginia opossums

Digestive recycling, *1:* 156
*See also* specific species

Dikdiks, Kirk's, *4:* 981–82, 981 (ill.), 982 (ill.)

Dingoes, *1:* 63

Dinomyidae. *See* Pacaranas

*Dinomys branickii. See* Pacaranas

Dipodidae. *See* Birch mice; Jerboas; Jumping mice

*Dipodomys ingens. See* Giant kangaroo rats

**Diprotodontia,** *1:* **99–104**

*Dipus sagitta. See* Hairy-footed jerboas

**Disk-winged bats,** *2:* 384, **388–94,** 396

Erinaceidae. *See* Gymnures; Hedgehogs

*Erinaceus europaeus. See* Western European hedgehogs

Ermines, *3:* 614, 616–18, 616 (ill.), 617 (ill.)

Eschrichtiidae. *See* Gray whales

*Eschrichtius robustus. See* Gray whales

Ethiopian wolves, *3:* 581, 584

*Eubalaena glacialis. See* North Atlantic right whales

Eurasian beavers, *5:* 1025

Eurasian wild pigs, *4:* 899–900, 899 (ill.), 900 (ill.)

European badgers, *3:* 615, 625–26, 625 (ill.), 626 (ill.)

European Community Habitats Directive, *5:* 1059

European hedgehogs, *2:* 219, 221–22, 221 (ill.), 222 (ill.)

European otters, *3:* 622–24, 622 (ill.), 623 (ill.)

European rabbits, *5:* 1202, 1214

European water shrews, *2:* 247

Eutherian mammals, *1:* 51

**Even-toed ungulates, 4: 848, 887–91**

Evolution, convergent, *1:* 170

## F

Fairy armadillos. *See* Pink fairy armadillos

Falkland Island wolves, *3:* 581

False pigs. *See* Pacaranas

**False vampire bats, 2: 323–29**

Family (Taxonomy), *1:* 173

Farming and wild animals, *1:* 72

Fat-tailed dwarf lemurs, *3:* 445

Feather-footed jerboas. *See* Hairy-footed jerboas

**Feather-tailed possums, 1: 102, 172–77**

Felidae. *See* Cats

Felou gundis, *5:* 1083

Fennec foxes, *3:* 583

Ferret badgers, Chinese, *3:* 629

Ferrets, *3:* 581, 614, 615

Filter-feeding whales. *See* Baleen whales

Fin-footed mammals. *See* Marine carnivores

Fin whales, *4:* 796, 797

Fingerprints, whale, *4:* 797

Finless dolphins, black, *4:* 715

Finless porpoises, *4:* 730

Fish and Wildlife Service (U.S.)
  on bats, *2:* 280
  on Buena Vista Lake ornate shrews, *2:* 216
  on Hawaiian monk seals, *3:* 700
  on kangaroo rats, *5:* 1042
  on manatees, *4:* 846
  on moles, *2:* 257
  on pocket mice, *5:* 1040
  on shrews, *2:* 249
  on solenodons, *2:* 242, 244
  on vespertilionid bats, *2:* 412

Fisherman bats. *See* Greater bulldog bats

Fishing bats, *2:* 280
  *See also* Greater bulldog bats

Five-toed jerboas, *5:* 1046

Flathead bottlenosed whales, *4:* 751

Flatheads. *See* Northern bottlenosed whales

Fleas, *5:* 999, 1000, 1004

Florida manatees. *See* West Indian manatees

Florida panthers, *3:* 658, 667

Flying foxes, *2:* 283, 284
  gigantic, *2:* 282
  Indian, *2:* 288–89, 288 (ill.), 289 (ill.)
  Malayan, *2:* 275–76
  *See also* Marianas fruit bats

Flying lemurs. *See* Colugos

Flying squirrels, *5:* 998, 1008, 1009–10, 1011–12, 1011 (ill.), 1012 (ill.)

Food, scatterhoarding, *1:* 125

Foreign species, *1:* 65

Forest elephants, *4:* 816, 817–19, 817 (ill.), 818 (ill.)

Forest hogs, *4:* 895–96, 895 (ill.), 896 (ill.)

Forest monkeys, *3:* 425

Fork-crowned lemurs, *3:* 444, 445

**Fossa, 3: 637–48, 644 (ill.), 645 (ill.)**

Foundation for Rabbit-Free Australia, *1:* 82

Fox squirrels, *5:* 1008

**Foxes, 1: 54, 65, 68, 134, 3: 583–92**
  *See also* Flying foxes

**Franciscana dolphins, 4: 719–23, 721 (ill.), 722 (ill.)**

**Free-tailed bats, 2: 278, 279, 399–408**

Fringe-lipped bats, *2:* 280

**Fruit bats, 2: 280**
  American, *2:* 345
  **Old World, 2: 277, 282–97**
  Salim Ali's, *2:* 315

Fulvous leaf-nosed bats, *2:* 340

Fungi, *1:* 131

**Funnel-eared bats, 2: 378–82, 380 (ill.), 381 (ill.), 384**

**Fur seals, 3: 673–83**

Furipteridae. *See* Smoky bats

*Furipterus horrens. See* Smoky bats

## G

Galagidae. *See* Bushbabies

*Galago senegalensis. See* Senegal bushbabies

Galápagos fur seals, *3:* 674

Galápagos sea lions, *3:* 674, 680–82, 680 (ill.), 681 (ill.)

Pteropodidae. *See* Old World fruit bats

*Pteropus giganteus. See* Indian flying foxes

*Pteropus mariannus. See* Marianas fruit bats

*Pudu pudu. See* Southern pudus

Pudus, southern, *4:* 946–47, 946 (ill.), 947 (ill.)

*Puma concolor. See* Pumas

Pumas, *3:* 658, 665–67, 665 (ill.), 666 (ill.)

Punarés, *5:* 1182

*Pygathrix nemaeus. See* Red-shanked douc langurs

Pygmy anteaters. *See* Silky anteaters

Pygmy fruit bats, *2:* 282

Pygmy gliders, *1:* 172–74, 175–77, 175 (ill.), 176 (ill.)

Pygmy hippopotamuses, *4:* 908, 909, 913–14, 913 (ill.), 914 (ill.)

Pygmy hogs, *4:* 892, 894

Pygmy marmosets, *3:* 423, 496, 505–7, 505 (ill.), 506 (ill.)

Pygmy mice, *5:* 996

Pygmy mouse lemurs, *3:* 423, 444

**Pygmy possums,** *1:* 101, 102, **149–53**

Pygmy rabbits, *5:* 1215

**Pygmy right whales,** *4:* **783–86,** 785 (ill.), 786 (ill.)

Pygmy shrews, Savi's, *2:* 246

Pygmy sloths. *See* Monk sloths

Pygmy slow lorises, *3:* 428, 431–32, 431 (ill.), 432 (ill.)

Pygmy sperm whales, *4:* 765–66, 765 (ill.), 766 (ill.)

Pygmy squirrels, *5:* 1008

## Q

Queensland tube-nosed bats, *2:* 295–97, 295 (ill.), 296 (ill.)

Querétaro pocket gophers, *5:* 1032

Quill pigs. *See* Old World porcupines

Quills, throwing, *5:* 1113

Quolls, spotted-tailed, *1:* 52

## R

Rabbit-eared bandicoots. *See* Greater bilbies

**Rabbits,** *1:* 82, *5:* **1200–1204, 1213–22**

Raccoon dogs, *3:* 583, 629

**Raccoons,** *3:* 578, 579–80, 581, **605–13**

Rainforest bandicoots. *See* Spiny bandicoots

*Rangifer tarandus. See* Reindeer

**Rat-kangaroos,** *1:* **129–34**
    *See also* Musky rat-kangaroos

Rat opossums. *See* Shrew opossums

Rato de Taquara, *5:* 1183

**Rats,** *5:* 996–1000, **1051–68**
    cane, *5:* **1097–1102**
    chinchilla, *5:* **1177–81**
    dassie, *5:* **1093–96,** 1094 (ill.), 1095 (ill.)
    kangaroo, *5:* 997, 998, **1036–43**
    plains viscacha, *5:* 1173
    Polynesian, *2:* 373
    rock, *5:* 1173
    spiny, *5:* **1182–87,** 1185 (ill.), 1186 (ill.)
    water, *5:* 998
    *See also* Mole-rats; Moonrats

Red-backed squirrel monkeys, *3:* 488

Red-billed hornbills, *3:* 638

Red colobus
    eastern, *3:* 537
    western, *3:* 537, 538–40, 538 (ill.), 539 (ill.)

Red deer, *4:* 940–42, 940 (ill.), 941 (ill.)

Red foxes, *1:* 54, 65, 68, 134, *3:* 584, 588–89, 588 (ill.), 589 (ill.)

Red howler monkeys, Venezuelan, *3:* 528–30, 528 (ill.), 529 (ill.)

Red kangaroos, *1:* 101, 140–41, 140 (ill.), 141 (ill.)

Red List of Threatened Species. *See* World Conservation Union (IUCN) Red List of Threatened Species

Red mouse lemurs, *3:* 446, 447–48, 447 (ill.), 448 (ill.)

Red pandas, *3:* 579–80, 605, 606, 610–12, 610 (ill.), 611 (ill.)

Red ruffed lemurs, *3:* 450

Red-shanked douc langurs, *3:* 537, 544–45, 544 (ill.), 545 (ill.)

Red-tailed sportive lemurs, *3:* 469–71, 469 (ill.), 470 (ill.)

Red-toothed shrews, *2:* 248

Red wolves, *3:* 581, 584

Reindeer, *4:* 951–52, 951 (ill.), 952 (ill.)

Rhesus macaques, *3:* 426, 546–47, 546 (ill.), 547 (ill.)

Rhesus monkeys. *See* Rhesus macaques

*Rhinoceros unicornis. See* Indian rhinoceroses

**Rhinoceroses,** *4:* 821, 848–50, 852, 853, **874–86**

Rhinocerotidae. *See* Rhinoceroses

Rhinolophidae. *See* Horseshoe bats

*Rhinolophus capensis. See* Cape horseshoe bats

*Rhinolophus ferrumequinum. See* Greater horseshoe bats

*Rhinopoma hardwickei. See* Hardwicke's lesser mouse-tailed bats

Rhinopomatidae. *See* Mouse-tailed bats

on western barbastelles,
2: 416
on western gorillas, 3: 570
on white bats, 2: 356
on woolly monkeys,
3: 534
on Xenarthra, 1: 181
World Wildlife Fund, 4: 797
Wroughton free-tailed bats,
2: 402

## X

Xenarthra, 1: 178–82

## Y

Yapoks. *See* Water opossums
Yellow-bellied gliders, 1: 163
Yellow-breasted capuchins,
3: 488
Yellow-footed rock wallabies,
1: 101
Yellow golden moles, 2: 226
Yellow-streaked tenrecs,
2: 237–38, 237 (ill.), 238 (ill.)
Yellow-tailed woolly monkeys,
3: 527
Yellow-winged bats, 2: 324,
325

Yellowstone National Park,
3: 587
*Yerbua capensis. See* Springhares

## Z

*Zalophus californianus. See*
California sea lions
*Zalophus wollebaeki. See*
Galápagos sea lions
**Zebras,** 4: 848–50, 852,
**854–64**
*Zenkerella* species, 5: 1069
Ziphiidae. *See* Beaked whales